R. GUPTA'S®

GROUP DISCUSSION

A PRACTICAL APPROACH FOR ANALYSING THE INNER ORIENTATIONS OF THE CANDIDATE

By:
RPH Editorial Board

RAMESH PUBLISHING HOUSE, New Delhi

Published by
O.P. Gupta *for* Ramesh Publishing House

Admin. Office
12-H, New Daryaganj Road, Opp. Officers' Mess,
New Delhi-110002 ☏ 23261567, 23275224, 23275124

E-mail: info@rameshpublishinghouse.com
Website: www.rameshpublishinghouse.com

Showroom
- Balaji Market, Nai Sarak, Delhi-6 ☏ 23253720, 23282525
- 4457, Nai Sarak, Delhi-6, ☏ 23918938

© Strictly Reserved with the Publisher

No Part of this book may be reproduced or transmitted in any form or by any means, electronic or mechanical including photocopying, recording or by any transformation storage and retrieval system without written permission from the Publisher.

Indemnification Clause: This book is being sold/distributed subject to the exclusive condition that neither the author nor the publishers, individually or collectively, shall be responsible to indemnify the buyer/user/possessor of this book beyond the selling price of this book for any reason under any circumstances. If you do not agree to it, please do not buy/accept/use/possess this book.

Book Code: R-194

26th Edition : 1912

ISBN: 978-93-5012-585-4

HSN Code: 49011010

ABOUT THIS VOLUME

Group Discussion Test is the most important and most popular technique of personality testing. It is used for selecting candidates for MBA, SSB, Airlines, UTI officers, Research scholars etc. It enables the examiner to assess candidate's leadership ability, intellectual level, communication ability, socialisation skill and an ability to motivate and influence others. The most important aspect of Group Discussion is its practical approach for analysing the inner orientations of the candidates. The enhanced leadership ability of the candidate has to be in the context of abilities and responses of other individuals of the group.

This volume would help to train the minds of the readers so that they could appear in the Group Discussions and emerge with flying colours. The volume comprises three parts—I, II and III—and covers the current topics with complete fidelity. It would inculcate the basic principles and values in candidates so that they could succeed in any examination.

What is a Group Discussion?

A Group Discussion is the process of conducting arguments over a subject in a group format. It tests the abilities of the participants in terms of power of thinking, leadership abilities and communication skills. Group Discussion is a mode of conversation among group members who have not been previously acquainted with each other. It is not pre-planned but is an extempore discussion.

Generally, participants of same age levels, similar educational qualifications, experiences and social backgrounds are grouped together and asked to discuss a subject in an uninhibited manner. A group of eight to ten participants is made to sit in a conference hall around a table or in conveniently arranged chairs. Only one topic is suggested by the examiner for the discussion. The participants consult one another and start speaking on the subject. Sometimes, a choice of two subjects is also given. The examiner could ask the participants to initiate the discussion (so that they decide their turns) or he could give them turn numbers in order to avoid confusion. Nearly thirty minutes are given for discussion over one topic and one of the participants speaks only for two or three minutes or so. Another participant either criticises or supports the topic of discussion after his predecessor has completed his speech. Everyone explains his point of view with the help of information supplied by all of the participants as well as with he help of the knowledge base acquired by him over a span of years.

At the end of the Group Discussion, conclusions and recommendations are necessary; the same are provided by one of the participants.

Group Discussion is a type of formal arguments on a particular topic. The participants discuss in a friendly manner without losing temper, shouting, condemning or using trite remarks. It may be the topic related to government, political parties, ministers, economy, arts and crafts, leisure, status of woman *etc.* For example, if a group of persons gets together over a cup of tea, they would not sit silent but would talk about various matters. Each one would express his views. In such a case, no one is required to be appointed as a leader of the group. There would also be no end of formal proposers, supporters or the leader of the opposition. None of them would be forced to take sides as is the case in a formal debate. Each individual would be liable to express his or her views in such a manner as he or she feels the best. We can conclude that Group Discussion in a railway compartment or at any public place is an informal debate and no results are expected from the same.

A note must be made here of discussions in conferences, assemblies and at political fora (including those in the Parliament). There is a Chairman of the house (or Speaker of the house) who conducts such debates. At one time, only one topic is discussed. The candidates prepare for many days prior to the discussion. A member starts the discussion and another member either seconds it or opposes it. The members speak one by one. Heated arguments could follow and the decision may not be forthcoming. The time limits would extend from 15 minutes to several hours for each speaker. This style is in total contrast with the style of Group Discussion for a competitive examination or for a post in a government department. There has to be a result, a conclusion or a brief summary of the discussion at the end of the same.

The main objective of Group Discussion is to analyse the psychological orientations of the participant. It has to be judged whether he or she has thorough understanding of the topic or whether he or she having superficial knowledge. The participant must have the power to carry out an analytical study of the topic immediately after the topic has been given for discussion. Such an approach gives better understanding and an assessment of the candidates who are in the fray for achieving an objective, a degree, a job or an increment. The Group Discussion process eliminates the 'fears' of the candidates (as the examiner recedes to the background). The candidates take off the veneer of formality and put up their best thoughts for either supporting or rejecting the topic. The participant has to remain composed and confident as these would be counted as his plus points. He can oppose but in a civilised manner. He can support but with a tinge of decency. Or we can say that there are no leaders in these debates; candidates have to catch the opportunities for becoming leaders, though for a few minutes only. The discussion would also judge whether he is sincere about his objectives, hardworking, knowledgeable and a person having an integrity of mind. Even if he does not state that he has (or does not have) these traits, his dialogues and interactions with other participants would reveal them to the watchful examiner who is judging each and every candidate on an analytical scale. If the participant is arrogant, boastful, selfish, monopolistic or aggressive, then his ratings would go down. All the actions, dialogues and speeches are carefully heard, seen and monitored by the examiner.

Another quality of the participant that the authorities would like to discover is clear thinking. A confused person would speak in circumlocuted language. His speech would be very long, involving the ideas that do not support or oppose the topic. The knowledge levels of an immature and unprepared candidate would be shallow and his personality would obviously be half-baked.

In sum, Group Discussion is a psychological technique that is used for judging the latent personalities of the candidates. It is a very effective and an efficient method and is practised in most of the competitive examinations and recruitment procedures.

How to Succeed in a Group Discussion?

Group Discussion Test is very simple and does not demand any equipment, machinery, computers or writing materials. So, participants' oratory power should be very good which includes speech, conversation with others, narration of an incident or an experience and arguing in favour of or against a topic. Further, good thoughts should be given top priorities. Good thoughts rule the world and those with good ideas are respected and revered by all.

Speaking is an art that can be acquired through regular practice. Most probably, one cannot speak on a subject unless he knows the subject thoroughly. Further, knowledge of the subject is a great asset but this asset can be put to use only when one possesses the power of expression. In a Group Discussion, one should have the capacity to make a favourable and a forceful impact.

Now, let us discuss the concept of an ideal strategy to elevate a candidate into the position of leadership. He has to remain good despite the gravest provocation and has to learn the art of bringing together all the persons with different temperaments. He has to help them come out with their own ideas and later, help them in hammering out a consensus that is appealing to all the participants.

After attaining a command over speech front, ideology front and strategy front, he must try to handle the discussion as a leader. But confusion reigns supreme in all the Group Discussions during the initial stages just because there is no chosen leader to co-ordinate the group members. It is usually observed that everyone argues with the other participant and thus works at cross-purposes, indulging in tense arguments, bickering and squabbling and doing everything except starting the Group Discussion about the topic prescribed to the group. A few points must be remembered which are as follows : (A) Success comes to those who are always hopeful and cheerful; (B) The best speakers are those who speak meticulously, to the point and use correct words and data; (C) The optimist sees the doughnut but the pessimist sees the hole; never be negative or pessimist while discussing.

The participants in a Group Discussion must possess not only the power to speech, but also a thorough understanding of the subject on which they are expected to discuss. Since the topic likely to be given is anybody's guess, it is good for every participant to familiarise himself with the most important topics under the heading of current affairs in magazines and periodicals. The best way to keep oneself attached to the latest developments is to get in touch with newspapers, magazines and television.

A group is a subtle simulation of a classroom where the atmosphere is replete with cross-talks, arguments and fireworks. However, a disciplined class monitor emerges on the scene to restore the decorum. That person could be having a pleasant smile. A person, cut out for leadership of the group, has to display such qualities of a dedicated motivator as initiative, thorough understanding, adaptability, co-operation, decision making ability, dynamism, determination *etc.* The group leader has to co-ordinate the discussion and has to see to it that through persuation and through dosages of firmness, the group settles down to conduct its business.

Despite the dismal and distressing situations, there are a few among us who can still radiate charm and confidence; they are the men and women who do not wait for opportunities but create them on their own terms. They are the energetic, bold and responsible people and are always ready to take the initiative. They watch the situation for a while and when they find that things are going haywire, they take the plunge to control the drifting situation. The leader in a Group Discussion has also the trump card unless they work properly, none of them is giving to win and they are there for a purpose and not for a gamble. Endorsed with all the quality that goes into the making of a true leader, the hero of the group can tackle any situation. He can guide Group Discussion to its successful finale. He would also conclude by stating the vital points (discussed by all the participants) and by giving the general trend of the discussion which could either be against the topic or in favour of the topic. The leader would do well to sum up the viewpoints of all the participants, though he himself may have either opposed or supported the topic.

Group Discussion can be held in an amicable atmosphere if all the candidates extend support to the same. Leaders are automatically identified within a few minutes. The sooner they are identified, the better it is for the entire group. If everyone tries to lead, there would be chaos. Even the followers have all the chances of getting full marks; after all, only a good follower would support a good leader.

In sum, success in a Group Discussion depends upon the abilities and communication skills of the participants. It also depends upon those participants who assume the leading roles and can win their battles with poise, knowledge and perseverance.

CONTENTS

TYPE-I

PSLV-C37 Launch with 104 Satellites 3
Brexit and its Impact 6
Union Budget 2017-18 10
Changing Face of Terrorism 13
Demonetisation of Indian Currency 16
Goods and Services Tax 20
Heart of Asia Summit – 2016 22
G-20 Summit–2016 24
Nuclear Security Summit–2016 28
SAARC Summit 31
Green Finance 35
Digital India Programme 38
India and the NSG 42

TYPE-II

Judicial Activism—Limitations 47
Reservation will lead to National Disaster 51
Peeping Tom Syndrome in Firms is Good for Employees 56
Environmental Control is the Responsibility of the Executive 62
Business vs Ethics 67
Internet Is Affecting Our Culture 70
How Far is Human Cloning Ethical? 75
Media Blitzkrieg is Nothing but a Ploy to Exploit the Mass Audiences 79
Does Modernisation Lead to Losing Values and Heritage? 82
Machines vs Men 86
International Politics Without Ethics—Boon or Bane 91
Sports Must be Separated from Politics 95
Should Army Training be Made Compulsory for the Youth 99
No Need to Send Large Contingents for International Sports Events 103
Satyagraha—Only Alternative to Remove Corruption? 107
Do Public Figures have Fight to Privacy? 112
The Mass Media Are the Tools of Societal Decay 116
IT Sector No Longer a Green Pasture 119
Satellite Channels are Creating Cultural Corrosion 122

Should We Punish Nations with Weapons of Mass Destruction 124
India Needs a Large Number of Small Firms 127

TYPE-III

The Aim of Cinema—Entertainment not Education 133
Should NRIs be Given Sops 139
Corruption is a Political Necessity 142
For Rapid Rural Development–Is Education more Important
 than Industrialisation? 145
To Stay United and Become a Super Power—Does India need a very
 Strong and Stable Central Government with Full Powers over the
 State Governments? 151
Indian Press—Is it Free? 157
Should Politicians Retire at the Age of Sixty 163
Unstable Democracies in Our Neighbourhood Can Harm Us 167
Politics, Business and Bureaucracy form a Fatal Triangle 169
A New Vision for the UN is Not a Pragmatic Idea 174
Will Limited Nuclear War Ever Remain Limited? 176
Lokpal Bill 182
Dangerous Debt Trap-Ultimate Outcome of ever Increasing Foreign Aid ... 187
Is Glorification of Violence and Crimes in Films and TV A Reason for
 A High Crime Rate? 194
Can Different Cultures Be Integrated to Evolve A Global Culture? 200
Will More State Autonomy Lead to India's Disintegration? 207
Press Freedom 212
Private Sector with Economic Liberalisation— India's Best Hope for
 Rapid Economic Growth 216
Rural India is not Developing Due to Resource Constraints 222
Should Our Sports Stars Earn Unlimited Wealth 230
FDI in Retail Sector—A Boon or Bane 234
Press Code—Is It Must For the Press? 239
Commercialisation of Education—An Avoidable Evil 244
Same Sex Marriage — Right or Wrong 249
Is Moral Policing Justified 253
Capital Punishment Uncivilized way of Punishing 257
Media Trial 260

Note 264

PSLV-C37 LAUNCH WITH 104 SATELLITES

Scripting history, India on February 15, 2017 successfully launched a record 104 satellites—all but three of them foreign—from Sriharikota (Andhra Pradesh) and put them into orbit in a single mission onboard its most dependable Polar rocket.

Recording its 38th consecutive success, ISRO's workhorse Polar Satellite Launch Vehicle (PSLV) injected India's weather observation Cartosat-2 Series satellite and 103 nano satellites into precise orbit in a gap of 30 minutes after a textbook lift-off from this spaceport, about 100 km from Chennai.

As the country seeks a bigger slice of the multi-billion dollar space launch industry, the Indian Space Researh Organisation (ISRO) bettered Russian space agency's feat of launching 37 satellites at one go in 2014. The previous highest number of satellites launched by ISRO in one mission was 20 in June 2015.

A majority of the satellites have earth-imaging capability while the Indian cartographic satellite is capable of taking high resolution images.

The launch of 104 Satellites in a single mission started off as a far less ambitious effort that would still have set world records. Initially, there was a plan to launch 68 satellites in a single mission, some time in late 2016 itself. An increasing number of satellites were accommodated into the PSLV-C37.

PSLV-C37 also known as Cartosat-2 series satellite. PSLV-C37 was the 39th mission of the PSLV program and its 16th mission in XL Configuration. It carried a total of 104 satellites including the 714 kilograms. According to ISRO, the 101 international satellites were launched as a part of commercial arrangement among several countries.

The launches started placing the satellites into a polar Sun-synchronous orbit one after the other, after a flight of 16 minutes and 48 seconds. It first injected the Satellite Cartosat-2D at an altitude of 510.38 km, with 97-46 degrees inclination, followed by the two ISRO nanosatellites INS-1A and INS-1B. All 104 satellites successfully placed in orbit. This is a significant step for India.

After separation, the two solar arrays of Cartosat-2 series satellites were deployed automatically and ISRO's Telemetry, Tracking and Command Network (ISTRAC) at Bangalore took over the control of the satellite. In the coming days, the satellite will be brought to its final operational configuration following which it will begin to provide remote sensing services using its panchromatic (black and white) and multispectral (colour) cameras.

The imagery from the Cartosat-2 series satellite will be useful for cartographic applications, urban and rural applications, coastal land use and regulation, utility management like road network monitoring, water distribution, creation of land use maps, change detection to bring out geographical and manmade features and various other Land Information System (LIS) and Geographical Information System (GIS) applications. The data sets could be used for urban planning of 500 cities under the Amrut Planning Scheme. The government initiative of 100 smart city programme in which these data sets could be used for master plan preparation and detailed geospatial data preparation for rural roads and infrastructure development.

Of the 103 co-passenger satellites carried by PSLV-C37, two – ISRO Nano Satellite-1 (INS-1) weighing 8.4 kg and INS-2 weighing 9.7 kg – are technology demonstration satellites from India.

The remaining 101 co-passenger satellites carried were international customer satellites from USA (96), The Netherlands (1), Switzerland (1), Israel (1), Kazakhstan (1) and UAE (1).

The large number of satellites in this mission demanded adopting innovative approaches in satellite accommodation and mission design.

Apart from conventional satellite adapters, namely, Payload Adapter (PLA) and Multiple Satellite Adapter (MSA), six numbers of custom made adapters were newly configured and used to house the nano satellites. Some of these adapters allowed multi-tier mounting of satellites and few of them were accommodated on the Vehicle Equipment Bay itself. This architecture enabled the optimal utilisation of the payload volume as well as capability.

Next requirement was managing safe separation of these large numbers of satellites within the constraints of limited visibility duration of ground stations and maintaining safe distance between the separated satellites over a longer period of time.

This was managed by designing a unique sequencing and timing for separating the satellites and with complex manoeuvering of PS4 stage to which satellites are attached. The separation sequence, direction and timing were finalised based on extensive study to ensure safe distance among the 105 objects (including PS4 stage) in orbit, which renders 5460 number of pairs.

The next major requirement was to ensure reaching separation command from launcher to respective satellites honoring the pre-defined sequence, which involves a complex electrical wiring scheme. Any error in the wiring may result in release of wrong satellite leading to undesirable situation of collision between them.

Another innovative feature in this mission was capturing all the separation events of vehicle stages and 104 satellites using a comprehensive video imaging system onboard.

This mission involved many technical challenges like realising the launch of a large number of satellites during a single mission within the time frame sought by the customers from abroad. Besides, ensuring adequate separation among all the 104 satellites during their orbital injection as well as during their subsequent orbital life was yet another challenge associated with this complex mission.

With this successful launch, the total number of customer satellites from abroad launched by India's workhorse launch vehicle PSLV has reached 180.

BREXIT AND ITS IMPACT

European Union was originally formed with six nations in 1957. Today, it is a gigantic transnational entity of 28 countries, including the U.K., which joined only in 1973. UK has a peculiar history with EU. Though part of EU, Britain has traditionally had a 'eurosceptic' stand. It continues to use the Pound as its currency, while most EU nations have moved to Euro. Neither does it participate in the Schengen border-free zone, which allows passport-free travel in EU. On June 23rd, 2016 UK voted to leave the EU. Let us examine the various aspects of this Brexit.

Sequence of Events

In January 2013, Prime Minister Cameron announced that a Conservative government would hold an in-out referendum on EU membership before the end of 2017, on a renegotiated package, if elected in 2015.

The Conservative Party won the 2015 general election with a majority. Soon afterwards the European Union Referendum Act 2015 was introduced into Parliament to enable the referendum. Despite being in favour of remaining in a reformed European Union himself, Cameron announced that Conservative Ministers and MPs were free to campaign in favour of remaining in the EU or leaving it, according to their conscience.

UK voted to leave the European Union. The 'Leave' side won decisively with 52 per cent of the vote in the high-turnout vote, which overturned opinion polls that predicted a slender margin for 'Remain'. PM David Cameroon was the architect of the referendum. He supported "Remain". As a result of the "Leave" verdict, he stepped down as PM. A stunned EU urged Britain to leave "as soon as possible" amid fears the devastating blow to European unity could spark a chain reaction of further referendum.

Reasons Behind the Result
The various people campaigning for "Leave" used the following issues to stress on the need for Brexit:
- **Economy and austerity measures:** There was public anger in Britain towards the status quo. Ordinary Britons, hit hard by the economic crisis, feel betrayed by their political leadership. The Conservative government's austerity policies have further alienated these sections.
- **Immigration:** As EU's membership expanded, more Europeans, especially from poorer EU nations, started migrating to U.K. using the "freedom of movement" clause. The anti-immigration parties argue this puts a severe strain on national resources and add up to welfare expenditure. The pro-EU members argue that EU migrants contribute more to the national economy than they take out.
- **Security:** The Remain side argues that in the era of international terrorism and criminality, cooperating with the EU will make the U.K. safer, while the other side says that the security risk will in fact increase if the U.K. does not have control over its borders.
- **Trade:** On trade, the Remain side says that access to the single European market, free of tariffs and border controls, is critical for the U.K. as 45 per cent of its trade is with the EU. The Leave side says that the EU needs British markets and individual trade deals with European countries can be easily negotiated.
- **Employment:** The Remain side argues that as three million jobs are tied to the EU there could be a jobs crisis if the U.K. leaves the EU; Brexiteers claim that there will be a jobs boom without the fetters that EU regulations impose.
- **Negative strategy:** The Remain campaign focussed mainly on the dangers of leaving the EU rather than making a case reasons for staying in EU and present a future vision. This alienated the people further, rather than convincing them.

Possible Implications For UK
- UK is currently in a situation of deep uncertainty post-leave vote. It remains to be seen whether the propositions of how the leave would benefit UK would materialise.

- **Turmoil in currency markets:** Pound dived to its lowest since 1985; Euro suffered its worst fall against the dollar.
- **Second Scottish referendum likely:** Scotland voted by a margin of 62 per cent to 38 per cent to remain in the EU in the referendum. Scotland sees its future in the European Union despite Britain's vote to leave. Hence, a second Scottish independence referendum is likely.
- **Exports:** 45% of UKs exports are to the Eurozone. Hence, the need to negotiate the relationship with EU is immediate.
- **Less influence in world politics:** The collective bargaining benefits enjoyed by Britain as a part of EU would no longer exist.
- **Hamper Joint efforts:** May hamper joint counter-terrorism, information sharing especially in context of instability in middle east.

For European Union and Rest of the World

- The members of EU make monetary contributions towards EU and UK is one the largest contributors.
- A British exit from the European Union would rock the Union — already shaken by differences over migration and the future of the Eurozone — by ripping away its second-largest economy, one of its top two military powers and by far its richest financial centre.
- Brexit would give rise more and more nations contemplating to exit the EU. Greece, last year held a referendum in which its citizens overwhelmingly rejected EU's bailout norms.
- **World economy:** World stocks saw more than $2 trillion wiped off their value as Britain's vote to leave the European Union triggered 5-10 per cent falls across Europe's biggest bourses and a record plunge for sterling.
- Such a body blow to global confidence could prevent the Federal Reserve from raising interest rates as planned this year, and might even provoke a new round of emergency policy easing from all the major central banks.

For India

- Though, Finance minister Jaitley claimed that India is well-prepared to deal with the consequences of the Bexit with strong macroeconomic situation, some issues still remain.
- Volatility in Indian markets triggered by Brexit- BSE Sensex fell by 4%.
- Indian companies in UK—There are 800 Indian companies in the UK—more than the combined number in the rest of Europe. Britain's exit from EU may affect Indian companies' appetite for investing in the UK, particularly those seeking access to the European market.
- The welfare of a nearly three-million strong diaspora of Indian-origin UK citizens is a major concern.
- The interests of a large number of Britain bound Indian tourists, business people, professionals, students, spouses, parents and relatives is also a concern.
- India-EU FTA—The FTA talks with EU will have to be modified in the event of Brexit. Much will depend of the future equation between EU and UK.
- If Britain gets the same treatment in terms of Free Tariff and Free Movement of persons, not much will change for India. However, if Britain gets the treatment as applicable to a non-member country, it may lead to positive impact on India's exports to EU as well as to Britain.
- Similarly, any restriction on movement of persons from EU to Britain will open opportunity for Indian service providers in wide range of services.
- The weakness in the currencies—Pound and Euro, may also lead to increase in imports to India from these countries.
- However, the uncertainties brought about by the referendum may benefit India too in some ways:
  - The drop in the pound will benefit Indian students bound for UK and Indian tourists.
  - Buying property in UK will be easier due to weaker pound.

UNION BUDGET 2017-18

Union Finance Minister Arun Jaitley presented Budget 2017-18 in the Parliament on February 1. He provided relief to the majority of taxpayers by halving the rate of personal income tax for those with annual income of as much as ₹ 5 lakh and cutting the coporate tax rate for medium and small enterprises with a turnover of up to ₹ 50 crore. The relief was aimed at ameliorating the consequences of the three-month-old demonetisation that has slowed economic activity especially in the small and informal sectors.

The Budget also proposed increase in allocations for a clutch of social sector programmes including the rural employment guarantee scheme, even as he stuck to the fiscal consolidation path. Affordable housing, a focus area of the NDA government, has been granted infrastructure status. Announcing a cap of ₹ 3 lakh for cash transactions, the Finance Minister pressed on with the government's anti-corruption theme, and set new norms for cash donations to political parties.

The digital economy would also get a big push, with steps announced to cut the cost of digital payments and discourage business expenses of more than ₹ 10,000 being paid in cash. Pursuing the Budget theme of 'Transform, Energise and Clean India', he promised a tough law to deal with "big time offenders, including economic offenders, fleeing the country to escape the reach of law." The government was considering legal changes to confiscate the assets of such individuals. As part of the effort to clean up the political system, the cash donation limit for political parties from a single person was slashed from ₹ 20,000 to ₹ 2,000, with the Minister asserting that this would bring transparency in electoral funding. Changes have also been mooted to the Reserve Bank of India Act to float electoral bonds that people could purchase from banks and political parties receiving them could redeem.

Other Highlights

➤ **Demonetisation:** • Demonetisation is expected to have a transient impact on the economy. • It will have a great impact on the economy and lives of people. • Demonetisation is a bold and decisive measure that will lead to higher GDP growth. • The effects of demonetisation will not spillover to the next fiscal.

➤ **Agriculture sector:** • A sum of ₹ 10 lakh crore is allocated as credit to farmers, with 60 days interest waiver. • NABARD fund will be increased to ₹ 40,000 crore. • Government will set up mini labs in Krishi Vigyan Kendras for soil testing. • A dedicated micro irrigation fund will be set up for NABARD with ₹ 5,000 crore initial corpus. • Irrigation corpus increased from ₹ 20,000 crore to ₹ 40,000 crore. • Dairy processing infrastructure fund wlll be initially created with a corpus of ₹ 2000 crore. • Issuance of soil cards has gained momentum. • A model law on contract farming will be prepared and shared with the States.

➤ **Rural population:** • The government targets to bring 1 crore households out of poverty by 2019. • During 2017-18, five lakh farm ponds will be taken up under the MGNREGA. • Over ₹ 3 lakh crore will be spent for rural India. MGNREGA to double farmers' income. • Will take steps to ensure participation of women in MGNREGA up to 55%. • Will allocate ₹ 19,000 crore for Pradhan Mantri Gram Sadak Yojana in 2017-18. • The country well on way to achieve 100% rural electrification by March 2018. • Swachh Bharat mission has made tremendous progress; sanitation coverage has gone up from 42% in Oct 2013 to 60% now.

➤ **Health Care for the Poor and Underprivilege :** • ₹ 500 crore allocated for Mahila Shakti Kendras. • Under a nationwide scheme for pregnant women, ₹ 6000 will be transferred to each person. • A sum of ₹ 1,84,632 crore allocated for women and children. • Elimination of tuberculosis by 2025 targeted. • Health sub centres, numbering 1.5 lakh, wilIl be transformed into health wellness centres. • Two

AIIMS will be set up in Jharkhand and Gujarat. • Aadhaar-based smartcards will be issued to senior citizens to monitor health.
- **Energy Sector:** • A strategic policy for crude reserves will be set up. • ₹ 1,26,000 crore received as energy production based investments. • Trade infra export scheme will be launched in 2017-18.
- **Railways:** • Total allocation for Railways is ₹ 1,31,000 crore. • No service charge on tickets booked through IRCTC. • Raksha coach with a corpus of ₹ 1 lakh crore for five years (for passenger safety). • 3,500 km of railway lines to be commissioned this year up from 2,800 km last year. • By 2019 all trains will have bio-toilets. • Five-hundred stations will be made differently-abled friendly.

New Tax Slabs

Individual Tax Payers

Up to ₹ 2,50,000	No tax
₹ 2,50,001 to ₹ 5,00,000	5%
₹ 5,00,001 to ₹ 10,00,000	20%
More than ₹ 10,00,000	30%

Senior Citizens who are 60 years old and above but less than 80 years

Up to ₹ 3,00,000	No tax
₹ 3,00,001 to ₹ 5,00,000	10%
₹ 5,00,001 to ₹ 10,00,000	20%
More than ₹ 10,00,000	30%

(Surcharge of 10% on income of all individuals above ₹ 50 lakh and less than ₹ 1 crore and surcharge of 15% on income above ₹ 1 crore.)

CHANGING FACE OF TERRORISM

Terrorism means an activity that involves a violent act or an act dangerous to human life, property or infrastructure. It appears to be intended to influence the policy of a government by intimidation and to affect the conduct of a government by mass destruction, assassination, kidnapping or hostage-taking.

Terrorism came into existence during the French revolution when the then king unleashed a reign of terror on his opponents and the revolutionary organisations. Our freedom fighters adopted the same measures against the British. During the struggle for independence in India, the militant groups and organisations cropped up to take up the struggle in aggressive and retaliatory methods. They used to get involved in bombing, killing and ambushing the ruling class. However, in free India, militancy started during 1960s when naxalite movement was initiated by Charu Majumdar.

Though a number of countries have been affected by terrorism since a long time but after the attack on the "Twin Towers" in USA (9/11 (2001) attack), and Paris attack on 19 November, 2015 terrorism came to limelight in the entire world. Almost all countries are now very much bothered with this problem. Terrorist groups like the Al-Qaeda or Hizbul etc. are very much advanced in their methods of operations. They have gone much ahead of the phase of the guerilla wars. They use suicide bombers, highly advanced artillery, they have very unique methods of communication amongst themselves using coded languages which are not very easy to decode.

The attack in Mumbai on Nov. 26, 2008 was a massive attack that the commercial capital has suffered in last 16 years. Likewise, in Delhi the public places were the main target. Indians can never forget the devastating bomb blast in Sarojini Nagar market in New Delhi. Yet it seems the people of Mumbai and Delhi have got used to militant attacks and hence once again they get on with their daily lives the very next day without any fear of attacks.

The alleged plot to blow up planes from the United Kingdom mid-flight involved the detonation of explosive devices smuggled in hand luggage on to as many as 10 aircrafts. One theory is that the attack may have involved liquid explosive being carried to a plane in either drink bottles or cans. An overpressure of just 10 per cent would wreck the aircraft and possibly kill the people in it.

Basically, no terrorist attack is possible without finance. Finance is the backbone of terrorism. These people need money at each and every point of their movement, may be for purchase of a vehicle, hire a house or may be to bribe anybody or may be for some specific purpose. After the 9/11 attacks in the United States, the governments of the world particularly the United States as well as the United Nations fixed their primary job to curb finances of terrorism. These terrorist organisations obtain money from a number of legitimate and illegitimate sources such as drug trafficking, smuggling, kidnapping and extortion.

Rich individuals are a critical source of terrorist financing e.g. Osama bin Laden charitable and religious institutions fund these terrorists in the name of religious works though the money is transferred to the terrorists groups to carry out operations. A number of rogue nations have been known to provide assistance, financial support and safe harbour to terrorist organisations. A prime example to this was Afghanistan under the Taliban regime.

Money is also needed to sustain media campaigns and win political support. They may transfer their money either by smuggling cash across borders, particularly through land crossings and sea shipments or through the traditional financial institutions. They also use the money laundering technique and the hawala to transfer their money.

Before September 2001 India has been raising voice against terrorism time and again but the western countries had not taken us seriously. Before 9/11 neither any tough resolutions were passed nor satisfactory actions were taken by the countries except countries like India which are facing the ugly face of terrorism. In the wake of September 11, 2001 terrorist attack in the United States, the United Nations Security Council adopted a resolution, which, among its provisions, obliges all states to criminalize assistance to terrorist activities, deny financial support and safe heaven to terrorists and share information about groups planning terrorist attacks.

India became a signatory to the International Convention for the Suppression of Acts of Nuclear Terrorism at the United Nations headquarters in New York on July 24, 2006. The Convention was adopted by the UN General Assembly on April 13, 2005. As per the Convention, states are required to make punishable as serious offences under their domestic law, terrorists acts involving the use of nuclear materials. The Convention enjoys upon the signatory states to cooperate in prevention, investigation and prosecution of these offences through the sharing of critical information regarding disruptive activities, extradition and mutual legal assistance.

Carnage in the name of religion will remain a threat as long as terrorists have access to the infrastructure needed to assemble large scale operations. If follows that security services should look not so much at the intention of individuals to execute violent acts as at the capabilities available to them. The terrorist threat is alive and kicking even with greatly increased security levels across the globe.

DEMONETISATION OF INDIAN CURRENCY

In a historical move that will add record strength in the fight against corruption, black money, money laundering, terrorism and financing of terrorists as well as counterfeit notes, the Government of India has decided that the erstwhile 500 and 1000 rupee notes will no longer be legal tender from midnight, 8 November, 2016. Prime Minister Narendra Modi made these important announcements during a televised address to the nation on the evening of 8 November 2016. He said that these decisions will fully protect the interests of honest and hard-working citizens of India and that those five hundred and one thousand rupee notes hoarded by anti-national and anti-social elements will become worthless pieces of paper.

Though the unprecedented financial measure may have come as a rude shock to many, Narendra Modi also gave enough opportunities and threw enough hints in this regard. However, he waited for the festival season of Dussehra and Diwali to get over. The first such initiative came when the Narendra Modi Government, in its very first Cabinet meeting, constituted a Supreme Court-monitored Special Investigation Team (SIT) on Black Money.

This was followed by the launch of the Pradhan Mantri Jan Dhan Yojana (PMJDY) on August 28, 2014. Prime Minister Narendra Modi took personal interest in the scheme. He made it a mission to ensure that the scheme was successful. The scheme would be of immense help in the present circumstances. Now, that ₹ 500 and ₹ 1000 currency denomination notes have been banned, transactions from banks will acquire importance. Opening of accounts even in the remote areas will help the rural villagers. They will not feel the pinch of demonetisation of the currency notes.

Had the bank accounts not been opened, the people would have faced immense problems. But not now, at least for those who have bank accounts. Roughly, 25.45 crore accounts have been opened and ₹ 45,302.48 crore has been deposited in these accounts.

A total of 4.30 crore accounts have been opened in the Regional Rural Banks with 3.70 crore in the rural areas and 0.60 crore in the urban areas. As far as the private banks are concerned, a total of 0.86 crore banks have been opened 0.53 crore in the rural areas and 0.34 crore accounts in the urban areas. Hence, a whopping 15.62 crore accounts have been opened in the rural areas and 9.83 crore accounts have been opened in the urban areas.

The government renegotiated the Double Tax Avoidance Agreement (DTAA) with Mauritius to impose Capital Gains Tax if such Capital Asset is situated in India. The Narendra Modi Government also negotiated an Automatic Information Exchange Agreement with Switzerland. Agreements are also being negotiated with other tax havens. From 2017, Organisation of Economic Cooperation and Development (OECD) countries have agreed to share information on foreign account holders with their home countries.

The scheme was launched to bring back black money stashed in foreign countries and tax havens. The scheme ended on 30 September, 2015. The Act also had various stringent provisions for penalty and prosecution of foreign black money holders unearthed during future investigation by the tax department.

The Income Declaration Scheme (IDS) which opened on June 1, 2016 gave a chance to black money holders to come clean by declaring the assets by September 30 and paying tax and penalty of 45 per cent on it. The Narendra Modi Government wanted to capture the entire parallel economy flowing in the system of ₹ 7 lakh crore in India. The government was upset with the output of IDS scheme. Though the Income Tax department had identified 90 lakh high value transactions without PAN, the final disclosure of black money was to the tune of ₹ 65,250 crore.

The Narendra Modi Government imposed a penalty of 20 per cent on all cash transactions exceeding ₹ 20,000 to purchase or sell a property (real estate). This was aimed at curbing the role of black money in real estate transactions. Another important step to check high value cash transactions and create an audit trail was to impose Tax Collection at Source at a nominal rate of 1 per cent on cash purchases exceeding ₹ 2 lakh.

The Parliament passed the Benami Transactions (Prohibition) Amendment Act, 2016 (BTP Amendment Act) in August. It came into force from November 1, 2016. The new law seeks to give more teeth to the authorities to curb benami transactions. The notification issued by the Income Tax department, stated that after coming into effect, the BTP Amendment Act, the existing Benami Transactions (Prohibition) Act, 1988, shall be renamed as Prohibition of Benami Property Transactions Act, 1988 (PBPT Act).

Narendra Modi is the second Indian Prime Minister to demonetise high-value rupee notes in independent India. But he will be the first to introduce the ₹ 2,000 note. In 1978, the then Prime Minister Morarji Desai had banned all currency notes above ₹ 100. In both instances, it was the menace of black money that had compelled the government to scrap the existing high-value currency notes.

The Prime Minister has time and again said that the Government is committed to ensure that the menace of black money is overcome.

Purple Patches of Indian Currency:

- The highest currency note ever printed by the RBI was a ₹ 10,000 note during the British Raj. It was printed first in 1938 and a new version came in 1954. These notes were demonetised in January 1946 and again in January 1978.
- When Morarji Desai came to power, banknotes of ₹ 1,000, ₹ 5,000 and ₹ 10,000 were in circulation. But Morarji Desai, who also held the finance portfolio, demonetised all these notes in January, 1978.
- During the Atal Behari Vajpayee era, the ₹ 1,000 note made a comeback. In November 2000, these notes were re-introduced on the ground that it would be easier for business transactions. The ₹ 500 notes had already returned into circulation in October 1987. The move was then justified as an attempt to contain the volume of banknotes in circulation due to inflation.

- Bank notes with the Ashoka Pillar watermark series in ₹ 10 denomination were issued between 1967 and 1992, ₹ 20 in 1972 and 1975, ₹ 50 in 1975 and 1981 and ₹ 100 between 1967-1979.
- The banknotes issued during this period contained the symbols representing science and technology, progress and orientation to Indian art forms.
- In the year 1980, the legend Satyameva Jayate was incorporated under the national emblem for the first time.
- In October 1987, the ₹ 500 banknote was introduced with the portrait of Mahatma Gandhi and Ashoka Pillar watermark. The Mahatma Gandhi banknote series-1996 were issued in the denominations of ₹ 10, ₹ 100 (June 1996), ₹ 50 (March 1997), ₹ 500 (October, 1997), ₹ 1,000 (November, 2000), ₹ 20 (August 2001), and ₹ 5 (introduced in November 2001).
- The Mahatma Gandhi Series-2005 bank notes were issued in the denomination of ₹ 10, ₹ 20, ₹ 50, ₹ 100, ₹ 500 and ₹ 1,000 and contained some additional/new security features as compared to the 1996 series.
- The ₹ 50 and ₹ 100 banknotes were issued in August 2005, followed by ₹ 500 and ₹ 1,000 denominations in October 2005 and ₹ 10 and ₹ 20 in April 2006 and August 2006, respectively.

GOODS AND SERVICES TAX

The One Hundred and First Amendment of the Constitution of India, officially known as The Constitution (One Hundred and First Amendment) Act, 2016, introduced a national Goods and Services Tax in India from 1 April, 2017.

The GST is a Value added Tax (VAT) and is proposed to be a comprehensive indirect tax levy on manufacture, sale and consumption of goods as well as services at the national level. It will replace all indirect taxes levied on goods and services by the Indian Central and State governments. It is aimed at being comprehensive for most goods and services.

An empowered committee was set up by the Atal Behari Vajpayee administration in 2000 to streamline the GST model to be adopted and to develop the required back-end infrastructure that would be needed for its implementation.

In his budget speech on 28 February 2006, P. Chidambaram, the then Finance Minister, announced the target date for implementation of GST to be 1 April 2010 and formed another empowered committee of State Finance Ministers to design the roadmap. The committee submitted its report to the government in April 2008 and released its First Discussion Paper on GST in India in 2009. Since the proposal involved reform/restructuring of not only indirect taxes levied by the Center but also the States, the responsibility of preparing a Design and Road Map for the implementation of GST was assigned to the Empowered Committee of State Finance Ministers (EC). In April, 2008, the EC submitted a report, titled "A Model and Road map for Goods and Services Tax (GST) in India" containing broad recommendations about the structure and design of GST. In response to the report, the

Department of Revenue made some suggestions to be incorporated in the design and structure of proposed GST bill. Based on inputs from GoI and States, The EC released its First Discussion Paper on Goods and Services Tax in India on the 10th of November, 2009 with the objective of generating a debate and obtaining inputs from all stakeholders.

A dual GST module for the country has been proposed by the EC. This dual GST model has been accepted by centre. Under this model GST have two components viz. the Central GST to be levied and collected by the centre and the state GST to be leived and collected by the respective States. Central Excise duty, additional excise duty, Service Tax, and additional duty of customs (equivalent to excise), State VAT, entertainment tax, taxes on lotteries, betting and gambling and entry tax (not levied by local bodies) would be subsumed within GST. Other taxes which will be subsumed with GST are Octroi, entry tax and luxury tax thus making it a single indirect tax in India.

In order to take the GST related work further, a Joint Working Group consisting of officers from Central as well as State Government was constituted. This was further trifurcated into three Sub-Working Groups to work separately on draft legislations required for GST, process/forms to be followed in GST regime and IT infrastructure development needed for smooth functioning of proposed GST. In addition, an Empowered Group for development of IT Systems required for Goods and Services Tax regime has been set up under the chairmanship of Dr. Nandan Nilekani.

GST Council Fix Taxes 4 Slabs from 5-28%

The GST council decided on a four-tier structure of 5, 12, 18 and 28 per cent for the Goods & Services Tax (GST) regime scheduled for roll-out next April. The tax rates would range from 5 to 28 per cent, with 12 per cent and 18 per cent as standard rates, steeper than the rates of 6, 12, 18 and 26 per cent earlier proposed by the government. The lower rates would apply on essential items and the highest on luxury and de-merit goods, which would also attract a cess. The fifth rate for gold and precious metals, which was earlier proposed at 4%, will be decided later.

HEART OF ASIA SUMMIT – 2016

The Heart of Asia - Istanbul Process was established to provide a platform to discuss regional issues, particularly encouraging security, political, and economic cooperation among Afghanistan and its neighbors. This region-led dialogue was launched in November 2011 to expand practical coordination between Afghanistan and its neighbors and regional partners in facing common threats, including counterterrorism, counternarcotics, poverty, and extremism. The United States and over 20 other nations and organizations serve as "supporting nations" to the process.

6th Ministerial Conference of Heart of Asia summit was held in Amritsar, India, from December 3 to December 4, 2016. The meeting was inaugurated by president of Afghanistan, Ashraf Ghani and Prime Minister of India, Narendra Modi, and co-chaired by Arun Jaitley, Finance Minister of India and Salahuddin Rabbani, minister of Foreign Affairs of Afghanistan.

Terrorism remained one of the important topics discussed at the Sixth Ministerial Conference of Heart of Asia in Amritsar.

The participating and supporting countries and their ministers signed a joint declaration stating the need to work to combat terrorism in Afghanistan and the region and to improve connectivity to it.

The declaration also sought for peaceful means to achieve its goal including bring an end to any kind of support and shelter to terrorism, and to create a fund to find forces of terror in the region.

Amritsar Declaration: Highlights

- Terrorism, particularly, state-sponsored terrorism was identified as a key challenge and members agreed upon a concerted effort to dismantle all kinds of terrorism. The regional meet unanimously named Terrorist groups in Pakistan and asked for action. The Express Tribune, a Pakistani English daily quoted Afghan president's statement "Taliban insurgency would not survive a month if it lost its sanctuary in neighboring Pakistan". The next day, Indian English daily Hindustan Times wrote an editorial saying "Ghani's criticism of Pakistan affirms India's portrayal of Islamabad".

- Members reiterated their belief in principles of sovereignty, independence, territorial integrity, sovereign equality of nations as enshrined in the United Nations Charter.
- Members expressed their commitment to the Universal Declaration of Human Rights.
- Members called up for leveraging the cultural heritage of the region to drive economic and social development.
- Members consented on eliminating non-tariff barriers to trade.

Side Developments

- India asserted financial aid to the tune of $1 billion to Afghanistan to improve infrastructure and fuel the socio-economic agendas of the later.
- India and Afghanistan also went for a bilateral meeting and a roadmap for air corridor was agreed upon, which is likely boost trade between the two countries. Afghanistan depends on the Pakistani port of Karachi for its foreign trade. It is allowed to send a limited amount of goods over land through Pakistan into India, but imports from India are not allowed along this route.

7th Ministerial Conference

The 7th Ministerial Conference will be held in Azerbaijan in the year 2017. Azerbaijan will be co-chairing the process.

G-20 SUMMIT-2016

The 2016 G20 Hangzhou summit was the eleventh meeting of the Group of Twenty (G20). It was held on 4–5 September 2016 in the city of Hangzhou. It was the first ever G20 summit to be hosted in China and the second Asian country after 2010 G20 Seoul summit was hosted in South Korea.

It is noted that Barack Obama and Xi Jinping announced the ratification of the Paris Agreement of the 2015 United Nations Climate Change Conference by their countries. After they did it, it is 26 countries which have ratified the agreement so far; the United States and China represent respectively 18 per cent and 20 per cent of global carbon dioxide emissions.

G20 is a forum for international economic cooperation amongst 20 major developed and developing economies of the world. It was founded in 1999, as a forum for finance ministers and central bank governors who met once a year, to discuss international economic issues. The global economic crisis in 2008 evolved the G20 into the premier Leaders' Forum for international economic cooperation.

Hence, the G20 was formally launched in 2008 in the USA. The G20 includes 19 individual countries, i.e. Argentina, Australia, Brazil, Canada, China, France, Germany, India, Indonesia, Italy, Japan, South Korea, Mexico, Russia, Saudi Arabia, South Africa, Turkey, the UK and the USA and the European Union (EU).

Collectively, the G20 economies account for around 85 per cent of the GDP, 80 per cent of world trade and two-thirds of the world population.

Annual meetings of finance ministers and central bank governors continue to take place, advancing the work of the G20 and contributing to the discussions at leaders' summits.

G20 Members Commit to Early Ratification of Paris Climate Deal

- The G20 members agreed to complete their domestic legal formalities for the ratification of Paris climate deal as soon as their "national procedures allow", a move which would provide more time to India to work out its own strategy keeping up with its developmental goals.
- The G20 communique, released in French before it was released in English, committed the nations to ratifying the Paris climate agreement. Leaders expect a rapid implementation of the agreement in all its dimensions.
- The push to bring the agreement into force this year was supercharged last weekend when the world's two biggest polluters, China and the US, formalised their acceptance together.
- That brought the number of countries joining the treaty to 26 accounting for 39.07% of global emissions. The triggers for the pact to become law are 55 countries and 55%.
- It is noted that India came under pressure to ratify the deal after China and the US—responsible for around 40 per cent of the world's carbon emissions—ratified the agreement ahead of the G20 summit and handed over their countries' instruments of joining the agreement to UN Secretary-General Ban Ki-moon.

PM Modi at G20 Summit : One Nation in South Asia Spreading Terrorism

- With a clear reference to Pakistan but without naming it, Prime Minister Narendra Modi told G20 leaders that "one single nation" in South Asia was spreading terror in the region, and that the international community should isolate those who sponsor and support terrorism instead of rewarding them.
- The PM urged the global community to speak and act together and urgently to fight terrorism and those who sponsor and support terrorism must be isolated and sanctioned, not rewarded.

- The Prime Minister's hard-hitting remarks extended his observations during the informal meeting of the Brazil-Russia-India-China-South Africa (BRICS) on the sidelines of the G-20. During that meeting, he had highlighted that terror groups "in South Asia and for that matter anywhere do not own banks and factories". "Clearly someone funds and arms them and the BRICS must intensify its joint efforts not only to fight terror, but to coordinate actions to isolate those who are supporters and sponsors of terror."
- The statements also form part of a larger effort on India's part to press the global community to move towards adopting a clear stand on terrorism. The lack of a globally-accepted legal definition of terrorism has often been faulted for double standards and inefficacy in dealing with terrorism and terror organizations and networks.

Highlights of the G-20 Summit-2016
- G-20 leaders have pledged to continue to work for a globally fair and modern international tax system, foster growth and refrain from competitive devaluation of currencies.
- They will continue the work on addressing cross-border financial flows derived from illicit activities, including deliberate trade mis-invoicing, which hampers the mobilisation of domestic resources for development.
- They vowed to go ahead on the ongoing co-operation on Base Erosion and Profit Shifting (BEPS), exchange of tax information, tax capacity-building of developing countries and tax policies to promote growth and tax certainty.
- They also vowed to use all policy tools to achieve the goal of strong, sustainable, balanced and inclusive growth.
- They agreed at the summit that refugees are a global issue and the burden must be shared. They called for strengthening humanitarian assistance for refugees.
- The 2017 G20 summit will be held in Hamburg, Germany from 7-8 July 2017.

The G-20 comprising of world's group of developed and developing countries represents over 85% of the world's economy and two-thirds of global population.

G-20 Finance Ministers Pledge to Boost Global Economy

The Finance Ministers from the Group of 20 (G-20) major economies have pledged to boost the global economy, which is showing a weak recovery. This announcement was made at the end of the two-day meeting of G-20 Finance ministers and Central Bank Governors meeting held in the Chinese city of Chengdu in July 2016.

Highlights of Meeting

- G-20 Finance ministers expressed concern about Britain's plan to leave the European Union and how Brexit will affect the world's economy.
- Member nations are well positioned proactively to address the potential economic and financial consequences from such developments.
- They vowed to reject trade protectionism, which became a prominent issue at the meeting.
- They expressed the importance of reducing the excess production of steel that has led to a glut on the global market.

India to Chair G20 in 2018

India is going to chair Group of Twenty (G20) nations forum in year 2018 and New Delhi could be the host of the prestigious annual G20 summit. This decision was taken by G20 forum earlier in September 2015 which was chaired by Turkey. Turkey handed over the Chair in the year 2016 to China and in 2017 Germany is going to chair it.

NUCLEAR SECURITY SUMMIT-2016

The Nuclear Security Summit (NSS) is a world summit, aimed at preventing nuclear terrorism around the globe. The Fourth Nuclear Summit was held in Washington D.C. on March 31 to April 1, 2016. Leaders including then British Prime Minister David Cameron, Canadian Prime Minister Justin Trudeau, French President François Hollande, Italian Prime Minister Matteo Renzi, Argentine President Mauricio Macri, Mexican President Enrique Peña Nieto, Chinese President Xi Jinping, Kazakhstan's President Nursultan Nazarbayev, Japanese Prime Minister Shinzo Abe, South Korean President Park Geun-hye and Indian Prime Minister Narendra Modi attended the Summit.

The first summit was held in Washington, D.C., United States, on April 12-13, 2010. The second summit was held in Seoul, South Korea, in 2012. The third summit was held in The Hague, Netherlands, on March 24-25, 2014.

The threat of nuclear and radiological terrorism remains one of the greatest challenges to international security, and the threat is constantly evolving. The leaders, gathered in Washington, D.C. on the first day of April, 2016 on the occasion of the fourth Nuclear Security Summit, observed that the Summits have since 2010 raised awareness of this threat and driven many tangible, meaningful and lasting improvements in nuclear security. The Summits have also strengthened the nuclear security architecture at national, regional and global levels, including through broadened ratification and implementation of international legal instruments regarding nuclear security. They underline the importance of the Convention on Physical Protection of Nuclear Material and its 2005 Amendment and the International Convention on the Suppression of Acts of Nuclear Terrorism and will continue to work toward their universalization and full implementation. They welcome the imminent entry into force of the 2005 Amendment to the Convention on Physical Protection of Nuclear Material and Facilities and encourage further ratifications.

The global leaders at the summit reaffirm their commitment to their shared goals of nuclear disarmament, nuclear non-proliferation and peaceful use of nuclear energy. They also reaffirm that measures to strengthen nuclear security will not hamper the rights of States to develop and use nuclear energy for peaceful purposes. They reaffirm the fundamental responsibility of States, in accordance with their respective obligations, to maintain at all times effective security of all nuclear and other radioactive material, including nuclear materials used in nuclear weapons, and nuclear facilities under their control.

More work remains to be done to prevent non-state actors from obtaining nuclear and other radioactive materials, which could be used for malicious purposes. They commit to fostering a peaceful and stable international environment by reducing the threat of nuclear terrorism and strengthening nuclear security.

Sustaining security improvements requires constant vigilance at all levels, and they pledge that their countries will continue to make nuclear security an enduring priority. They, as leaders, are conscious of their responsibility. Actions taken today can prevent tomorrow's nuclear security incidents. Where they choose to take such steps visibly, in light of national conditions and while protecting sensitive information, they contribute to strengthening and building confidence in the effectiveness of our national nuclear security regimes.

Countering nuclear and radiological terrorism demands international cooperation, including sharing of information in accordance with States' national laws and procedures, International cooperation can contribute to a more inclusive, coordinated, sustainable, and robust global nuclear security architecture for the common benefit and security of all.

They reaffirm the essential responsibility and the central role of the International Atomic Energy Agency in strengthening the global nuclear security architecture and in developing international guidance, and its leading role in facilitating and coordinating nuclear security activities among international organizations and initiatives and supporting the efforts of States to fulfill their nuclear security responsibilities. They, welcome and support the Agency in convening regular high-level international conferences, such as the December 2016 international conference on nuclear security including its Ministerial segment, to maintain political momentum and continue to raise awareness of nuclear security among all stakeholders.

They seek to maintain the international network of officials and government experts who have supported the Summit process and to incorporate the broader community of States, as well as encourage the continued engagement of relevant partners in nuclear industry and civil society.

In their continued collective determination to ensure political momentum and to continuously strengthen nuclear security at national, regional, and global levels, they resolve to implement the attached Action Plans, in support of the international organizations and initiatives to which they respectively belong (the United Nations, the International Atomic Energy Agency, Interpol, the Global Initiative to Combat Nuclear Terrorism, and the Global Partnership Against the Spread of Weapons and Materials of Mass Destruction), to be carried out on a voluntary basis and consistent with national laws and respective international obligations. These plans reflect the political will of participating States.

They concluded, "The 2016 Summit marks the end of the Nuclear Security Summit process in this format. We affirm that the Communiqués from the 2010, 2012 and 2014 Summits and the Work Plan of the 2010 Summit will continue to guide our efforts as we endeavor to fully implement them."

SAARC SUMMIT

A two-day 18th Summit of SAARC was held at Kathmandu, Nepal on November 26-27, 2014. The 8-nation bloc was represented by their respective heads. Prime Minister Narendra Modi represented India in this summit. While addressing the summit PM Modi promised India's willingness to take a lead in increasing connectivity and trade among the countries of the region.

Articulating his SAARC vision, the Prime Minister said: Ours is a region of thriving democracy; of rich inheritance; the unmatched strength of the youth; and a strong thirst for change and progress. He recalled endless pain of the lost lives in the 26/11 Mumbai terror attack on the day in 2008 and urged the need to work together to fulfil the pledge taken to combat terrorism and trans-national crimes. He added India wanted to set up a Special Purpose Facility to finance infrastructure projects in the region and promised to ensure that the facilities at the border would speed up trade. He also announced that India would give a business visa for three to five years for SAARC suggesting SAARC Business Traveller Card by all member-states. In health, medical visa would be issued for a patient and an attendant to travel to India.

SAARC countries resolved to build an economic federation in 15 years. Pakistan decided to clear the energy pact, which facilitates trade of electricity among all SAARC nations. The Kathmandu summit was to witness three agreements—on road connectivity, railways and a framework for energy cooperation.

Foreign Ministers of the eight member states signed an agreement on energy cooperation namely 'SAARC Framework Agreement for Energy Cooperation (Electricity)' in the presence of their heads of state and government during the concluding ceremony of the 18th SAARC Summit on 27 November. Although Pakistan stalled, citing insufficient internal preparations, signing of two other agreements on Vehicular Traffic and Railways respectively. Pakistan successfully blocked all efforts to promote road and rail connectivity across South Asia because it intends to deny India access to the markets of Afghanistan and Central Asia.

Pakistan was compelled not to render the Kathmandu Summit a disastrous failure. It reluctantly agreed at the last minute to promote electrical connectivity. Nepalese Prime Minister Sushil Koirala, current SAARC Chair, expressed his hope that the 'Regulation of Passenger and Cargo Vehicular Traffic amongst SAARC Member States', and 'SAARC Regional Agreement on Railways' would be signed later after the Transport Ministers of these countries reviewed them. It was also decided that Pakistan will host the next summit in 2016.

China, which holds an observer status in the group, was represented by Vice Foreign Minister Liu Zhenmin, seen actively promoting a more active role for itself in the region including infrastructure funding through its proposed 'Asian Infrastructure Investment Bank' (AIIB) and extending its ambitious Maritime Silk Road project to South Asian nations. Pakistan, China's all weather friend, also vouched for a more participatory role for the observer nations in the summit process, indirectly advocating for a more Chinese involvement. Although no such proposal was accepted because of India's reservation.

History

The South Asian Association for Regional Cooperation (SAARC) is an economic and geopolitical organisation of eight countries that are primarily located in South Asia. The SAARC Secretariat is based in Kathmandu, Nepal. The combined economy of SAARC is 3rd largest in the world in the terms of GDP(PPP) after the United States and China and 8th largest in the terms of nominal GDP.

SAARC nations comprise 3% of the world's area and in contrast having 21% (around 1.7 billion) of the world's total population. India makes up over 70% of the area and population among these eight nations. All non-Indian member states except Afghanistan share borders with India but only two other members, Pakistan and Afghanistan, have a border with each other.

During 2005-10, the average GDP growth rate of SAARC stood at an impressive 8.8% p.a., But it slowed to 6.5% in 2011 largely because of slowdown in India which accounts for nearly 80% of SAARC's economy.

The idea of regional political and economical cooperation in South Asia was first raised in 1980 and the first summit was held in Dhaka on 8 December 1985, when the organisation was established by the governments of Bangladesh, Bhutan, India, Maldives, Nepal, Pakistan, and Sri Lanka. Since then the organisation has expanded by accepting one new full member, Afghanistan, and several observer members.

The SAARC policies aim to promote welfare economics, collective self-reliance among the countries of South Asia, and to accelerate socio-cultural development in the region. The SAARC has developed external relations by establishing permanent diplomatic relations with the EU, the UN (as an observer), and other multilateral entities.

The SAARC Declaration

The 18th Summit of the SAARC concluded on November 27, 2014 with issuing a 36-point declaration of the future actions to be performed either independently or jointly by the member countries. The member states signed an energy exchange deal aimed at boosting up energy generation and consumption in the region that has enormous potentials for the same.

The Summit adopted the Kathmandu Declaration with the theme of 'Deeper Integration Peace and Prosperity' to deepen cooperation in core areas of trade, investment, finance, energy, infrastructure and connectivity. The Summit decided to accelerate the process of creating free trade in the region and formulation and implementation of projects, programmes and activities of SAARC in a prioritised, focussed and result-oriented manner.

The leaders also agreed to utilise youth power for socio-economic development, especially through creation of employment opportunities at home and building collective positions for their security and welfare while on employment outside the region. The declaration called for combating terrorism in all its forms and manifestations and having effective cooperation among the member states for preventing the trafficking of people arms and drugs and exploitation of children for forced labour.

Increasing agricultural productivity and ensuring food and nutritional security is also the part of the Kathmandu Declaration. Providing quality education, eliminating illiteracy, providing vocational education and training and making South Asia an attractive common tourist destination by promoting public-private partnership, are also mentioned in the declaration. The leaders agreed to hold henceforth the SAARC Summit meetings every two years, or earlier if necessary.

The 19th SAARC Summit was originaly scheduled to be held in Islamabad, Pakistan on November 15-16, 2016. The summit was to be attended by the leaders of the eight SAARC member states and representatives of observers and guest states. But following the rising diplomatic tensions after the Uri terrorist attack, India announced its boycott of the 19th SAARC Summit alleging Pakistan's involvement in the same. Later, Bangladesh, Afghanistan, Bhutan and Sri Lanka also pulled out of the summit culminating in an indefinite postponement of the summit.

GREEN FINANCE

The term green finance has gained a lot of attention in the past few years with the increased focus on green development. The Rio+20 document clearly states what green economy policies should result in and what they should not. While there is no universal definition of green finance, it mostly refers to financial investments flowing towards sustainable development projects and initiatives that encourage the development of a more sustainable economy. Green finance includes different elements like greening the banking system, the bond market and institutional investment. Several working definitions and sets of criteria of green finance have also been developed. Examples include the China's Green Credit Guidelines, the Climate Bonds Taxonomy of Green Bonds, the International Development Finance Club's (IDFC) approach to reporting on green investment, the World Bank/International Finance Corporation's (IFC) Sustainability Framework and the UK Green Investment Bank Policies. An initial review of the current definitions in use reveals sizeable intersections of the various definitions in thematic areas such as clean energy, energy efficiency, green buildings, sustainable transport, water and waste management, as well as areas of controversy such as nuclear and large-scale hydro energy, biofuels and efficiency gains in conventional power.

Over the past decade there have been advances in mainstreaming of green finance within financial institutions and financial markets. Voluntary standards such as the Equator Principles have enhanced environmental risk management for many financial institutions. The World Bank Group has set up an informal "Sustainable Banking Network" of banking regulators, led by developing countries, to promote sustainable lending practices. In 2015, green bonds issued by governments, banks, corporates and individual projects amounted to US$42 billion. Globally, more than

20 stock exchanges have issued guidelines on environmental disclosure, and many green indices and green ETFs (exchange-traded funds) have been developed. The Financial Stability Board (FSB) has established a climate-related financial disclosures task force that is expected to complete its first stage of the work by end-March 2016. A growing number of institutions, including the Bank of England and Bank of China (Industrial and Commercial Bank of China), have begun to assess the financial impact of climate and environmental policy changes. Germany, the US and the UK have developed interest subsidy and guarantee programmes for green financing, and over a dozen government-backed green investment banks are operating globally. The G-20 has also recently set up a green finance study group (GFSG).

One topical issue in the context of green finance is that of enhancing the ability of the financial system to mobilize private green finance, thereby facilitating the green transformation of the global economy which has been widely discussed in different fora including the G20. However, for developing countries like India, private finance will not readily be forthcoming and public finance both international and domestic needs to be used to leverage private finance.

Green development is also important for India though green finance is yet to pick up. Attaining the ambitious solar energy target, development of solar cities, setting up wind power projects, developing smart cities, providing infrastructure which is considered as a green activity and the sanitation drive under the 'Clean India' or 'Swachch Bharat Abhiyan' are all activities needing green finance. India has created a corpus called the National Clean Energy Fund (NCEF) in 2010-11 out of the cess on coal produced/imported ('polluter pays' principle) for the purpose of financing and promoting clean energy initiatives and funding research in the area of clean energy. Some of the projects financed by this fund include innovative schemes like a green energy corridor for boosting the transmission sector, the Jawaharlal Nehru National Solar Mission's (JNNSM) installation of solar photovoltaic (SPV) lights and small capacity lights, installation of SPV water pumping systems, SPV power plants, grid-connected rooftop SPV power plants and a pilot project to assess wind power potential.

So far four banks have issued green bonds in India. Proceeds from these bonds are mostly used for funding renewable energy projects such as solar, wind and biomass projects and other infrastructure sectors, with infrastructure and energy efficiency being considered as green in their entirety. The Securities and Exchange Board of India (SEBI) has also recently approved the guidelines for green bonds.

While mobilization and effective use of green finance is of primary importance, there are some issues which need to be taken note of.

- For a developing country like India, poverty alleviation and development are of vital importance and resources should not be diverted from meeting these development needs. Green finance should not be limited only to investment in renewable energy, as, for a country like India, coal based power accounts for around 60 per cent of installed capacity. Emphasis should be on greening coal technology. In fact, green finance for development and transfer of green technology is important as most green technologies in developed countries are in the private domain and are subject to intellectual property rights (IPR), making them cost prohibitive.
- Green bonds are perceived as new and attach higher risk and their tenure is also shorter. There is a need to reduce risks to make them investment grade.
- There is also a need for an internationally agreed upon definition of green financing as its absence could lead to over-accounting.
- While environmental risk assessment is important, banks should not overestimate risks while providing green finance.
- Green finance should also consider unsustainable patterns of consumption as a parameter in deciding finance, particularly conspicuous consumption and unsustainable lifestyles in developed countries.

DIGITAL INDIA PROGRAMME

Right from the day of assuming power, Digital India and Make in India have been two big USPs of Prime Minister Narendra Modi. The first steps were taken with the launch of MyGov.in portal. Prior to this Narendra Modi launched his mobile app to connect further with the netizens.

Over the last one year, several initiatives have been taken for introduction of Information Technology to empower people in areas relating to health, education, labour and employment, commerce etc. Digital India Week has been launched with an aim to impart knowledge to people and to empower themselves through the Digital India Programme of Government of India.

The Programme Structure

Digital India comprises of various initiatives under the single programme each targeted to prepare India for becoming a knowledge economy and for bringing good governance to citizens through synchronized and co-ordinated engagement of the entire Government.

This programme has been envisaged and coordinated by the Department of Electronics and Information Technology (DeitY) in collaboration with various Central Ministries/Departments and State Governments. The Prime Minister as the Chairman of Monitoring Committee on Digital India, activities under the Digital India initiative is being carefully monitored. All the existing and ongoing e-Governance initiatives have been revamped to align them with the principles of Digital India.

Vision of Digital India

The vision of Digital India programme aims at inclusive growth in areas of electronic services, products, manufacturing and job opportunities etc. It is centred on three key areas:
- Digital Infrastructure as a Utility to Every Citizen
- Governance & Services on Demand, and
- Digital Empowerment of Citizens

With the above vision, the Digital India programme aims to provide Broadband Highways, Universal Access to Mobile Connectivity, Public Internet Access Programme, E-Governance: Reforming Government through Technology, eKranti - Electronic Delivery of Services, Information for All, Electronics Manufacturing: Target Net Zero Imports, IT for Jobs and Early Harvest Programmes.

Key Projects of Digital India Programme

Several projects/products have already launched or ready to be launched as indicated below:

1. **Digital Locker System** aims to minimize the usage of physical documents and enable sharing of e-documents across agencies. The sharing of the e-documents will be done through registered repositories thereby ensuring the authenticity of the documents online.

2. **MyGov.in** has been implemented as a platform for citizen engagement in governance, through a "Discuss", "Do" and "Disseminate" approach. The mobile App for MyGov would bring these features to users on a mobile phone.

3. **Swachh Bharat Mission (SBM) Mobile app** would be used by people and Government organizations for achieving the goals of Swachh Bharat Mission.

4. **eSign Framework** would allow citizens to digitally sign a document online using Aadhaar authentication.

5. **The Online Registration System (ORS)** under the eHospital application has been introduced. This application provides important services such as online registration, payment of fees and appointment, online diagnostic reports, enquiring availability of blood online etc.
6. **National Scholarships Portal** is a one stop solution for end to end scholarship process right from submission of student application, verification, sanction and disbursal to end beneficiary for all the scholarships provided by the Government of India.
7. DeitY has undertaken an initiative namely **Digitize India Platform (DIP)** for large scale digitization of records in the country that would facilitate efficient delivery of services to the citizens.
8. The Government of India has undertaken an initiative namely **Bharat Net**, a high speed digital highway to connect all 2.5 lakh Gram Panchayats of country. This would be the world's largest rural broadband connectivity project using optical fibre.
9. BSNL has introduced **Next Generation Network (NGN)**, to replace 30 year old exchanges, which is an IP based technology to manage all types of services like voice, data, multimedia/ video and other types of packet switched communication services.

Policy Initiatives

Policy initiatives have also been undertaken (by DeitY) in the e- Governance domain like e-Kranti Framework, Policy on Adoption of Open Source Software for Government of India, Framework for Adoption of Open Source Software in e-Governance Systems, Policy on Open Application Programming Interfaces (APIs) for Government of India, E-mail Policy of Government of India, Policy on Use of IT Resources of Government of India, Policy on Collaborative Application Development by Opening the Source Code of Government Applications, Application Development & Re-Engineering Guidelines for Cloud Ready Applications

- BPO Policy has been approved to create BPO centres in different North Eastern states and also in smaller/mofussil towns of other states.

- Electronics Development Fund (EDF) Policy aims to promote Innovation, R&D, and Product Development and to create a resource pool of IP within the country to create a self-sustaining eco-system of Venture Funds.
- National Centre for Flexible Electronics (NCFlexE) is an initiative of Government of India to promote research and innovation in the emerging area of Flexible Electronics.
- Centre of Excellence on Internet on Things (IoT) is a joint initiative of Department of Electronics & Information Technology (DeitY), ERNET and NASSCOM.

Impact

The estimated impact of Digital India by 2019 would be cross-cutting, ranging from broadband connectivity in all Panchayats, Wi-fi in schools and universities and Public Wi-Fi hotspots. The programme will generate huge number of IT, Telecom and Electronics jobs, both directly and indirectly.

Success of this programme will make India Digitally empowered and the leader in usage of IT in delivery of services related to various domains such as health, education, agriculture, banking, etc.

INDIA AND THE NSG

Recently, India rejected China's contention that it must sign the NPT to get membership of the Nuclear Suppliers Group, saying France was included in the elite group without signing the Non-Proliferation Treaty.

What is NSG?

Nuclear Suppliers Group (NSG) is a multinational body concerned with reducing nuclear proliferation by controlling the export and re-transfer of materials that may be applicable to nuclear weapon development and by improving safeguards and protection on existing materials. Interestingly, the NSG was set up in 1974 as a reaction to India's nuclear tests to stop what it called the misuse of nuclear material meant for peaceful purposes. Currently, it has 48 members.

Background

India sought membership of the NSG in 2008, but its application hasn't been decided on, primarily because signing the NPT or other nuclear moratoriums on testing is a pre-requisite. However, India has received a special waiver to conduct nuclear trade with all nuclear exporters.

India, Pakistan, Israel and South Sudan are among the four UN member states which have not signed the NPT, the international pact aimed at preventing the spread of nuclear weapons.

Recent Controversy

China had opposed India's bid to get NSG membership on the ground that it was yet to sign the NPT. It had said all the multilateral non-proliferation export control regime including the NSG have regarded NPT as an important standard for the expansion of the NSG. And hence, members of the Nuclear Suppliers Group should be party to NPT.

How India Defends its Move?

It says, the NSG is an ad hoc export control regime and France, which was not an NPT member for some time, was a member of the NSG since it respected NSG's objectives. Also, the NPT allows civil nuclear cooperation with non-NPT countries.

Why India Should be Granted NSG Membership?

In this game of developing nuclear weapons India has not indulged in any dubious/clandestine activity and its programme has been developed solely by years of hard work indigenously. By this single act India has shown that developing a credible nuclear weapons programme through honest and civilian means is possible for any country having high-level scientific manpower and materials.

Besides, by declaring a voluntary moratorium on further underground nuclear tests India has effectively acted in sense and spirit of NPT/CTBT provisions. By steering its programme only as a minimum deterrence and pledging NFU unless faced with an attack of weapons of mass destruction (WMD), India has established itself as a responsible nuclear state.

Benefits associated with NSG membership:

- Timely information on nuclear matters
- Contributes by way of information
- Has confirmed credentials
- Can act as an instrument of harmonization and coordination
- Is part of a very transparent process.

NSG membership cannot be linked with NPT. But, it can be linked with International Atomic Energy Agency (IAEA). And India has closely cooperated with IAEA. Therefore, India's case should be judged independently without prejudice or on requests to block it following lobbying from other countries. In 2008, China was among the last few countries to lift its objection to clean waiver by NSG to India. During then American President Barack Obama's visit to India in January 2015, the US had announced that India was ready to join the NSG. This position was reiterated by the US recently.

- However, to build support in the NSG, which operates by consensus, India will need to take additional steps to demonstrate its commitment to nonproliferation. India's case is being pressed by the US and other influential countries based on the India's record in non-proliferation and the India-US civil nuclear accord.
- Also, India is actively eyeing membership of the MTCR, the Wassenaar Arrangement and the Australia group along with the NSG.

India's nuclear doctrine is non-proliferation-oriented and is both sensible and responsible. Having accepted IAEA safeguards and Additional Protocol and having effectively subscribed to and practised the principles of non-proliferation, it is immaterial if India has formally signed the NPT, CTBT or any other such treaty. India has already acquired high-level expertise in the peaceful use of nuclear energy in industry, power, agriculture and health care. India's membership of the NSG shall not only benefit it but also encourage civil nuclear trade globally without compromising on world peace and harmony.

JUDICIAL ACTIVISM—LIMITATIONS

Mr. Vijay: Before we start the discussion, let me put the term in proper perspective. The term "judicial activism" has begun to be used quite recently. With the executive weak and corrupt, the Supreme Court took it upon itself to put right several things on which there was no action. These ranged from directions to the Civic authorities for disposing garbage on Delhi roads to asking government to have its bungalows vacated from those who occupied it, even though they had long ceased to hold public office. But perhaps the most famous example of judicial activism was in the hawala case when the Court directed the CBI to complete an enquiry and report to it on the progress on a daily basis. It was felt that the Court was exceeding its jurisdiction after all, how many departments could the court control given the fact that few of them actually did the jobs they were supposed to do? Moreover, in certain cases the judges were passing wide, uncalled for remarks, which could well have been avoided. They were issuing summons to famous politicians for which there was no real need. It thus, started appearing that the judiciary was exceeding its limits. Thus the term *judicial activism* was born. Personally, I am not in favour of judiciary taking over day to day governance.

What is the Government then for? I would rather have it discharging the functions it is supposed to. The courts are for dispensing justice and certainly not for governance.

Ms Ruchi: We all are forgetting that we live in extraordinary circumstances where practically every leader is corrupt and his bureaucrat Secretary is a conduit for bribes. Even the names of a former Prime Minister and his son are appearing prominently in a number of scandals.

How can we trust them any more? In these circumstances, I don't think there is no any harm in overactivism by the judiciary. Extraordinary situations call for extraordinary solutions. I agree that the judges' comments are unnecessarily harsh and may have been unceremonious in the case of Rajan Pillai, but no amount of harshness is enough for a politician, who has betrayed public trust in order to amass wealth of his own. Perhaps the harsh comments and the summons issued by the judges will act as a warning to other politicians and prevent corruption. Corruption is afterall the most important issue that faces the country today. I support the judges and do not find it objectionable if they go overboard.

Ms Ritu: Your anger is justified but then how can you justify summons issued to the public figures on frivolous complaints? Issuing summons to the PM has already been mentioned. Surely a petition about his appointment can be heard without his being present. In criminals cases, yes, the person must be summoned, but certainly not in civil cases. Similarly people like Mr. KPS Gill are being called in cases where personal appearance is not necessary. I agree that summons may be issued by judges with an eye on publicity. But what is the future of this overactivism? The judges will be involved in activities like having the garbage cleaned and taking day to day decisions. We may be heading towards "judocracy". Where judges are assuming the role of rulers. Is this a desirable situation, especially when thousands of undertrials languish in jails and lakhs of cases are pending in courts all over India? Who will give them justice if the judges are busy with other things? We can say goodbye to justice and the courts will assume the status of the state secretariat. I am sure that we do not want such a situation. At the same time, I would not want that judges turn a blind eye to the evils of society. I would like to suggest that there should be judicial activism tempered by common sense. The judiciary has to work with the executive. Usurping the powers of the executive can be justified today, but what of the future? If the judiciary really starts interfering in all policy decisions, the future will be very grim. It might lead to loss of democracy. I, therefore, think that judicial activism is not a very good thing and it has serious repercussions on the future of the country.

Mr. Virendra: I agree with Vijay that the courts are for dispensing justice and that it is the government that should actually do its job. But what if the government does not do what it is supposed to? Who is going to look after the interests of the common man? Unfortunately, the situation today is that the executive is very weak. Practically every politician is corrupt and the rot has spread to the bureaucracy too. In such a situation, the common man finds that he is at the receiving end. In such a situation, the judiciary has come to the rescue. Frankly, I don't think that judicial activism or overactivism are proper terms at all. The judiciary is just doing what should be done by the people in the government. If they don't do what they are supposed to, someone else will take over by default.

Ms Seema: It is true that the executive has surrendered its powers to the judiciary out of its own weakness. But the objection is not courts taking action to help the common man but their going overboard in their judgments. For example, in the Rajan Pillai case the judge made some cruel, personal remarks against the industrialist and even denied medical aid leading to his death. Is this judicial activism? Then again, a judge of the Allahabad High Court issued summons to the Prime Minister to appear before it on a petition challenging his appointment. Surely, there was no need for the PM's personal appearance in this case. But it seems that the judges are enjoying the publicity that comes out of sensational cases. It is their going overboard that is termed as judicial activism and which is objectionable.

Mr Vijay: I think that the remarks of the judges, that we find objectionable, should not be taken at face value. What they reflect is the anger of the society against those whom it placed its trust on. Any person with even a little love for his country would have reacted in this way. I think the judges cannot be blamed. But I still feel that day to day governance should not be left to courts. They should maintain their distance and maintain their position in which they can judge the executive if something goes wrong. Now, if the CBI still does not take action in spite of the court making it responsible. Who can we turn to? In fact, the CBI is dragging it feet in the hawala case where only some selective chargesheets have been filed. Should we blame the Supreme Court for this inaction? It would have been better if the court maintained its distance and kept pressurising the government to take action in the case. The present situation suits no one else but the leaders who have been involved. So judicial activism is not the solution to all that plagues our society.

Mr Virendra: I agree with Ruchi that the situation has become extraordinary. It is amazing that the new CBI director should go to the former PM for *"guidance"*, knowing well that cases are pending against him. The court was right in reprimanding him. In a situation where the CBI is willing to be guided by the accused politicians. Which agency will see that the CBI merely does its job? It goes to the credit of the judiciary that they have taken it up. To a certain extent the judiciary is performing its constitutional role. When the government is weak, it gives up its constitutional obligations. We really cannot blame the judges if they take over.

Ms Ritu: While it may be accepted that the judiciary is doing a role that is necessary in the Indian condition. What is objectionable is the sweeping statements made by some of the judges in discharging their duties. Judicial activism does help the common man in the sense that government agencies start to show results. What the courts are ensuring is that they merely do their job. If judicial activism be curbed, then the elected representatives must be strong and do what they are supposed to do. Today, we are grateful that someone is taking interest in the affairs of the country. But for the judiciary we would have become a banana republic, where corrupt are never punished.

Ms Seema: I think we have reached a consensus that judicial activism is not a bad thing in the present circumstances. I am sure that the common man appreciates it too. But the judiciary must do an introspection about its future role. There is also a real danger that the courts may become all powerful. Moreover to whom will the judges be accountable? The problem of corruption within the courts cannot be ruled out. Some judges have already come under a cloud due to this. In cases involving celebrities, judges have to be careful that media attention does not influence what they say. Secondly, there must be some restraint in cases involving national leaders. There is no doubt that if corruption is the issue. They should be summoned and treated like any accused. But in frivolous complaints such as the one challenging election of the Prime Minister. There is no need to show undue heroism. The judges must be practical when such complaints are received. Finally, I would like to conclude by saying that judicial activism has served an important role now that we are seeing the collective depravity of the ruling class. But can it or should it continue? For that an introspection is required and leaders have to really live morally to avoid their powers being usurped by the courts. Is that too much to ask?

EXPERT COMMENTS

Mr. Vijay shows his knowledge about the issue. He has deep understanding and is capable of expressing it with diligence. He has a balanced approach as he is not bitter or a crimanious towards anyone.

—*He will be an asset to the organisation.*

Ms. Ruchi expresses her anguish and personal grievance. She does not express facts. She is bitter towards politicians and this shows that she does not have balanced approach towards the topic. This shows that she has a biased approach which is detrimental to an organisation.

Ms. Ritu shows good knowledge. She has a balanced approach as she doesn't castigate either the executive or the judiciary. She has a harmonious personality. She has a pragmatic approach towards the controversial issue. She understands her colleagues' sentiments.

—*She will be an asset to the organisation.*

Mr. Virendra is an informed speaker. He participates in the discussion with ease. He incorporates the ideas of his colleagues and harmonises them. He is a good listener as well. He remembers what his colleagues have spoken.

—*He will be an asset to the organisation.*

Ms. Seema comes up with a new idea. She is an informed speaker. She is aware of pros and cons of the topic. She harmonises between the executive and the judiciary. Thus, she shows a balanced psyche. She also takes up the task of bringing all the ideas to their logical denouement as she is able to conclude the consensus among the group members. She has a pragmatic approach.

—*She will be an asset to the organisation*

RESERVATION WILL LEAD TO NATIONAL DISASTER

Mr Ahlawat:—Morning friends, we are about to discuss the controversial topic of "Reservation", which has also been debated at the national level. In my opinion the concept of reservation spells doom for the nation. The moment we think or talk about reservation, we immediately bifurcate the society and this means that we create a partisan attitude, which can snowball into violence. The question arises "Why reservation ?" By creating quotas we are snatching away the rights of the other people and dividing the society on caste-lines. The government should definitely create an atmosphere where even the economically-weaker sections should have access to education, but then not at the expense of the people who really deserve. By doing so, a bad blood is created between those who get the privilege to reservation and those who are not privileged and in this way the government has to do with mediocre officials who ultimately prove to be a failure. Reservation is the infringement of the basic human rights and this is very much against the Constitution. Given the same academic qualification, everyone should be provided an equal field to compete where the best comes out with flying colours. Thank you.

Ms Kanappan:—Friends, in order to discuss this controversial topic, it is important to understand as to why reservation was created in the first place. After independence when we decided on a democratic constitution, we saw that those who have been downtrodden and under-privileged, over the centuries cannot really enjoy equality before law and equality of opportunities provided by the democratic set up due to their age-old handicaps. In other words, our Constitution makers realised that Scheduled Caste and Scheduled Tribe people will not be able to compete with their brothers on equal footing. The social and economic inequalities and ignorance would always work against them. Hence, reservation to the extent of their population ratio was provided in the Constitution for educational institutions and Government jobs. It was thought that with the spread of literacy and the betterment of economic status, the Scheduled Tribes and Scheduled Caste would be in a convenient position within ten years. Since this target could not be fulfilled, these reservations had to be extended every ten years and they are still in vogue. But even after more than 40 years, there has been no improvement in the educational and economic levels. Moreover, no action has been taken to delete those Scheduled Castes and Scheduled Tribes who have become economically well-off from the purview of the reservation provision. Instead of social and economic criteria, birth and caste have become the major guiding factors and this definitely is not in conformity with our objectives of reservation. Moreover, instead of abolishing caste divides, this policy has perpetuated it. Hence, I would like to make it clear that reservation is definitely good, but the misutilisation of this policy should be stopped. Thank you.

Mr Atwal:—Well friends, if, as stated by my previous speaker, the aim of our government is to bring up the standard of the under privileged and downtrodden people both socially and economically, then the best way is to make education free for them and appoint them to important social positions. Reservation in jobs and seats in education and other institutions is not the answer. The very mention of the reservation and castes perpetuates them. On the contrary, we should appoint Harijans as priests in temples. They should be given scholarships, and other inducements to educate themselves. Above all positive effort should be taken to uplift them economically. The best way to promote social equality is to abolish reservations because till today reservations have done more harm than good and have constantly reminded an untouchable that he will always be one. So in the broader context, I would like to opine that reservation should be abolished. Thank you.

Mr Verma:—In addition to what my previous speaker has said reservation is being extented to promotions also. As we all know that promotion is more performance-oriented or seniority-oriented. If promotion is based on caste then surely the performance is bound to suffer. Once a candidate from Scheduled Caste has been deemed fit and appointed on a job, there is no doubt that it will improve his social and economic status. Moreover, there are some professional fields like scientist, engineers, doctors and computer programmers which need an intensive study. For these studies, the best and the most talented candidates should be selected as the progress of a nation depends on them. Regarding this the agitations which have taken place in the various parts of the country is quite valid. In today's politics, reservation has become a gimmick of catching vote banks which will later on lead to a larger disaster, so reservation should be scrapped. Thank you.

Ms Dogra:—In my opinion, the country had been divided into caste by just one word uttered by Gandhiji 'Harijan' and I still believe that he in one shot perpetuated the caste system. Later on Mr. Ambedkar, who belonged to the Scheduled Caste wanted their well-being, and initiated the reservation. Frankly speaking, reservation is a Frankenstein of Indian politics, which aims to uproot the very basis of the society and create a national catrastrophe. In no other country, one can find such a system which makes a mockery of democracy. By snatching the rights of others, one cannot bring social equality. Thank you.

Ms Aggarwal:—This topic of reservation is actually disgusting. In my opinion, by uplifting an individual on social and economic platform, one cannot change the mentality. When the "Varnas" *i.e.,* Brahmin, Kshatriya, Baniya and Sudras were created; they were divided according to their functions. So, when one of my friends said that a Sudra should be made the priest of a temple, he attacked the sensibilities of the Brahmin community. Today all the problems in the society is because we have started to change the nature through our whims and fancies and the day is not far when a social upheaval will occur. Thank you.

Mr Shamim:—Friends, I'm amazed at all your misinformed fulminations, which are perhaps a result of caste prejudices with which we tend to look at the issue. Ambedkar accepted this much-riled and vilified concept of social justice to save Gandhi's life, who was willing to concede the Muslims a separate homeland of Pakistan, but was dead against granting the Dalits an equal space in the economic and socio-political life of an Independent India, which Ambedkar and other leaders sought from the British before they left India. Gandhi feared this would sever the Dalits from Hindu fold and sat on fast till death. Reservation is not about jobs alone, it is about granting a democratic space to the aspirations of the deprived sections, which comprise one fourth of India's population, and which still cannot afford two meals a day let alone education. If reservations have failed to uplift them, it is because of the system and larger society. However, unpalatable they may be for us, reservations are a necessary evil in an India where a low caste but bright final year medical student is forced to commit suicide after she is publicly humiliated for her origin by her professor. Do you know a country like the US too has this mechanism, called affirmative action, firmly in place to bring all the alienated and deprived communities like the blacks, Red Indians and other minorities into mainstream? And this policy even extends to the private sector? In my view, reservations are only a small way of offsetting centuries of wrongs done to the Dalits. Thank you very much.

Mr George—I feel that this 'reservation' is nothing but a political gimmick by the different parties to increase their vote banks and neither will it improve the plight of the Scheduled Castes and Tribes nor is it going to benefit them in jobs or education. Thank you.

Expert Comments

Mr. Ahlawat shows understanding of the topic but doesn't appear to be a well-informed speaker. Facts are missing from his speech. He raises a question but does not attempt to explore its answer. He has the courage to initiate a discussion and speak up his mind. He is able to look into the negative aspects of 'Reservation' but lacks balanced approach. Inspite of his deficiencies, he may be selected for his leadership quality.

—But he is not a strong candidate

Mr. Kanappan has deeper understanding and profound knowledge. He explores the historical context of the issue. He has a balanced approach and is able to find out the real problem. He is not against the system but is aware of the deficiencies of the system. He has a positive attitude.

—He is a strong candidate

Mr. Atwal is not a well informed speaker. He comes up with his suggestions without exploring the real issue. He lays down only normative statements, which shows that he is an imposing kind of person with rigid point of view. He has actually digressed from the topic.

—Not a strong candidate

Mr. Verma is not a well informed speaker. He just beats about the bush. He is not at all innovative. He starts his speech with a statement that is irrelevant for the issue in question. He finds only the negative aspect of 'reservation', i.e., political gimmick but he forgets that the issue is 'reservation' and not its political misuse.

—Not a suitable candidate for the organisation

Mr. Dogra is an uninformed speaker. He is disrespectful towards the two well personalities who are revered by all. He is a pessimist and cantankerous individual—a mal content.

—He is an unsuitable candidate

Mr. Aggarwal engages in irrelevant rhetoric. He speaks for the sake of speaking. He tells a personal anecdote about his friend, which is unnecessary. He doesn't have ideas. *—Not a suitable candidate*

Mr. Shamim is disrespectful towards well known and respected personalities. What he speaks about Gandhiji, is irrelevant to the topic. He just beats about the bush. Facts are missing. Though he mentions a suitable concept of 'affirmative action' but doesn't carry it forward. He shows superficial knowledge. He doesn't come up with logical arguments.

—Not a suitable candidate

Mr. George has nothing to speak. He appears to be a pessimist as he cannot see the brighter aspects of the topic. He is not an informed speaker—shows lack of knowledge. He completely failed to participate in the discussion. *—Not a suitable candidate*

It may be noticed that no one comes forward with a harmonious conclusion. This shows that the group discussion was not all organised and everyone spoke wantonly. No one showed the required leadership quality. Mr. Kanappan, who appears to be a rational speaker, also disappoints by lack of the leadership quality.

PEEPING TOM SYNDROME IN FIRMS IS GOOD FOR EMPLOYEES

Mr. Dongre : The Peeping Tom syndrome relates to the actions of a firm that help its top bosses keep a watchful eye on its employees. There are many devices that can be used to monitor the working of an employee. The examples of such devices are GPS tracking, CCTV, Radio Frequency Identification (RFID), presence of a personal spy of the management in the employee group etc. My view is that this policy of the management helps the employee. He is always on his toes because he knows that the big brother (his immediate boss) is watching him in the office (or at his desk). The monitored employee would work harder that way. He would not waste his time. He would deliver concrete results. His phone conversations are also tracked. They are analysed to judge whether he is spending time on company's work or on his personal affairs. Hence, due to this strict discipline, employees would contribute more effectively to goal achievement in their firm. Therefore, I fully support the topic.

Ms. Roshanara : I do not agree with my friend, Mr. Dongre. Probably, he has come from a remote village of India. He does not know that employees do not perform when they are subjected to such painful vigilance exercises by their bosses. How can a firm become productive or efficient if its employees are scanned and monitored that way? Don't you think that it is an attack on the privacy of an employee?

Mr. Singh : I also agree with the views of Ms. Roshanara. We are not buffaloes and cows that should be herded into an office space and monitored through sophisticated workplace surveillance equipment. As employees, we would know what is to be done. Then, why should we be humiliated by our employers? It is a sad development of corporate history. Let the employee work sans restrictions.

Ms. Kadambini : I would like to support the views of Mr. Dongre. In my view, people do not want to perform in office because they are working to achieve their objectives, not those of the firm. They ought to be put under the vigilant eyes of Peeping Tom. A business firm works to gain profits. If its employees do not work hard to contribute to its objectives, what is the use of having them?

Ms. Roshanara : If you do not like an employee or the quantum or quality of his output, fire him. But do not monitor his activities in the bathroom. You should know that Article 21 of our Constitution grants personal liberty to Indian citizens. In case of government organisations, this Article can be invoked as a defence against snooping on an employee (of a government organisation).

Mr. Dongre : The clauses of Article 21 and the law of tort are so general that an individual would not be able to make a solid case in any Indian court. Further, if an individual is found indulging in some wrong doing, he can be fired. The examples of BPO employees are before us. Thus, an employee—if he is sacked—would not get damage money through the court (from his employer). Even a judge would not understand the issue of privacy, as it is a subtle issue.

Mr. Singh : Mr. Dongre, you are telling us to rely on the law that has not defined privacy till date. No problem! We shall re-define the law.

We can file a PIL and get the ruling of the SC. We can also tell the Parliament to get a law passed to this effect. But we shall not tolerate Peeping Tom at any cost. We can be sacked, not humiliated. You should know that if the police want to search a home or office, they require a search warrant from a court. In this case, the person is being interrogated in an indirect manner through electronic surveillance systems, which is objectionable. Ms. Roshanara has stated that if someone is found to be guilty of misconduct, dishonest in dealings and of loose moral character, he should be sacked. Why should he be tortured?

Mr. Dongre : Here you are, Mr. Singh. How would the firm learn that he is corrupt, dishonest or of loose moral character? There has to be a mechanism to find out where he stands in the organisation. He would not dare to go on the wrong side of operations (of the firm) if he knows that he is being watched. This would keep him on the right track at all times. Firing an employee would not solve the problem. Good employees are difficult to find. The firm would not like to throw them away, as they would join its competitors. Hence, electronic surveillance is an ideal control tool, especially in the IT sector.

Mr. Singh : I oppose the topic. It is against human dignity to work in an office that has the Peeping Tom syndrome. This is an immoral act of the management.

Ms. Kadambini : Mr. Singh, things dont't work in the manner described by you. In real life situations involving private firms, it is possible that the employees may be leaking information to the competitors of their firm. They must be controlled, especially those who are handling classified sets of information. Recently, a BPO firm had faced a crisis when one of its employees had leaked vital data. Don't you think such an employee should be monitored? Once an important set of data is leaked, the loser firm stands to lose business worth billions of rupees. How would the firm survive under such circumstances, given that every employee wants to work for his interest?

Ms. Roshanara : What about human rights? What about the privacy of an individual at the work place? If an employee is monitored even in a bathroom, who would work for such a firm that has put cameras at places in the office (including bathrooms)? This is a heinous crime against humanity. If you do not trust an employee, tell him to leave.

Note that organisations work (and prosper) because of the feeling of trust between the employer and employees. We are not machines that should be monitored through digital surveillance equipment. If Article 21 is not strong enough to protect the rights of an employee, we shall go to the Parliament to get another law passed. I fully support the views of Mr. Singh in this context.

Mr. Singh : Now that Ms. Roshanara and I think along the same lines, both of you should also align your views with ours.

Ms. Kadambini : How did you find out that we would align our views with yours?

Mr. Singh : That is because our views are rational and human oriented.

Ms. Kadambini : In that case, you would not be able to work in any firm. I have told you that organisations want their employees to perform. A small degree of vigil should not hurt their ego sets.

Ms. Roshanara : That is the crux of the issue. The level of vigilance is so high in some companies that their employees cannot even breathe. Did you know that? In the BPO sector, an employee is a slave, literally!

Ms. Kadambini : That is quite right. But you should know that there is a need to be extra vigilant in some firms. You have given the example of Peeping Tom in the context of the BPO firms. Even in some production units, the phenomenon of Peeping Tom is alive. It should not be called a syndrome, as the topic of this group discussion session suggests. Some liner-level cadres deserve to be controlled that way, else they would not deliver results.

Mr. Singh : You are in the wrong, Ms. Kadambini. You cannot get work out of anybody if you monitor his activities on a minute-by-minute basis. This is a crude way of controlling an employee. There are production targets, QC norms and directives of the boss to take care of the quality and quantity to be delivered by an employee. The MBO technique is also in vogue. Under this technique, the junior sets his targets in consultation with his boss. In a way, he himself sets these targets. Then, he would work at his work place and try to do his best. The question of electronic surveillance should not arise, given that he is accountable to his boss for his actions and performances.

Mr. Dongre : I agree with you but there is a problem. Targets are revised quite often, especially for the operative staff. They do not want to work. They waste time and indulge in useless gossiping. This gossiping leads to grapevine. This grapevine, in turn, leads to the strengthening of an informal organisation. Quite often, this informal organisation works against the interests of the formal organisation. In the end, there is conflict between formal and informal organisations. Due to this conflict, the formal organisation—which is supposed to deliver various types of products and services to the markets—suffers. Its competitors take an edge over it and get additional market shares. Hence, the purpose of creation of an organisation is defeated when the employees are not controlled. Peeping Tom is a blessing for the top brass of any firm. You should align your views with ours. We are on the right track.

Mr. Singh : Do you want to state that you are on the right track and we do not have the ability to think? What a judgement!

Ms. Kadambini : He does not want to state that, Mr. Singh. He only wants to tell you that we are supposed to arrive at a result.

Mr. Singh : So, you would put your words into my mouth. How can you dictate your terms?

Mr. Dongre : This fighting would not help us arrive at a result.

Ms. Kadambini : We must arrive at a result in any case. Hence, we must co-operate with one another to reach a consensus.

Ms. Roshanara : I think we should submit the gist of our discussion. Then, we can take a decision.

Ms. Kadambini : Ms. Roshanara, it would be more appropriate to submit one's own gist of views first. Then, we can make an amalgam of the views and reach a consensus. Constant surveillance makes an employee uncomfortable, overly conscious and apprehensive. Moreover it inhibits the relationship of trust between the employers & employees.

Ms. Singh : Peeping Tom is not liked by any employee. But you can give the consensus statement. I will agree with group's consensus.

Ms. Roshanara : Now, the group must arrive at a consensus quickly. Mr. Dongre can deliver the result now.

Mr. Dongre : Thank you, friends! The group has concluded that Peeping Tom is not a very acceptable phenomenon, as far as the corporate conditions of India are concerned. We must not forget that we are living in a liberal era. Every person has the right to personal liberty. Article 21 of the Constitution also confirms this fact. However, the Indian law system does not have any code that would check an employer snooping on his employees. We hope that such a law would be delineated in the future. We have also decided to carry on electronic surveillance of all those employees who can damage the financial position, information sets or markets of a firm they work for. Such rogues must be monitored on a constant basis.

Some senior employees, who are senior managers or achievers of a unique kind must not be managed or controlled by Peeping Tom. They have their targets. They are responsible too. They can be told to be more careful about their performances. But they must not be subjected to electronic surveillance systems' roving eyes.

Finally, the appointment of detectives for monitoring employees is a bad concept. Further, the electronic surveillance systems must be non-evasive. They should not hurt the privacy of employees. No employer should install electronic surveillance systems in bathrooms, green rooms and private areas meant for women.

With this statements, I come to the conclusion of this group discussion session. Thank you!

All : Thank you!

Expert Comments

Mr. Dongre is a well-informed speaker. He doesn't hesitate from being the first speaker. He doesn't speak anything that is not related to the topic. He has the knowledge but lacks socializing skills. He doesn't greet his colleagues and takes a flying start. This shows that though he has courage and knowledge yet he is not a suitable sociable group organism and cannot elicit group co-operation. He is still a strong candidate as he strikes balance towards the topic.

Under Consideration (decision of the examiner)

Mr. Roshanara starts by disagreeing and pointing out lacunae in Mr. Dongre's argument. A direct reference to a colleague's deficiencies, without greetings or compliments, will offend him. She lacks behavioural skills and not a suitable group-organism. —Rejected

Mr. Singh also lacks socializing skills and convincing ideas and presenation. —Rejected

Ms. Kadambiri appears to be a balanced candidate. She has positive views and approach. She can be a suitable candidate and group organism though she also lacks socializing skills as she did not greet anyone in the start of her statement. She is a strong candidate for her balanced approach.
—Under consideration

ENVIRONMENTAL CONTROL IS THE RESPONSIBILITY OF THE EXECUTIVE

Mr Naushad:— Friends! You are aware of the fact that a healthy and clean environment is needed for the development of any country. In India, this issue is being addressed to deliver a good standard of living to her citizens. During the past sixty years, industrialisation and growth in population levels led to environmental decay. Our cities have become the garbage centres of the world. Our rivers are polluted. The quality of air in cities has deteriorated. Thus, pollution of water, food, air and soil led to a decline in the standards of living despite rapid industrialisation and urbanisation. That is why, the government took several initiatives to curb this decay. Pollution control norms were defined under Bharat-I system, which was based on Euro-I system. Later, Presently BS III norms have been implemented, norms for control of emissions from automobiles were also defined. The same are in force now. The government also took up several projects to clean and maintain India's river systems. It also made it mandatory for every vehicle owner to get his vehicle tested. The vehicle that emits the minimum quantities of NO, CO_2, CO and SPM is given a Pollution Under Control (PUC) certificate, that is valid for a period of three months. What does this mean? It only points out that the executive of our country is responsible for the control of environment.

Hence, all the policies and procedures must flow from the executive. The same ought to be followed by the citizens of the country so that it could become a better habitat.

Mr Agarkar:— Mr Naushad has forgotten to mention that India is a democracy. The will of the people is selected in the policies and decisions of the executive that governs such people. Hence, the real power lies in the hands of our people. Naturally, those who are powerful, ought to be responsible too. Hence, the masses of India must be motivated to protect the environment. For this purpose, efforts would have to be made at the grass-root level to control the environment. The garbage cans must be cleaned and removed in tune. Households must not throw garbage out of their homes on the roads. Industries must emit pollutants according to stipulated norms. Scooters, cars, trucks and other vehicle must also conform to pollution control norms. The people are responsible for taking steps to check environmental decay. That is because control and maintenance of environment would keep them escape the wrath of many a disease. Moreover, the country would also be neat and clean, just like those of the West, if the masses take active part in environmental control exercises. Hence, the executive can play the role of a guide or mentor. The actual tasks are to be performed by the masses themselves. That is why the masses are deemed more responsible than the executive in this context.

Mr Khan:— I do not agree with the views of Mr Agarkar. In this context, the views of Mr Naushad are based on rationale. How can the masses be given such a big responsibility? The state defines the laws and procedures. It enforces the same through law-enforcing agencies and organs of the bureaucracy. It provides technologies and equipment for controlling pollution. I can quote an example in this context. In Delhi, the CNG bus service has been started. It is the largest pollution-free state transport service in the world. The masses can never organise the resources and manpower to start a service of this kind. The government of NCT of Delhi and union government collaborated to start this service.

CNG was made available to the DTC through Indraprastha Gas Limited (IGL). All the buses running on diesel were replaced by CNG buses. After a lot of toil and hullabaloo, the bus service was started. The masses can only use this system. They cannot be told to participate in the process of its installation. Hence, I would like to align my views with those of Mr Naushad. The executive is responsible for the control of environment of our country. The simple logic is—the executive is powerful, authorised and resourceful and that is why, it takes necessary actions in the interest of the masses.

Mr Sharma:— If Mr Khan bluntly refuses to take the role of the masses into account, it would lead to a chaotic situation. The masses must be trained to control the emission of harmful pollutants. As stated by Mr Agarkar, the households of our country are squarely responsible for controlling pollution. That is because they are required to dispose off the garbages which is a nuisance in large and medium cities. If these households put garbage in cans and dispose it off in a careful manner, our cities can become beautiful and disease free.

Hence, every household is responsible for controlling pollution. Similarly the industries would also be held responsible for spewing out minimum quantities of pollutants into the air, water or soil. The executive can only follow the procedures. The judiciary can only ensure that laws are adhered to. The actual conformance has to be effected at the grassroot level. What is the fun of passing a law related to pollution control if no one follows it? I do not underestimate the power of the executive but the laws made by it would have a meaning only if the masses obey such laws. Hence, I conclude that pollution control is the exclusive responsibility of the subjects of our country and not of the executive that governs these subjects.

Mr Johnson:— All my friends are overlooking an important aspect of the debate—we have to control the environment of our country to achieve a better quality of life. The masses must control pollution. The executive must create conducive conditions to control pollution. Both are equally responsible. Why should we shift the onus to the masses or the government?

Mr Naushad:— Mr Johnson, you have to choose one option. Either you can support the executive or you can support the masses. Do not give a subtle amorphous answer. Be clear in your thoughts.

Mr Johnson:— If that is the case, then I would like to state that the executive is responsible for controlling and regulating the environment of our country. After all, it is more resourceful, financially stable and powerful than the masses.

Mr Agarkar:— You are foregetting that the masses, as a collective whole, are also a powerful entity. Moreover, the executive is a product of the mass movements (general elections and state elections). Don't you think that the demands of the masses would have to be met?

Mr Johnson:— You are absolutely right, Mr Agarkar. However, the masses are spread across the length and breadth of India. Pollution control is not on the agenda of the people of our country. Rather, problems of the family, business development, social interactions, entertainment and other issues remain the priority areas of most of the people. They may not be able to devote time to environmental regulations, pollution control or adoption of technologies to ensure that they breathe fresh pure air. In such a case, the government, as a democratic administrator, ought to be given this Herculean task. It would define rules and laws and get them enforced through the law-enforcing agencies and Judiciary. This is the appropriate *modus operandi* which is being followed around the world.

Mr Agarkar:— However, the masses have installed the government and its policies and rules reflect the will of the masses. Why should the masses not be made responsible for controlling the environment? They are going to be benefitted due to their own actions. The executive is only a regulator in this context. If the masses do not have the will to check pollution, how can rules and laws be effective? The responsibility has to be defined at the individual level. Hence, I do not agree with your viewpoint.

Mr Naushad:— Mr Agarkar, you are trying to bypass the executive by allowing the masses to take decisions. In every democratic set-up, the masses choose the executive. The executive defines the laws for the masses and implements the same through its law-enforcing agencies. Why do you forget that the executive has been created to serve the masses. In order to manage a large number of masses, some rules and regulations ought to be framed. And the executive is one such authority that defines these rules and regulations. In every country, there is a government. It manages the country in an efficient manner. Naturally, the management of the environment of the country is also a task to be undertaken by the government. I wonder! why you are in favour of the masses?

Mr Agarkar:— Perhaps, we are sitting at two different poles.

Mr Johnson:— That way, we would not be able to arrive at a consensus.

Mr Sharma:— The responsibility of the masses is prime in this context. However, I am willing to accept that the executive has also to play several roles to control and regulate the environment. After all, the resources and infrastructure belong to the executive.

Mr Agarkar:— You are right, but in the wake of the arrival of a market-dominated system, the masses would be allowed to control the resources as well as the technologies related to pollution control. Private sector participation in government-owned PSUs is inevitable. Hence, you need not change your previous stand.

Mr Sharma:— I am with you but, the views of the opponents must also be incorporated in the final consensus.

Mr Agarkar:— They would be incorporated if they have some rationale or logic behind them.

Mr Naushad:— Mr Sharma is right. Let us declare a consensus view that should incorporate the views of all the participants. Who would take the initiative?

Mr Khan:— If all of you agree, I can do it.

All:— Please go ahead.

Mr Khan:— The group has concluded that the executive has the responsibility of defining laws and procedures for controlling the environment. At the same time, the masses are supposed to adhere to such laws and procedures so that our country becomes a better place to live in. The joint and active participation of the masses and the organs of the government (including the Judiciary and law-enforcing agencies) is required to address the complex issue of environmental control in India.

Expert Comments

Mr. Johnson fails to take a stand initially. But when prompted, he takes a stand but not with conviction. This shows, he has a confused and amorphous personality. He just balances the two aspects but doesn't come up with express arguments to substantiate his opinion. He fails to stem by his opinion, as he changes that because of promptings by others. Not a suitable candidate. —*Rejected*

Mr. Khan has the courage to express his opinion and to expressly disagree with a colleague. He takes a stand in favour of one of the colleagues and comes up with additional arguments to support his view. He cites an example from real life. This shows he is observant and is aware of the contemporary circumstances. The best in him is his ability to recapitulate and conclude by incorporating the views of all his colleagues. He has an aptitude for 'harmony of disparate things'. He may turn out to be a good decision maker—a quality essentially in all leaders. He himself overtures to take up the task of concluding. —*Selected*

BUSINESS VS ETHICS

Mr Ravi:—I would like to say that ethics is a personal question, since companies too are managed by people. It is likely to be faced by all of us at some time or the other. So it is important to have our own priorities right and be well prepared to face the situation when it arises. It is time we faced our morals or lack of them. For example, if we worked in a company where, illegal things were taking place. Would we speak against it or let it go? Considering that employees are put in jail for violations. This question assumes great significance. If one lives honestly in one's life and does what he thinks is right, chances are that the person would be happier and have less tensions. In the long run, that is what matters.

Ms Yamini:—Ethics is a trickly subject and clearly has no answers. A sense of values is important, but these are imbibed rather than taught. We can, in fact, learn something from other nations. In South Korea, corruption does rule but capital punishment overrides it. Business houses had better see what is happening to politicians in our own country. Before business crimes are taken to court, it would be better of they started subscribing to ethical behaviour. We should remember that we are citizens of a free country and companies are corporate citizens too. Correct behaviour should become the rule rather than the exception. Let us not forget that in management, as in real life, there are no short cuts.

Mr Ravi:—This topic has assumed great significance these days, considering that many companies have been found to break laws and behave unethically. ITC Ltd. has been involved in cases of excise evasion and *"FERA"* violations. There was large scale fraud at Indian bank rendering the bank almost insolvent. Raids by the income tax department on companies and individuals have revealed immense wealth. The question arises as to why those who are prosperous should indulge in breaking the law to save some amounts of tax. It also raises the question of ethics and morals. Why is it that a senior manager, should stoop to illegal things when he has the power to put his foot down and stop the illegal acts? I think that these days there is a crisis of values and nobody knows what is right and what is wrong. The leaders, who are looked upon as examples, themselves have been shown to be a greedy bunch. An individual has no reference points, nothing to fall back upon exact the values thought to him by his family. Unfortunately, even that is not saying much, going by the recent disclosures. It is not surprising that our Engineers, Doctors, bureaucrats and Chartered Accountants have no idea how to deal with ethical issues when confronted with them. Many take the easy way out by accepting something bluntly immoral by saying, "Everybody is doing it, so what is the harm if I do the same? " I think a person takes naturally to immoral acts since he has no strong values to guide him.

Ms Sonu:—You are right, but ethics is important today, even though there is a crisis of values. Simply because there is so much generation around, we need people who can uphold values of honesty and decency. And indeed there are such people and even companies with a high sense of values. Take the Tatas, for instance, a business house which has never been involved in a controversy. Business has to operate within the laws of the country, but managers of some companies think that management is all about circumventing laws. Chartered Accountants devise ways of reducing tax liability for their clients. Everybody wants to be clever these days. Surprisingly, the companies in controversy are blue chip companies, which hire people from the best institutes of India at fat salaries. One would expect that a person from Indian Institute of Management (IIM) or a Chartered Accountant (CA) employed by a company like ITC should have a better sense of values. Moreover, a highly paid person should have more guts than a low paid employee. It seems that education has failed us. Even the topmost institutions, it seems, just award degrees and do not impart values. In the case of ITC, no less than a Chairman was involved, no doubt, with help from other employees. In the Indian Bank Fraud, too, bank officers must have turned a blind eye to wrongdoings. In both cases, the Auditors too must have been incompetent or corrupt. The point is; when our best people behave in this way, what can be expected from people lower down the line?

Ms Yamini:—I think you are ignoring an important point and that is the context, in which unethical practices take place. First, where there is corruption all around us, why blame only the Auditors and Managers? Secondly, tax rates are so high in our country that a company or a person has no alternative but to avoid tax somehow or the other. Thirdly, when you have to pay bribes to carry on your legitimate business—everyone from a Telephone lineman, the Postman to the labour inspector—what will the company do? There has to be a way to generate black money to pay all these people. If one is to pay all the bribes and pay high taxes too, no business would be viable and all business activity would stop in the country. Perhaps that is why no progress takes place in spite of high sounding speeches by politicians. The whole discussion on ethics has to be seen in the proper context. I think that ethics have a relevance only in rich nations. In our country, ethics really has no meaning.

Ms Priya:—I agree with you. The environment in our country is one which encourages corruption. Improving ethics will result only from an improvement of general conditions all round. That seems difficult at this stage. You mentioned about our education failing us. I think a discussion on ethics should be introduced in business schools and other professional courses. Some business schools do offer a paper on ethics influenced, no doubt, by institutions of the west. Unfortunately, in India it is treated as an esoteric subject since there are no trained teachers for it. Students learn to mouth the right platitudes, but when it comes to crunch, do they have the courage to live up to their beliefs? Is it right to expect them to behave ethically when there is so much corruption all around? Treated as an exam, students will learn to say all the right things but will not hesitate to do exactly the opposite in real situations. For instance, almost everyone will say that employing child labour is bad, but still we see every other factory employing children, simply because children cost cheaper. So there is a world of a difference between theory and practice. Another thing is that jobs are not available easily in India. Even highly paid employees have to do what the employer demands. If they oppose some wrong in their company, they may just be fired. The best thing would be to go along with what is demanded. If one is in a job, the only way to succeed is to kill your conscience otherwise you may be unemployed. Let us face the fact that being too honest in today's world is not a virtue.

Ms Bharati:—Unfortunately, that is the thinking which prevents many people from speaking out against a wrong but that is a bogus argument. If we have no sense of right and wrong, what kind of a life would we be leading? The question of ethics is not limited to business only but to our private lives too. Without a sense of right and wrong. We would become a nation of thieves and cheats and our lives would degenerate. We would only sink into a greater mess of we allowed this kind of thinking to continue. Further, the argument of bribes as being necessary for survival is wrong. Many business houses continue to operate ethically even in today's climate. Bribes are often given to have a wrong thing done, to bend a low or to get undue benefits. The bribes paid in the Jharkhand Mukti Morcha scandal by reputed business houses were certainly not for survival. They were paid to get maximum benefits out of the corrupt leaders. I think it is possible to do business honestly in our country, in spite of what you say. But there is no way to fulfil greed, which has no limits. If everyone refused to pay bribes, public servants would perforce become honest themselves.

INTERNET IS AFFECTING OUR CULTURE

Ms Bhavika:— Friends, before we discuss this topic, let me tell you my experience when I worked on the Internet. It is a wonderful thing :

almost everything under the Sun is available on it. One can access any set of information on it. One can sent *E-mail* to any part of the world. It increases our mental horizons and is a means through which, one can easily learn new techniques. The Internet is a world without borders and one is not controlled by the national boundaries or time. However, I spent several hours on it and did not realise how much time, I had spent on various web sites. I had seen a lot of information and pictures but much of it was not very useful to me in my life. May be, I would have been better off reading a book. But the Internet helps many other people who spend time on it exploring information from all sources. It is exciting and attractive also. People may spend their entire time staring at computer screens and live in their make-believe worlds. This may lead to cultural erosion. Unrestricted information may also result in the erosion of our cultural identity. In many countries, there is a move to restrict access to the Internet as it affects their culture.

Mr Pramod:— You may be right. One can easily access newspapers, video and graphics on the Net. The whole debate about allowing entry of foreign media has become ridiculous. One can get anything that one wants on a computer screen. But I would like to say that one should not be scared of cultural erosion. How long can we rely on censorship? Easy access to information is a boon and we may become more modern in our approach discarding the negative values of our culture that make us backward. We Indians really have a wrong sense of protecting our culture. Moreover one should have the freedom of accessing information and it should be up to the individual to decide which data one should access. I would also like to say that there is no need to oppose the advancements of technology. Satellite television is already a part of our lives. The Internet has come to stay. Let us take all these developments in our stride and mould ourselves rather than try to protect ourselves from it.

Mr Nirmal:— I would like to say that every technological advancement comes with its uses and drawbacks. The Internet has its own uses. One can send messages to anyone across the world in seconds. Indian companies and exporters can set up their home pages on it and this will give them worldwide exposure. Although we get programmes from all over the world. Yet many people have become couch potatoes. Their only activity is to watch television. Internet may do worse. It may cause people to live in virtual worlds, losing contact with real World. For a country like ours, it will be a real bad thing as productivity will reduce further. People will spend time in front of monitors of computers without producing anything. Public sector and government employees will spend time surfing the net rather than doing their work. It will give them a means to spend their time and to access entertainment when they should be working. Now a days, Internet Addiction Disorder (IAD) is taking a toll on human health.

Mr Rajeev:— This is a real danger but the answer lies in using the technology responsibly. I would like to quote Mr Bill Gates on this. He has written that some people waste time in front of computers, but that doesn't mean that technology is holding us back. Unfortunately, many Indians are not able to use the tools of modern technology well. They get enamoured of technology and begin to misuse it. You mentioned about government employees wasting time in offices. This is indeed a very great danger. Already they do not work. Computers installed for official purposes are used to play games. The Internet will make them worse. We really have to be more disciplined and not to get involved in the useless information available but use the tool effectively for our development. Hence, we have to use the technology and not to be driven by it.

Ms Bhavika:— We have discussed about the effect on lives of individuals. Let us also see the impact of Internet on our culture. Like television and other foreign media, the Internet will also have an impact on culture. Other countries too are trying to control easy access to the *Net*. Don't you think that in India too much a control is required? Already, we have seen the impact on our culture due to software of television; girls have started smoking, thinking that it is modern. The Internet may only accelerate the process started by other media, especially by TV. Our people are not responsible enough. We must make them aware of the ill effects of the Net.

Mr Pramod:— I find such arguments very wrong. How long should we act as cultural policemen and say that this is right and that is wrong. People should be allowed to make their own choices. May be, some people will waste time on the Internet. Gradually, however, they will become mature enough to utilise this new technology-based tool. Take the case of satellite television. Though initially there was a craze for it, people have taken it in their stride. Broadcasters like Tehelka, who had to bear the wrath of the high handedness of the state, can go freely on the Net. I would say that foreign media has actually helped Indians get out of the age old beliefs, which have given unnecessary power to our leaders. The Internet will give exposure to Indian writers and musicians.

Mr Nirmal:— Mr Pramod, you are right. Many of us are unduly worried about culture. That is why, we raise bogies about foreign media. Already, we are talking about convergence of technologies of ICE- Information communications and entertainment. In the future, a single optical cable will carry all the signals to our homes. The cost is also decreasing day by day. We will not need expensive computers, but our televisions would suffice. When technology is expanding at such a rapid pace, it is foolish to introduce a Broadcasting Bill. Assuming the satellite television can be controlled, how can the government control the Internet or future technolgical advancements that promise to make everything cheaply available? I think we need to grow up. Instead, let us look at new technologies and find ways how they will help us. Culture, in any case, is not static. It has changed in the past and it will continue to change in the future too. It would be better to take part in the process of facing the Herculean challenges that technology brings forth. So let's join the progress and stop looking back.

Mr Rajeev:— I think that all of us are agreed that our culture is not under threat from foreign media or even the Internet. We have to discard our outdated thinking. Instead, we have to start looking at ways to use the technology for our benefits. The Internet brings forth a challenge to integrate the entire World. True, it may have its disadvantages too, but we cannot stop it or ponder over its negative points. The challenge is to use the technology. Even the countries, which speak of cultural imperialism, have not really imposed a strict censorship on the Net. Only dictatorship in Myanmar or China can do so. Fortunately, we live in a democratic nation. The cultural policy may try to impose its norms upon us and would like us to go the Taliban way. It is our good fortune that good sense prevails in the end and we are not pushed into the Medieval Age.

Expert Comments

Ms. Bhavika starts with a personal anecdote. It may make a group discussion more interesting, but she speaks more about Internet and its advantages than its effect on our culture. She loses sight of the topic. Suddenly she takes a reverse turn and states that Internet may lead to cultural erosion. She leaves this unexplained. Her statement is contradictory to her anecdote. She has a confused aptitude. She has a digressive attention, in the beginning. She comes back to the main issue in the second round, but in a group discussion one should start with the main issue because a second chance may or may not be possible. She presents both the aspects—good & bad—of the Internet but her stand remains unclear because she does not conclude with an unambiguous statement of her opinion. She does not greet her colleagues—every first speaker must do that. —*Not a strong candidate.*

Mr. Pramod has also lost sight of the topic. Instead of speaking on the effects of Internet he takes the direction of highlighting the ills of our culture. He fails to explore the details of the issue. But unlike Bhavika, he takes a stand and has arguments to support it. He supports Bhavika once but doesn't hesitate to object to her argument in the 2nd round. Thus, he shows a strong aptitude. In spite of his deficiencies, his candidature may be considered. He is able to see the larger perspective of the issue.

Mr. Nirmal does not have original ideas. He beats about the bush. He misses the topic. He has nothing to say about culture. He also fails to explore the details of the topic as whether our culture is adversely affected or not. He makes an abrupt turnaround in his second speech. Thus his stand is ambiguous. He is neither a good thinker nor a good decision maker and cannot make out his stand by assessing both his speeches together. —*Not a suitable candidate*

Mr. Rajeev has not explored the details of the topic. But he has a balanced approach towards the topic. He can see and appreciate both pros and cons of the issue; as well as he can take a stand. Moreover he incorporates and harmonises the views of the whole group in his concluding speech. He may be considered for selection in comparison to most of the members of the group.

—*May be considered for selection*

HOW FAR IS HUMAN CLONING ETHICAL?

No. 2 :—Morning Friends, today the topic is "How far is Human Cloning Ethical? Whether it is frightening or not hardly matters. The foremost point is whether humans should have the power to play God or not. Cloning, by definition implies exploration. It means creating life forms for economic or other benefits. Perhaps cloning of crops is acceptable, but cloning of animals and human being is disgusting. Raising only animals that deliver high yields of milk or meat is not only unethical, it is deplorable. What will we do to animals which are not as efficient as the clones? Kill them? Apply the dame to human cloning. A person may want to clone himself to acquire immorality or someone may want to clone himself for his intelligence or for his cruel qualities. The idea is absolutely repulsive because the clone is as much a citizen as anyone else. Further, consider manufacturing people from those who are better looking and more intelligent than we are; what will happen to the rest of us with our shortcomings? Perhaps the better race will make us, into their slaves or may be kill us. So, we should ban all further experiments and leave our biological future in the hands of God.

No. 5:— The issue of cloning or genetic duplication, has existed in human imagination since Frankestein. 'Dolly', a sheep cloned in Scotland, has the same genetic make up as her mother. This really is remarkable thing, something which was not thought to be possible decades ago. In terms of importance, it equals the creation of the atomic bomb and the consequences will change our lives forever. But, frankly, I don't think that man should have the power to play God in this fashion. Such research is unethical and goes against the laws of-God. Reacting to the news the former U.S. President Clinton said that, *"Each human life is unique, born of a miracle that reaches beyond laboratory science"*. He had banned the use of government funds for human cloning, and I think he had done right. I dread to think what we might do with this technology: breed human hybrids, clone armies or even slaves or a superior human race that subjugates all other humans. We have already seen the evils that this kind of thinking that they were the superior race.

No. 7:—It is true that cloning opens many evil possibilities, but human cloning has not been done yet and perhaps never will be. Many countries have laws that prohibit cloning of human beings. The US and the European Union have said that they will review the ethical implications arising from cloning. In Denmark, cloning of cows was stopped as it was felt that to mass produce cattle for slaughter would be the worst kind of exploitation. So, I think fears are unfounded. The main thing being that what we see in space movies or read about in books may remain a work of fiction, nothing else. I don't think that the Brave New World or even a Frankenstein can ever be created. Let us not be carried away by popular imagination. I think that human age is perfectly capable of dealing with this. Let us not create a hue and cry about something which may never turn out to be true.

No. 1 :—I agree with No. 5 and No. 7 but the truth may lie somewhere in between. Laws cannot stop the advancement of technology so it would be wrong to assume that the lid can be put on cloning by enacting laws alone. What prevents the technology from falling into wrong hands? The potential for evil is infinite. Frankly, there is nothing that prevents someone from breaking the law and start experimenting on human beings. At the same time, it seems highly improbable that someone will be mad enough to raise a clone army, the men so created will have to be fed and clothed too. On the other hand, there may be hope for infertile couples, who may now clone themselves and experience parenthood. Think about animals that are endangered today or clone crops that are disease resistant. Farmers could clone cows that yield more milk and this would lead to higher productivity in the farm sector. We cannot stop technology, but the challenge is to use it properly. Take the case of the atomic bomb. The technology has helped to create power plants and has also been used after its destructive powers were seen. The technology has not fallen into wrong hands and the world ensures that. Similarly, the cloning technology may result in some benefits while the evils may be controlled by the World.

No. 2:—I agree that halting the progress of science is impossible, so instead of enacting laws needlessly we should accept that this technology is available with humans now. Today we can have *'test tube babies'* and do many things that were not thought possible before. Now we should define moral boundaries so that technology is not misused. But frankly the possibilities are frightening. Can we create a human being from the cells of a dead person? What would happen if someone decided to clone some one like Hitler or Saddam Hussein? Of course, one can say that personality is not a matter of having the same genes, it depends to a large extent on upbringing and environment. Even identical twins brought upon in the same environment may turn out to have different personalities. A clone of Albert Einstein, for instance, will be very intelligent, but may not produce the same spectacular results again. For all we know he may turn into a brilliant stock broker this time or go into a life of crime, who knows?

No. 5 :—I am afraid that the dangers are very real and greater than we care to admit. Cloning places the ability to produce life forms in human hands. This is too dangerous. It is not a question of creating intelligent beings alone. Even if we limit the research so as not to include humans, I fear that we may be subjecting all life forms to the worst form of exploitation for cloning endangered species. Will, the reason that they become endangered in the first place was that we killed indiscriminately for their skin or something else in their bodies. What will happen now that we know that animals can be cloned as well? I am afraid that we will go about slaughtering them without giving them a second thought. Tiger and Elephants would be cloned and will be either skinned alive or slaughtered. No I don't think that cloning is such a good idea.

No. 1 :—I think No. 5 is right. I think that scientists who are doing cloning experiments in many parts of the World have not gone into these issues at all. Nor do I agree that the technology can be safe-guarded as we have safe-guarded nuclear technology. Today, there are fears of nuclear proliferation. Cloning is a simple technology in the sense that it can be copied without much equipment. Since, it is not a destructive technology as such, there will not be safe-guards against it. World opinion can be swayed by just one infertile couple who may want to clone themselves. And once cloning starts somewhere, there may be no stop to it. Egotistical people with visions of immorality would want to clone themselves. Kidnappers may simply clone us from a few hair and hold the clone for ransom. Truly, the possibilities are mind boggling. There is a really no saying what people might do. Of course their would be no guarantee that the clone may turn out exactly the way that we want it to be. At best, it may just be an identical twin with the same looks but different personality. Yet, there is no stopping people from ordering their clones.

No. 7 :—I disagree with No. 1. Whenever some new technology has been created or made, people have responded with fear. When Copernicus said that the World was round and not flat as was then believed, he was denounced as a heretic. Similarly, we have treated everything—the Steam engine, the Telephone, the Internet with disdain, in the beginning at least. It is almost as if we are scared of any new thing that comes along. The same is the case with cloning. Here we are fearing what may happen- without realising that each scientific discovery has enriched to any new technology, but history has proved that mankind is able to harness technology for its benefits and the dangers are relatively small by comparison. When experimenting with genes and hybrid crops started, there were visions of mutants who would take over the earth. Nothing of the sort has happened. On the other hand, the science of genetics has given us disease resistant crops and new medicines. So let us not worry about cloning too.

No. 2 :—You may be right No. 7 but I don't think that cloning is anything like the technologies that we have discovered till now, except perhaps the nuclear bomb. There are too many implications of it. I don't think that mankind has yet come to terms with them. Technology, at least in the field of bio-technology, is very exploitative. Take the example of how we produce meat. The industry is, too cruel for words and animals are subjected to the worst forms of torture. Cloning too is part of that technology. Yes, we have the power to play with life but do we have the responsibility? The answer, unfortunately, is no.

No. 3:— There were many issues raised about cloning. After listening to arguments on both sides, I think we can conclude that the technology represents a giant-stride for mankind but there are no clear answers. Some of the fears are genuine and do not arise from blind beliefs. But at the same time, there is no way that technological progress can be stopped by individuals or governments. It is next to impossible. Will mankind come to terms with this extraordinary advancement? Only time will tell.

All:— Thank You.

MEDIA BLITZKRIEG IS NOTHING BUT A PLOY TO EXPLOIT THE MASS AUDIENCES

Ms Richa: Thank you, friends, for allowing me to start this group discussion session. The topic for today's discussion is—media blitzkrieg is nothing but a ploy to exploit the mass audiences. I do not agree with the statement. Hence, I have decided to oppose this concept. I can cite many reasons for doing so. Firstly, the media serve the audiences; the audiences consume the media and not vice versa. Secondly, the media provide information to the masses. This information may or may not be used by the masses to buy products, services and/or concepts. The final decision of a buyer is not affected by the advertising campaigns on TV and in the print media. If a product is liked by a person, he buys it. A TV ad merely tells that person about the presence, quality and price of that product. The media do not force a person to buy things. They only motivate and inform them through their thrilling content. Thank you.

Mr Gattu: It is my turn to speak, as has already been decided. I do not agree with the views of Ms Richa. The media exploits the mass audiences. They deliberately force the masses to buy such products as the latter do not need. They waste the time of the audience. All of you know that time is more important than money. The media supply information from a commercial viewpoint. They want the masses to 'buy' information. Thus, the media expert that the masses would buy particular products, visit particular showrooms or commit themselves to particular ideologies. Such products or ideologies may not smite the masses. But the media force the masses to take certain actions, many of which might go against the interests of the masses themselves. This is a bad trend by any norm. Thank you.

Mr Yadav: I agree with the views of Mr Gattu. I wonder why Ms Richa has chosen to oppose this topic. Corporate firms use the media to sell products and services. Hence, these corporate firms are exploiting the masses by making them media addicts. The media also exploit the masses by altering their opinions. They are squarely responsible for effecting cultural homogenisation in the nations of the east. After the fall of the Imperialist empire during the last century, the West adopted the mass media. It used the mass media to spread such content as should not have been consumed in the eastern societies. Nevertheless, it was consumed because the media had thrust such content on the masses of the east. This is a bad trend and ought to be reversed. Thank you.

Ms Kashyap: I have been listening to the views of those who have spoken so far. After carefully analysing these views, I can conclude that the media are not to be treated as a villainous demon that is out to demolish or degrade the mass audiences. In today's world, every person knows what content is good or bad for him. If a mother learns that her children are watching obscene channels, she can lock such channels. The discretion of the mass audience depends upon mass morality, not upon media blitzkrieg. If you do not like a content, reject it. If a media content disturbs your moral values, do not consume that content. But some others could consume that content because they might like it. Today, we have all types of media content. We have to choose according to our needs, moral values and commercial aspirations. Hence, I oppose the topic.

Mr Stephen: I do not support the viewpoint of Ms Kashyap. She wants to state that the children and the youth of today would be able to choose media content according to their needs. In all probability, they would choose to watch a blue film and not a film devoted to religion, if these two choices mere given to them. The media have created such a content that sells easily. Naturally, it would be spicy and raunchy, else it would not sell so easily. Therefore, the media would exploit the mass audience because the latter would always like to consume raunchy content. It is natural predisposition of man to enjoy and have a whole of time. The media provide such outlets as would help him forget his agonies. In this process, he becomes a media addict. He forgets who he is. He buys products and services that are advertised on TV and the Net. He watches adult movies. He surfs through Internet websites and reads all kinds of books. The media make him a slave. He pays money to buy the content that he loves. He is exploited by the media. The consumer of today is not left with many choices, as we normally think. The media thrust products, services and concepts on the consumer. Thank you.

Mr Singh: I agree with the views of Mr Stephen. The media are directly responsible for effecting moral decay in society. They thrust new products and services on us. They provide obscene content and spoil the youth and children. Thus, the media are exploiting the mass audiences. The media compaigns of today are not designed to make people literate, aware or enlightened. Rather, they are designed to get money out of the pockets of viewers, readers and listeners.

This trend must be reversed, as someone has already stated. I fully support the topic. Thank you.

Ms Richa: Let us try to arrive at a consensus statement. Some candidates have opposed the topic while some others have supported it. Who would like to merge these two opposite views?

Mr Gattu: Please allow me to do it.

Ms Richa: Should Mr Gattu conclude?

All: Yes!

Ms Richa: All right. Mr Gattu can conclude now.

Mr Gattu: Thank you for allowing me to give a final conclusion.

Mr Yadav: Your conclusion should merge the views of all the candidates.

Mr Gattu: I shall do in that way, my friend. The group has concluded that the media have been exploiting the mass audiences. This is a bad trend. It can hurt the moral codes of conduct of our society. In fact, it is already affecting our youth and children in an adverse manner.

Ms Kashyap: I think Mr Gattu has repeated what he had said earlier. This is not the group consensus. He has not taken care of the views given by me or by my supporters.

Mr Gattu: I was about to conclude that the choices made by the youth and children must be rational and sans immoral insinuations. But you interrupted me.

Ms Kashyap: No! You were probably keen to impose your views on the group. You may not be able to conclude. Let me give a group statement.

Mr Yadav: Do not create chaos here. We have to conclude quickly as time is running out.

Ms Richa: All right, let Mr Singh decide. He should include the views of all the participants. Do you agree?

All: We do.

Mr Singh: Thank you, friends. The group has concluded that the media are responsible for effecting decay in our society. They exploit the mass audience. At the same time, the satisfied consumers (the audience) are also responsible for choosing and consuming the content spread by the media. Media blitzkrieg has dirty insinuations because the audience want the media to spread obscene or horror-based content. Violence, sex, pornography, thrill, boredom and other features of the media content are a part of the media's blitzkrieg because the audience of today demand such features from the media. Hence, the media are giving what the audience are expecting from them. Both are equally responsible effecting the decay in our moral values. Viewer's discretion is quite often touted as the solution for solving such problems. But this discretion is not exercised by any consumer of today. Media blitzkerieg is a tool to exploit the masses. The media are more responsible for it and the masses are somewhat less guilty in this context. That is because they are vulnerable to this blitzkrieg. Had the media been more responsible and accountable to their clients (the audience), the masses would not have been exploited. Hence, there is a *prima facie* case against the media, although content consumers also cannot be exculpated from the blame. Thank you for your kind co-operation.

DOES MODERNISATION LEAD TO LOSING VALUES AND HERITAGE?

Mr. Naresh : This is an interesting topic which, I am sure, is on the minds of most people. Our society is witnessing sweeping changes; the attitudes are also changing. We seem to be following western ideals in many ways. Today we do not even dress in our traditional way but follow the *'fashion designers'* who give us clothes which may be all right for the west but are impractical in our country. Our music is westernised. Our language and mannerisms are increasingly becoming western. We are supposed to drink liquor and be sexually free if we want to show ourselves modern. If we do not have any of these things, we are not modern and are fit to be merely villagers. It appears that to show ourselves modern, we must become some sort of westernised nuts. I think this is sad. We have a rich culture, yet all we do is mindlessly follow an alien culture. It thus appears to me that modernisation means losing our traditions and our values.

Mr. Rajesh:—Mr Naresh had a point, imitating west in respect of sexual behaviour and consuming liquor. Surely you cannot defend that? Today we have western style parties where young people, including girls, show that they have no long ups. I take your points that wearing a jean is very convenient and even English is the language which connects us to the rest of the world. But how can you defend these things? Society is opening up and many of the influences are indeed very harmful. We can well do without these things as they are not part of hour heritage.

Ms Shalini:—The argument that I have heard often. What is it about sex and liquor that worries us? Remember, India had one of the most open societies in the World, as can be seen from our ancient texts. Prudery was imposed upon us by the British. It is ironical that, though Britain has been able to shake off its prudery. We are left with the colonial baggage and continue to defend to this day our suppressive society. Perhaps you are scared that young people will be corrupted by these things. There are two aspects of this. First, our people are only now coming out of their self-imposed prudery and it is natural that they might overdo something. We too find it shocking, but this will decrease in the future, as has happened in the west. Secondly, young people always have done what they liked. Now things are simply coming out in the open. I think we should be happy that youth can be free with their parents and confide in them rather than do tilings hidden from them. We should not worry too much about outside influences. Moreover, there are other things in our tradition that are best discarded. For instance, there is the blind faith of people in "Sadhus" and godmen. Many of them are charlatans and do not deserve the respect we give them. Then there is the dowry and the related problems of bride burning and female infanticide. Are these the values we should be proud of? The sooner we get rid of such traditions the better is it for all of us.

Ms Princy:—I agree that our society is undergoing a tremendous change. A number of influences have come in with liberalisation. The culture of the west appeals to a lot of young people since it is based on the principle of personal freedom. Whereas, in the west this freedom resulted in young people becoming economically independent, thereby fuelling economic growth, what we are imitating are the outside trappings of freedom. Nobody wants limitations on how you dress, talk or behave. There is no harm in being modern, but what we are witnessing today is that we are taking the negative aspects of the western culture without its positive aspects. At the same time, we are forgetting our own values, which have suddenly become unfashionable.

Mr Atul:—Let us define the values which, we say, are Indian and are supposedly being discarded. What are those values? Youth have never been given the authority to do things, leave alone starting business ventures like one started by Bill Gates. Our society has held the individual back for too long. Now, if they take up values of the west and try to "*break free*" what is the harm? Why to be scared about wearing a saree or dhoti when it is convenient to wear these things in day-to-day life? In the fast life of today when have to run and catch buses and so on. Wearing jeans is much more convenient. It is not merely the desire to be modern. To say that we should wear out traditional dresses just for the sake of keeping up our tradition would be foolish. Similarly, I do not see what is wrong in speaking English, though it is a foreign language. English is the language of modern technology and communication. If we use any other language, we will cut-off ourselves. Therefore, I find it wrong that you criticise our imitating modern clothes and speech. It is not merely imitating, it is taking the best of both the worlds for no other reason than our own convenience.

Mr Atul:—The argument that I fully agree with is that there is no point worrying too much about the loss of certain negative aspects of our own traditions. It is not as if our culture is better than others. In fact certain aspects of it have made us under achievers backward looking.

While other countries advanced. We remained stuck in our *"Hindu rate of growth"*. I also agree that we should not worry about outside influences too much. Indian society has the ability of assimilating the best of each of the cultures that came here. Many invaders come, but Indian society and traditional values were able to take the best out of them. I have no doubt that the same will happen even now. Our society will take the best elements from the west but its good traditions and values will remain untouched.

Mr Naresh:—I do not agree with the view expressed by Mr Atul. What happened in the past was that invaders brought their customs which were limited to certain geographical areas. Thus, society as a whole was never influenced. What is happening now is an invasion of values as never before. We, no longer celebrate Indian festivals like *Baisakhi* and *Holi* as we used to. But look at Valentine's Day and New Year's Eve! I fear, we are forgetting our own traditions and imitating western traditions without even comprehending what they are and what they stand for. What is alarming is that we have begun to mistake western values as fashionable and Indian values as unfashionable. In an effort to keep up, we are forgetting own root. Gandhian values of austerity and non-violence have become unfashionable, in favour of violence, revenge and materialism. We do not even value honesty and human virtues. I am afraid that we are heading towards anarchy, with little to guide us in personal and professional matters. It is no wonder that corruption in public life has increased like never before.

Ms Princy:—There is a point in what has been said by Mr Naresh. Have you seen some of our young people speak Hindi and other languages? It is one thing to defend English but the genteel way of speaking local languages is truly bugging. But it is fashionable to speak like that. Let me also point out that forgetting everything, that we have cherished is not a good idea. Even in Europe some countries jealously guard their traditions from the onslaught of the American culture. In France and Germany, they do not argue in favour of English the way we do. In fact, they are proud of there language. But in India we have begun to speak Hindi like English! We go to ridiculous length to appear modern. It is good to be modern but it certainly should not mean sacrificing our values and heritage.

Mr Rajesh:—I think the argument is misleading. Suppose we say that we should not sacrifice our heritage, can we really stop the trend? The fact is that we cannot. Technology makes sure that outside influences are bound to come and trying to stop them is foolish. In France and Germany there is national pride in values. Here we don't have that pride. In fact, self-criticism is a national hobby. If we do not have pride in our traditions and values who is going to protect them? In all fields of life we have taken the British system and we have also ensured that the ruling class is westernised. How can we then stop the masses from trying to copy them? It is no wonder that people want to send their children to English medium schools. Once we do that, how can you stop youngesters celebrating western festivals? We cannot say that we must speak and behave like the Englishmen but remain Indians at heart. It is quite an impossible thing to do. I would say that we should not worry too much and let matters take their own course. If people realise themselves that they are doing wrong by discarding Indian values, there is hope that will survive. But if people do not have pride, then the values are best discarded, the sooner the better.

Ms Shalini:—The discussion has thrown some interesting points and some heated debate. It is good to be modern, but I would say that we should maintains our own values. The danger is that we may forget them. No doubt, India has a way of assimilating outside influences. Perhaps we, can assimilate some good things from the west's cultural invasion. At the same time, there are certain traditions that are best discarded, Indian society would do well to get rid of things that take us backward. But what is required is that people develop a respect for our customs. That can only be developed over a long period of time, and there is need to modify our education system so that the sense of pride is inculcated otherwise, perhaps there is no way that we can stop our people from forgetting our basic values and heritage.

MACHINES VS MEN

No. 3 :—Thank you, friends for allowing me to start this group discussion session. The topic for today's discussion is 'Machines vs Men'. If you look at the evolution of computers, you will find that smaller machines and laptops were developed keeping in view the needs of people. Artificial Intelligence will also be developed if it finds any practical use. Rather than replacing man, it will also remain a tool for man. Let us not go back to the times of the industrial revolution and repeat the arguments that people raised at that time. Development is a law of nature and we will continue thinking of newer things and smarter machines. Each of these will make life easier for man and help him in exploring new vistas. Man has something more in him, and that is consciousness. Even when he sleeps, his mind is at work. But if you switch off a computer, it just becomes a dead object. So, even though computers may mimic humans, they remain only machines. They have raw powers of computation, but do they have 'a sense of what is right or wrong? Of happiness and sorrow? Of doing things on their own? Let us not forget that a computer or a railway engine, was created to help man, not to replace him.

No. 6 :—Man's inventiveness knows no bounds. In every field, newer and sophisticated things have been made. Computers are now available that can do things much faster and more efficiently than any human. Robots have been developed that can do things almost like humans. They are not only replacing workers in factories but redefining how work is done in organisations, for example, earlier it required an army of accountant and auditors to make the balance sheet of a large organisation, now one or two persons can do it with the help of computers. Computers do many things these days, including playing games. Slowly, machines are going to replace men in many spheres of activity. People are going to lose jobs and already unemployment rate in the country is alarming.

No. 1 :—I do not agree with No. 6. While it is true that computers are doing things and are getting smarter, yet they can never replace man. Even if they become smarter, they will always require man to run them. They can not do jobs on their own. Rather than take away jobs, they have helped economies to grow and created new jobs in a way that could not be imagined. In some areas, fewer people may be required to do the same job but at the same time, new employment opportunities have been created. So, it is wrong to say that the computers have taken away jobs and have replaced men. In banks, for example, computers have helped work to be performed efficiently but the number of jobs has not reduced. On the contrary, systems experts are required which has increased the number of people employed. Thus, there is a shift in the kind of jobs that are available. Man has been freed from doing routine, repetitive jobs which are delegated to machines. He can use his mind on more creative pursuits instead. A bank accountant can provide service faster to customers as the routine task of updating ledgers is done by computers. In addition, some totally new industries have opened up. In India, the software industry has picked up and jobs have been created in thousands. So a computer is only a tool and cannot replace man.

No. 4 :—If we look in a slightly different perspective then, there is no fear that machines will replace man. A robot will be as smart as the software given to it. Will it be able to take decisions on its own? In fact, getting it to do things that are not programmed into it, will be impossible. The ultimate decisions to be taken will still be man's. Science fiction writers portray the scenario that machines will be able to control man. To my mind, this is impossible. Man has a certain curiosity that makes him try different combinations. He will look at things and try new inventions and discoveries. It is doubtful that a robot will ever develop that kind of intelligence. Can it look at the moon and want to develop a rocket? Can it look at itself and want to reproduce? The fear that machines will ever replace man is misplaced.

No. 6 :—But let us not forget that computers do things faster and more efficiently. If more and more powerful computers are installed, fewer people will be needed. This may be all right for western countries where population is limited, but for a country like India, we need labour intensive technologies that are able to use the manpower available. There is no point following the west blindly. This was the point of the unions that have opposed computerisation in banks and other organisations. They were worried that the workers would lose their jobs and the fears were not misplaced. Today people are losing jobs because of automation. In developed countries there are factories where cars can be produced almost entirely by machines. While productivity per worker has increased because of the machines, a lot of jobs have been lost also.

No. 3 :—That is one of the most backward ideas I have ever heard. Trade unions in India have behaved in a most irresponsible way when it came to automation. They have opposed computers based on their lack of knowledge and also to protect their own positions. Actually it has made the job easier for them. Moreover, though productivity per worker has increased and fewer workers may be required to do certain jobs, employment has increased because volumes have increased. For example, now more people want to invest money because of better services offered, thanks to computers. The information technology has also opened up jobs in other areas. Machines have not led to loss in jobs at a macro-level, but resulted in more jobs being created. We cannot stay with outdated manual technology simply for the sake of keeping people busy. The challenge is to look for more job opportunities that new technology throws up.

No. 1 :—India has remained backward because of our distrust of new technology. It is also wrong to say that computers are better for developed nations and not for us as they replace labour. In fact, computers help in economic development of a country. A higher growth rate will result in more jobs. Simply remaining backward in the hope of protecting jobs will never achieve anything. I would also like to say that the quality of work life has also improved with smart machines. A worker need not be present at places where certain hazardous processes are taking place, a robot can handle the work at such a work station. Infact while sitting at home, individuals can play (deal) with shares and bonds with the help of a computer and not go necessarily to the share market. The fear of machines replacing man arises because we think that the machines have intelligence of their own. Indeed, there is a race to build Artificial Intelligence. Can we have a *"digital biology",* for instance, a small self-reproducing program that can be put on the Internet; which may evolve by itself and begin to do things on its own? At present these things may sound futuristic but nobody knows whether this can actually happen. If it does, there may be a possibility of machines dominating mankind.

No. 2 :—I think the fear arises when we see computers performing tasks which we find amazing. When a computer plays chess, we are overwhelmed and think that the machine has intelligence of its own, because chess requires a great amount of intelligence. But actually this may not be so. A computer works as commanded by the software which is loaded on it. The software may have millions of chess positions in its database. A computer merely compares the position in its memory and selects the best move according to the rules of the software loaded on it. A clever software will be able to win games, whereas a bad software will not. So it is wrong to talk about the machines intelligence. What is amazing is that a human mind can match and still win against a computer which can analyse 50 billion chess move in 3 minutes. A human mind could only analyses 4 or 5 moves in that time. Yet, a man who plays by the *feel*" of the game is able to win against these massive odds. Now that is real intelligence. A computer is only as smart as the software it has. Even if the computer wins–as it is bound to be in the future–it hardly proves anything. In the words of Bill Gates, "It shouldn't offend, human dignity any more than the realisation that a person with binoculars can see distant objects better than a person without binoculars."

No. 4 :—I think that the fear of people being replaced by computers has arisen because of lack of understanding and knowledge. The argument is similar to the time of the industrial revolution. At that time, people thought that machines would replace man. They did, but different jobs were created and the revolution actually fuelled economic growth. There was a shift in jobs. The same thing is happening now. The information revolution will also cause shift in jobs. Though the machines are smarter and do new things now, they can never replace man. Machines yet are invented to help man do something in a better manner. The smart computers care also something that man will use to do his work. That a machine will do his work and replace him is wrong idea. Like the industrial revolution, the revolution taking place today will help man achieve his ends.

No. 2 :—That is still a futuristic scenario. But, even then I doubt that artificial intelligence can match human ingenuity. If computer virus are created which could reproduce on their own, so were programs to detect and destroy them. Similarly, artificial intelligence could be countered too, if it gets out of hand. But the real fear of the people is not artificial intelligence but whether computers could take away their jobs. Since India has seen how computers assist workers. I don't think any body has fears today that their jobs will be taken away. And since they have led to faster service in most organisations, everybody wants to work with them.

Thank You.

ANALYSIS : Selected Speakers No. 2, 6, 4, 3

Speaker 2 : Sound Knowledge

Speaker 6 : To the point.

Speaker 4 : Logical Arguments

Speaker 3 : Solid treatment of the points.

INTERNATIONAL POLITICS WITHOUT ETHICS—BOON OR BANE

Mr. Subir:—The nexus between politicians and criminals brings forth its own dangers. Why do you think the social evils continue to exist in the country in spite of our best intentions? Surely, a criminal who pays the politician or one who comes to power himself, will use it for his own benefit. Drugs, trafficking in women, smuggling and other evil acts or realms have flourished because the criminals have godfathers among politicians. A tip of the iceberg was exposed when our foreign minister was found to be a beneficiary in the Oil for Food Scam (of the UN) in Iraq. It is all very well to say that it does not affect us but it definitely does. Society is being pushed into a morass. This is surely not right, nor can we say that it will not lead to disaster. It is just a matter of time that something explodes and we may be pushed into anarchy. That is a very real danger. If politicians continue to act unethically, we may well end up being like the failed countries of Africa. Everyday, on TV, we watch poverty, hunger and civil war and the disastrous consequences of selling national interests. I have the fear that India may be following the same path of destruction. Unethical global practices in politics have to stop.

Mr Suresh :—Friends, the topic we have today is very relevant in the present context. Politics has really degenerated in our country and there seems to be no morals or principles left in political life. Getting votes is all. What happens after that seems to be nobody's business. If democracy is a will of the people, we have witnessed complete subversion of what we stand for. Things cannot continue like this and may well result in a disaster. The world over, politicians have come to grief whenever they resorted to unethical practices and there is no reason why the same should not happen in India too. The Volcker Report is out. Nearly 2000 International firms are said to be involved in the OFFP Scam of Iraq. These firms acted like criminals and colluded with Saddam Hussein to mint millions. The peoples of Iraq are suffering while these firms have amassed large fortunes. This is shameful. The culprits must be brought to book and punished.

Mr. Vicky:—I do not think Mr Suresh is right. By definition, politics is the art of manipulating people. The politician has to gain the seat of power by hook or crook. He has to misguide the electorate and then, he has to look for allies. Constant realignments can, therefore, be made. Being in power is important because no benefits are obtained by staying out of power. The actual concept is that of profit maximisation. An industrialist does the same and so does each one of us. It is a law of economics. What does the industrialist do when he finds that operating a machine is not profitable? He sells it. Similarly, if he finds that a worker is not adding to his profits, he will certainly get rid of him. The politician too does the same, using and discarding allies. Why should he stick to people when they do not help him make money? What is the ideology? What are morals? I think it is a simple thing—maximising profits. Note that any international politician is not in the game for altruistic reasons. He is a human being, like any other. He has the right to form his alignments. Of course, there are safety checks as well, as he can be booted out by his people.

Mr. Subir:—That is the modern outlook, but I don't think that it is right. The principle of profit maximisation works only to some extent. I agree that money plays an important role today, but a leader has no right to be in politics if he is in its solely for money. He should start a business if he is looking only for profits. Being a leader, implies for looking after the needs of the people. It is a public job involving public trust. Look at Italy, a nation that was ruled by mafias. Attempts to clean up resulted in brutal murders. People lost faith in politicians and finally, some order is returning. The point is that unprincipled politics just cannot work for long. Unethical doings result in violence and even our society has been witnessing scams and violence of all genres. Two of our Prime Ministers were allegedly involved in scams. This trend will continue if people lose faith in politicians. The public cannot be taken for granted. How can they respect a minister who is involved in scandals and corrupt practices? If the system fails to punish him, it would not be surprising if people resort to violence. It would lead to anarchy and disaster and the cause of this would be unprincipled politics. I think that politicians should read the writing on the wall. Keep global polity clean.

Ms Jayanti:—I think Mr Subir is missing an important aspect. People often feel powerless against the system. Most people in the country never vote—the percentage of people casting votes is nearly 50 per cent. They want to go on with their lives and work without being bothered by the evil plots of politicians. There is a kind of apathy in the air. So, what disaster are we talking about? I think things will continue as they are till the politicians get tired of their own games. For example, no party is able to get on absolute majority these days because people have stopped trusting the politician. We have seen the consequences at the centre, where no Prime Minister will last for long in an era of coalition politics. Either the coalition partners will start fighting or somebody will withdraw support. In Kashmir, no government could be formed for some time and then, two rival parties had to support each other in a unique system of government by rotation. Slowly, I think, the politician will realise that all he can get is power for a short term only. He can be motivated to act in an ethical manner. But it will certainly not lead to disaster if he does act in that manner.

Ms Neelu:—I disagree with Ms Jayanti since uncertainty will result in delayed decisions. Often, it may be in the matters of international importance such as defence and foreign relations. It is very well to say that things will continue till the politician learns his lesson. But that allows a foreign country to take advantage of the situation and attack India? It will be a walkover for any country if we have a government that is not able to take decisions and is more keen to satisfy the coalition than look after the national interest.

Mr Suresh :—India did not protect the nuclear interests of Iran in a crucial meeting of the IAEA. This is an ugly facet of international politics. India should have supported Iran, not the USA. This is also a kind of corruption. We are being forced to toe the line of the USA and its allies. We are also interacting with foreign agencies to get aid. God knows how many new scandals would be unearthed. If we were told to analyse the details of such transactions with foreign funding agencies, we would be able to unearth many scams. These agencies do not give money to recepient nations free of cost. For instance, why should any foreign agency give money to a politician without expecting something in return? I am afraid that the interests of the country have been sold off in many matters. The country has become a dumping ground for toxic wastes of the developed nations. But it is done so secretly that not many know about it. We are importing polluting technologies from the West but do not know about them. Our plants and genetic wealth are being destroyed by companies of the developed world.

Mr Vicky :— That may be too pessimistic a scenario and I oppose it. After all, unethical politics have existed in the country since the age of Mahabharata. But, we have remained as we are and no disaster has happened. So, I think we are getting irritated without any reason by the Volcker Report. As he has been mentioned earlier, the leaders will themselves realise the consequences of their unethical dealings and learn a lesson. Common people have really nothing to worry about. We have lived through many foreign invasions and even a foreign rule but we are not as badly off as many other countries. Let us not, therefore, talk about disasters. One great advantage we have in our country is that we are a democracy. Politicians too know that if they lose the trust of the people, they will not be able to come back to power. So, we have adequate safety checks within our system. Let us not be pessimistic, friends. Let us see if we can set the system right. If we cannot, let us not bother about it. We should do our work and let the leaders reap the consequences of their actions. There is something called natural justice too and our leaders know about it too well. As surely as a person who lives by the sword will die by it, a person, who lives unethically, will not be able to escape from the wrath of his actions.

Ms Jayanti :—That, I am afraid, is too fatalistic. You are in the wrong in saying that unethical global politics does not lead to disaster. The first World War and the second World War bear destiny to the fact that unethical global politics leads to disaster. It also depends on how you define disaster. I think that if our independence gets taken away or we have to toe the line of other nations, it would be a disaster. Unfortunately, our interests are being sold off by our leaders. Patents have already been mentioned and there are reports that neem and basmati rice have been patented. Slowly, our independence and self-sufficiency are being taken away from us and we are not even realising it. Being complacent will not help. We have to realise what is happening and prevent unethical global politics if we are supposed to save ourselves.

Ms Neelu :—Many views were expressed on both sides but I think there is a consensus that global politics without ethics is definitely a disaster. There may be many things that we may not realise today but there is a danger that the selling of India by politicians will land us in a disastrous situation. We must make global trade transactions totally transparent. We must unseat corrupt politicians too. On this note, we end discussion, which has given all of us quite a lot to think about. Thank you!

All :—Thank you!

SPORTS MUST BE SEPARATED FROM POLITICS

Mr. John : India's sports scenario is beset with many problems. Firstly, our sports stars do not perform well in the national-level and international-level tournaments. Secondly, they do no get adequate daily allowance and good accommodation when they go for their training schedules. Thirdly, they do not have secure jobs, which would help them survive after their heydays are over. Fourthly, the political bodies like the BCCI indulge in political bickerings and wars over trifles and slow down the tempo of sports movement in India. The last factor discussed by me is probably the chief causative factor that is hurting our sports. If it is eliminated, all the other (three) factors would become conducive to the sports movement in India. Politicians play their own games in India's sports arenas. Medals cannot be won if politicians act like spoilsports. They should be told to move away from every sports arena.

Ms. Preeti : My friend has given nice views about the topic. But little does he know that sports management has become a professional realm nowadays. Every team requires a professional coach, manager, physiotherapist, sponsors and other operational staff. These people are not seen in the sports arenas but are the ones who conduct the show. Work is done both inside the sports arena and outside it. This operation—in the context of every sport or game—has to be executed with perfection. If this is not done, the players do not play well and the spectators do not come to watch them (the players) perform in the sports arena. Therefore, some non-sporting bodies are created. They take care of the management of a particular team. The BCCI is an example in this context. All professional teams have professional non-sporting bodies that govern the managerial operations behind the scenes. We are watching the game and are in front of a scene. Little do we know that behind the scene, a lot needs to be done. Now, some sports bodies have to be elected through election process. In such processes, every person can participate. Naturally, politicians also take active part. That is because they think they can do well in the managerial process of a particular sports body. So, let them take part in the election process of such a body. When they are selected—there are democratic procedures to do so—they must manage the sport or game behind the scenes. If they do not, they are replaced by efficient managers. This is a free market system. A politician is also a part of it. Hence, politicians should be allowed to dabble in sports. It is just possible that they may do well in the particular sports arena chosen by them. Hence, I support the concept that politicians should indulge in sports management activities. Hence, I oppose the topic.

Mr. Khan : My friend has given nice views about the topic. I also agree with her on many accounts. However, she has overlooked an important aspect of the management of sports. Politicians do not join such bodies to help the sports stars or managers. They want to cling to power at any cost. If the cricket of India is a star performer, they want to get into the BCCI. If our hockey stars do well, these politicians make a beeline to join the IHF. The same fact is true for other sports bodies as well. They are not going to serve the sports discipline. Rather, they create obstructions on the way to good performance of sports stars. Further, the recent spate of bickerings in the BCCI has nothing to do with the game of cricket. Cricket players are supposed to get their dues, training, other facilities etc. to do well. They are the highest paid sports persons of India. The BCCI is the richest cricket control body of the world. Politicians want to join it because of the prestige tag attached to it. They want to be those stars that live to be associated with any rising sun. They do not intend to serve the interests of cricketers. They would join any other professional sports body if they are given an opportunity to do so. Hence, I do not like the idea of mixing sports with politics because this combination would hurt any game.

Ms. Saxena : I think Mr. John and Mr. Khan have given the right views. I would also like to align my views with their politics and sports must be separated. This combination can spell disaster for the particular game. We cannot afford to take any risk in any national-level or international tournament. As far as the management of sports is concerned, the particular sports team can be managed by a professional team, not politicians. Such professionals are available in the markets. Government officials may not be able to perform (behind the scene) to deliver good results. So, we can appoint professional managers, from the private sector to organise and execute a sports event. In any case, private players are already involved in almost every sports discipline. They include sponsors, stadium managers, coaches, suppliers of illumination equipment, caterers etc. The government can appoint private parties to manage the players as well as these private players. But politicians should be kept outside the sports arenas of the world. They have already caused enough damage in other walks of life. They can spare the sports arenas of the world. At least one or two realms of human operations should be spared by them. We are tolerating them in other fields. At least give us a reprieve in the field of sports and games. So, I support the topic.

Mr. Jacob : Thank you, Ms. Saxena but I would like to oppose the topic. Our opponents want to state that politicians are a rotten lot. They have taken ones from the internal bickerings of the BCCI to support the topic. Politicians can also prove to be good managers. Rather, they may prove to be better managers than other professional managers of a game. Let us not be cowed down by the expertise of the present-day sports managers. Even such managers can fail under a given set of circumstances. A person with the tag of politician is also equally competent if we compare him with others. He can even prove to be a better performer if he loves the sports discipline he is supposed to manage. If any person fails to manage an event or sports discipline, he is told to leave. Hence, a politician can also be told to leave, if he is unable to contribute effectively to the field in which he has been given a position of responsibility. Power is always associated with responsibilities. Politicians are no exception to this rule.

Mr. Rajashekhar : I have decided to oppose the topic. In my view, politicians have equal chances of entering a sports body. They can also prove to be better managers than others who do not know anything about politics. They are likely to take the particular sports or game to new heights. The BCCI is an example in this context. Because of the efforts of the BCCI, Indian cricket has touched many unscaled peaks. I suggest that other sports disciplines also have similar professional bodies. A politician is a better manager than a sportsman. If a sports star is allowed to manage the affairs of a team, he would try to concentrate on the technical aspects of the game. He would not take care of the managerial aspects of that game. You should know that matches are won by combining technical and managerial skills. A politician is a better manager than a sportsman, whose knowledge is limited to his game. Hence, politicians should be allowed to enter the realm of sports and games and manage it.

Mr. Khan : Thank you, friends! Now, I will give the consensus statement. The group has come to the conclusion that sports and politics cannot be separated, at least in our country. Politicians are needed to manage the non-sports aspects of sports and games. Professional players need such sports bodies as would make the players comfortable in so far as their performances are concerned. But these politicians should be elected through proper electoral procedures defined by the law of the land. They should not be allowed to indulge in back biting and evil machinations to dethrone other members of the body, who are also politicians in most of the cases. They should be encouraged to promote the game in India and abroad, not work against its broader interests. Corrupt politicians should be thrown out of the sports bodies. Only honest and hardworking politicians should be allowed to hold powerful seats in sports bodies.

However, all the politicians and sports specialists must join hands to promote the game. They cannot work in isolation. A politician should take care of the managerial aspects of the sport or game. A player or former player should take care of the technical aspects of the sports or game. We should invite foreign coaches to take care of the technical training of our sports stars. These coaches must not be bothered by the politicians or the holders of powerful offices. I hope you will agree with me on this account.

Ms. Preeti : But the coaches would have to report to the sport body or federation of which they are a part. Politicians would rule the roost in such a body. Then, how will you determine that they are doing their best, given that a politician is likely to head the sport body or federation in question?

Mr. Rajashekhar : Your point has been well taken. I think the politician should guide the coach only when there is a need to do so. A politician can only give suggestions to a coach because the latter knows more about the game. The politician can give only subtle, broad suggestions. The coach is the real guide of sports stars, not the politician. The latter should provide adequate facilities and resources to the former to make training programmes successful and effective.

Mr. Saxena : We now come to the end of this GD session. We had a nice time discussing such a vital issue with one another. With these words, I would like to come to the end of this GD session. The examiner has also given us the signal that the GD session is over. Thank you very much for co-operating.

SHOULD ARMY TRAINING BE MADE COMPULSORY FOR THE YOUTH

Ms Pratima:—Good evening, friends! The topic of today's discussion is—should army training be made compulsory for the youth. I would like to reply in the affirmative. Army training should be imparted to all the youth after the completion of the ten-plus-two class. They should be given this training because it would make them physically sturdy and mentally sound. We all know that armed forces accept cadets and convert them into perfect gentlemen. These gentlemen join the cadres of armed forces and defend the country during peace or war. Our youth would become better individuals after getting army training. Thank you.

Mr Ramesh:—I think this proposition is ridiculous. If a person is not physically fit to get such a kind of training, would you force him to join the barracks? I do not want the youth to get such a kind of training, given that there is no better teacher and educator than life itself. Do not impose army training, or for that matter, any kind of training on the youth of today. They can decide what is best for them. Thank you.

Mr Madan:—Some people oppose this concept and some others support it. In fact, this concept has picked up as a trend in some countries only recently. I would like to support this concept. It is important to give training to the youth so that they could be prepared for life. If army training is also a part of their training schedules, there is no harm in accepting as a national norm. After 10+2 class, every youth should join such training schedules for a period of six months. Then, he can choose a career of his liking. Thank you.

Ms Asha:—I think this is a ridiculous concept. I would like to align my views with that of Mr Ramesh. No one is giving any consideration to the training of young girls. We are considering only boys for the purpose in their late teens get this kind of gruelling training? Army Jawans are made of different stuff. A girl would become a women later. How can we put her health to risk? Thank you.

Mr Kapoor:—Friends! This is an interesting topic. But I don't know who to support. I think Ms Pratima is right. But Mr Ramesh is not wrong either. I would like to align my views with the collective group opinion.

Ms Pratima:—But we have not decided anything yet.

Mr Kapoor:—It's OK, whenever you decide, please tell me.

Mr Roy:—That's ridiculous who told you to come here?

Ms Kannan:—Please, Mr Roy. Do not attack him. He has the right to say anything when his turn is due. You give your views now.

Mr Roy:—All right. My view is that army training should not be made compulsory. Those, who want to get this training, should be given such training free of cost. Girls should not be forced to get this kind of training. The period of this training schedule must never exceed one year. If some youths are able to make up their mind and eager to join the armed forces, they should be accepted by the armed forces.

Mr Madan:—Should they join the armed forces without going through tests and interviews?

Mr Roy:—Yes! That is because they would already have gone through the tough schedules of training during the training period. It is not at all necessary for them to face those tough conditions again, given that they would be really in the armed forces after they decide to join. Thank you.

Ms Kannan:—It is my turn now. Thank you for analysing the topic from two perspectives. A group discussion session must look at both the sides of the coin. In my view, there is no harm in making army training for the youth compulsory after the 10+2 level of education. The youth must go through these gruelling schedules at least once. That way, they would be better prepared for life. One of my friends has pointed out that the youth should be allowed to decide whether or not they would join such a course. But my contention is that no one would join this course voluntarily. Army training is a tough job for every one of us. We would have to be trained per force. After we are through, we can come back and start a normal life. Nevertheless, this gruelling training schedule would become a pleasant memory of our life. It would make us physically fit, emotionally stable and mentally alert. A friend of mine has also given similar arguments and I fully support him.

Mr Ramesh:—What about the training of girls?

Ms Kannan:—Let the group decide. In my views, girls are equally competent, in physical terms, if we compare them with boys. Women are flying fighter aircraft. They are also working in the cadres of the army. A girl of 16 or 17 years of age would love to be trained. That is because she would make herself physically fit that way. Once she gets married, she cannot keep herself physically fit. Thus, this training would prepare her for life. There is no second chance for her in this context.

Ms Asha:—Let us discuss the issue in detail. I have already stated that women are not fit for this kind of training. Why should we make it compulsory for girls in their teens? Further, boys should also be allowed to decide whether they would like to get this kind of training or not. Some one has rightly stated that every youth should be allowed to choose his mode of education. The circumstances surrounding a youth decide what he would do and become. My parents want me to get settled in my life. They would probably despise the idea that I am sweating in the remote jungles and learning how to detonate a landmine. This knowledge is of no use to me, given that I am not on joining the armed forces. Even if I were, I would certainly get training after clearing the NDA, CDS or other related examinations. I want to imbibe life one sip at a time. Why should I go through a gruelling training schedule even before actually taking up armed forces as my career? Everything seems to be perfect when its time comes and also, when there is an interest in its intricacies. The modern generation is more keen to dance in discotheques. How would you convince them to get such kind of training? Hence, I oppose the topic, as I did earlier.

Mr Madan:—What is your opinion, Mr Kapoor?

Mr Kapoor:—Oh! Please don't involve me in this debate. I am already too tired to concentrate on the topic. Moreover, I would abide by the consensus statement, as has already been promised by me.

Ms Asha:—It is important for us to evolve a final consensus statement. Would anyone come forward and try to align the thoughts of group members?

Ms Pratima:—I can do it.

Mr Madan:—So can I.

Ms Asha:—This would lead to chaos. Please co-operate, friends.

Ms Pratima:—If that is the case, let Mr Madan sum up the debate and evolve a consensus view.

Ms Asha:—Does every one agree with the proposal of Ms Pratima?

All:—Yes!

Ms Asha:—Mr Madan, please consider the viewpoints of every member and give a final consensus statement.

Mr Madan:— I am not giving the final statement right away. You can alter it, if need be. The tentative group decision is that the youth should be given army training. Those, who are not willing to take it, should not be forced to take it. Girls should be allowed to decide whether they would like to have this training or not. The youth should voluntarily take up such gruelling schedules because they would prepare them for life. However, no one from among the government, educational institutions and parents—would force the youth to take up this training. Such training schedules should develop the physical and mental abilities of the youth. They should also help them explore avenues in the armed forces. After the completion of such schedules, the youth should take up careers of their choice. Infact, their stint in the army, howsoever brief, would help them remain agile, efficient and nationalist to the core. They would realise how much difficult life is for our *Jawans*. Hence, their demands from life would be based on rationale. Thank you for your co-operation.

NO NEED TO SEND LARGE CONTINGENTS FOR INTERNATIONAL SPORTS EVENTS

Mr. Govind : Our country has not done well on the global sports front. We send a team of 80–odd sports stars. Nearly 40 managers, coaches and physiotherapists accompany them. The total number of sports contingent—as far as international sports are concerned—exceeds 100. We spend nearly one crore Rupees on every sports person in a year. Add to this cost, the costs of transportation, participation fee, boarding and lodging and sundry expenses. So, one sports person costs nearly Rs. 1.5 crore when he is sent abroad. On the training of Major Rathore, nearly 1 Crore Rs was spent. He was the only medal winner of India in the Altanta Olympics. This is shameful on our part. Why should we send other sports stars to an international event if they are not even close to the national marks? So, we should choose a limited number of sports stars who satisfy the international sports parameters. All others would do well to stay back.

Mr. Nagar : Did you know that Gavaskar, Tendulkar, PT Usha, Bahadur Singh, Milkha Singh and KD Singh Babu became all-time greats due to international exposure? If we face the storm, we would be able to tame it. If we sit at home, we would not be able to do any thing, despite our talent and ability. Lord Krishna said that we must do our duty. We must not bother about the results.

Ms. Lata : That is not a nice idea, as far as international sports events are concerned. In such events, only the best can survive or win. Just doing our bit of job and taking part in an event would not help India. International sports is not a child's play. I align my views with those of Mr. Govind. So, Mr. Govind and I are supporting the topic.

Mr. Kadam : This topic deserves careful analysis. We have to train our sports stars first. Then, we have to invest money on them. They would start delivering results (in international sports arenas) only if they get the inputs of training, good sports gear, good facilities and sponsorship. Currently, only a few sports disciplines are receiving the attention of private sponsors, spectators, trainers and government agencies devoted to the promotion of sports. If the number of performers is less in our country, we should spend money and other efforts only on star performers. We should not send sports contingents to foreign countries simply because we want to be called a "sports nation." All of you know that sports is not a career in India. We are struggling to survive. Our country became independent only 66 years ago. We are trying to cope with the problems of poverty, illiteracy, social chaos and development. Hence, our sports contingents should be small in terms of size. The resources are limited; they ought to be spent with care. Therefore, I support the topic.

Ms. Shagufta : Mr. Kadam is not trying to understand one basic fact—our progress and achievements in sports are as important as our survival and socio-economic growth. Do you think that we should not aspire to win medals in international sports events till the time we become a fully developed nation? This is not a nice idea. Some people are born sportsmen or sportswomen. Kapil Dev, Gavaskar, Vijay Hazare, Dhyan Chand, PT Usha, Shiny Abraham and Anju Bobby George are the examples in this context. They as well as other sports stars did not wait for India to become a socio-economic superpower. They worked hard in their respective sports disciplines. So, in the future, many more Gavaskars, Ushas and Abrahams would be born in India. What about them? They must do their part of the job, irrespective of the fact that they remain come home sans medals. We must allow the new-generation youth to participate in international contests. Some of them would do well while some others would lag behind the international players. But that is not an issue. We also want to participate to promote the spirit of sports. If the government or private players do not earn due to the failure of our players, let them not lose their heart. In sports, there are always ups and downs. No one can be sure that one will always win. No one can be confident if one will always come out with flying colours in an international sports contest. In chess, to quote an example, people like Anatoly Karpov, Viswanathan Anand and Bobby Fischer have also failed many times. But they are counted among the great chess players of the world. They have earned money. They have won many trophies and awards too. If we do not support the rising stars of sports and games, how would we find out who is competent and capable in an international sports arena? We must work hard to achieve results in the international sports arenas. We must not be afraid of participating in such competitions.

Mr. Govind : Ms. Shagufta, you have deviated from the topic. We want to discuss the issue of participation of large sports contingents (of India) in international sports contests. We are not opposing the concept of success or failure of any sports star in a sports event or game. We have tried to prove that most participants of the Indian contingent prove to be white elephants. They are a burden on the national exchequer too. We want to send only those sports stars (to international sports events) who are likely to win medals and honour for the country. If the selected stars fail, we do not mind. This phenomenon is a part of every game. But look at the performance of the Indian sports contingent in Atlanta. Only one person—Major RVS Rathore—won a silver medal. Don't you think it is ridiculous? How can we take a risk in any international sports event, given that our resources are very limited? We are trying to become rational and not emotional, as far as international sports contests and games are concerned.

Mr. Kadam : I am fully supporting Mr. Govind in this context. Ms. Shagufta has really gone in the wrong direction, as pointed out by Mr. Govind. First of all, we must train our sports stars and other players. Then, we can invest money on them, as sponsorship fees and other promotional expenditures, and send them abroad. But if they are not up to the international marks, they do not deserve to be sent abroad. Take the example of Narain Karthikeyan. He has taken part in many grand prix rallies but he has not won any prize. The selectors would give him a few more chances. Then, they might show him the door. We are happy to learn that he is the only Indian in Formula One Circuit of the world. But the world wants him to do a Hakkinen or Schumacher in his sports discipline. Imagine how difficult it is to join the Formula One circuit. If he is told to leave, the Indians would not be able to produce another F–1 racing specialist to the international circuit for many years to come. But our hockey stars, cricket players and athletes go to international events and come home empty-handed. Why are they not accountable for their actions or performances? Let us not live in Utopia, as far as international sports events and other games are concerned. In any international sports contest, the player should go with loads of enthusiasm and the killer spirit. Those, who do not have the guts and will power to win the tough contests, must not be sent abroad. Needless to state that the number of such sports persons would be very limited. So, if only the right kind of stuff is selected, the size of the sports contingent would be automatically reduced. That would mean less money to be spent, less complications and better results. So, we must concentrate on high-quality performers, not chaff. I hope all of you would agree with me on this account.

Ms. Shagufta : I fully agree with Mr. Kadam and Mr. Govind. So, all three of us support the topic.

Ms. Tarangini : But I have good reasons to oppose all three of you, friends. If we follow your policy, India would never be able to become a sports power in the future. How will we produce all-time greats if we keep on sitting at home? We should not worry about the expenses if we aim for gold and silver medals in international sports competitions. Not all the participants can win medals. It is not possible for any country of the world. We have to keep on sending a large number of sports persons abroad so that they could be exposed to the gruelling schedules and performance parameters of international competition. What I suggest is that corporate players send sports stars by spending money on them and sponsoring their sports itineraries.

Mr. Govind : Ms. Tarangini, the corporate sector would not spend money on novices. After all, millions of Dollars are at stake in any sports event at the international level. A private player would invest his money on the best horse, not on an untrained mule.

Ms. Lata : Friends, we can conclude that India should send only competent sports stars for taking part in international sports competitions. We should send moderate-sized contingents, not large ones, to foreign countries due to cost and sponsorship constraints. Nevertheless, the Indians must continue to take part in global sports competitions, for that is the only way to grow in the realm of international sports and games. Now, Ms. Tarangini can give final views on the topic.

Mr. Kadam : Ms. Lata, our view should prevail. We are in the majority.

Ms. Shagufta : That is bad, Mr. Kadam. We are not in the middle of a battlefield. Ms. Tarangini is also a friend. Moreover, she is mature enough to give an acceptable, logical consensus statement. Friends, should we allow Ms. Tarangini to go ahead?

All : Yes, go ahead.

Ms. Tarangini : Thank you friends. The group has decided that India should send its sports stars abroad so that they can take part in tough international competitions. But the Indian selectors must take adequate care to send only those sports stars abroad who are very near international sports parameters. The contingent should be limited in the sense that its members should have more sports stars (direct performers). The people out of the sports arena need not be large in number. If need be, the contingent's size can be cut down if the talented sports stars are not available to meet the demands of the sports competition. Only probable winners should be allowed to go. "Wannabe athletes" or "also ran stars" should be dropped from the contingent.

SATYAGRAHA—ONLY ALTERNATIVE TO REMOVE CORRUPTION?

Mr Rajneesh : It is a very strange situation that the President and the Prime Minister, two of the most powerful men in the country, are pleading their helplessness and want the people to start a national movement. I want to ask you two basic questions; first, against whom should the *"Satyagraha"* be, and second, what can a common man really do? I think it is very foolish to ask the common man to take up a task which essentially belongs to the government. A common man can merely complain. The complaint is usually never looked into, since the seniors too have their fingers in the pie. In most cases, the investigating agencies ask for proof – how is anyone to gather evidence in a transaction which is essentially verbal? It is the government, on the other hand, which has the power of investigating agencies do their job? Ironically, the same PM who wants us to launch a *"Satyagraha"* also has the dubious record of transferring the CBI Chief when crucial investigations were under progress and also did nothing when the Bihar government should have been dismissed. The message is clear. The government will shield the corrupt while the Indian people may get involved in a movement so that they do not have time to question the actions of the government. This is a very dishonest approach and needs to be condemned.

Mr John: —I agree with Mr Rajneesh. Politicians often make slogans to keep the junta pre-occupied. We have seen the "*garibi hatao*" campaign in the past which did not do anything to remove poverty but it kept the people busy for a while. I am afraid that this "*Satyagraha*" business is also an insincere attempt of the wily politician, to show that he is sincere while actually not being so. And look at the impractical advice being doled out to us, that we should start a national movement. Does this mean that we should take the law in our own hands and mete out justice to the corrupt? How is one to do that, when the government shields those very people? Even if we complain about the corrupt officials, no action is ever taken. Enquiries drag on, if they are constituted at all. The corrupt officials, on the other hand continue to harass the common man by not doing their job unless bribes are paid. If they come to know that someone has complained about them, they will only make life more difficult for the complainant. The PM says that we should be ready to bear hardships and refuse to pay bribes. It is all very well to give such advice from his office. Has he cared to see the amount of hardship that the common man is bearing anyway? Why should he bear more hardships while the political class and the bureaucracy live like parasites and suck the nation's vitality?

Mr Mohit:—Recounting the achievements of the nation on completion of the 66th year of independence, both the President and the Prime Minister mentioned the most oppressive thing that pulled India down; corruption. It has indeed become a very big problem in India. From small jobs like getting a ration card or a driving licence to a big job like dealing with the Income Tax Department, government officials accost you with their hands out, like little beggars in the street. For such a huge problem, the luminaries had a common solution; the President called for a social movement or national movement and the Prime Minister wanted the people to launch "a new kind of Satyagraha". It seems that the government has virtually given up in this matter and that is why such suggestions are being made. There may be some merit in the suggestions, since everybody is corrupt in the system. A people's movement was able to throw out the British from the country. Why can it not do the same with corrupt officials? I think that if we all refuse to pay bribes and are able to bear the hardship, this problem would be reduced to a very great extent. So the ball is in our court, really.

Mr John:—Let us not dismiss the PM's suggestion off-hand. I think he is a well-meaning individual and unlike the others who just accepted things. He has dared to say something about the widespread problem. Let us look at the reason why such a suggestion has come about. It has been floated because the government is unable to fight corruption because of lengthy court procedures, the insistence of documentary evidence and the clout of the corrupt. While honest officers can be transferred, the corrupt can afford to pay bribes to have the orders issued in their favour. Thus, there really cannot be any real evidence of corruption, except for checking the assets of an official's family. Further, there can be no action against politicians because of weak governments. Under such a situation, the PM is right when he says, that the people should come forward and start a movement against corruption. After all, if all of us stopped paying bribes and complain about those who demand money from us, things would certainly improve. We need to have a Gandhian approach and launch a movement of non-cooperation with those officials who demand bribes from us. If people organise *"dharnas"* outside and force the work of the administration to stop, it will look at why people are protesting.

Ms Swati:—It is easy to say such things but difficult to implement them. What Mr John is saying is that people should coerce the administration to act. Does it not amount to taking the law in our own hands? How will the administration respond? It will call the police and throw us in prison. So the problem can not be solved by the people, but by the government itself. Today, the people are disgusted and do not want sermons on corruption. They look for a lead. I will take a guarantee that if any PM takes on corruption head on and takes strong action against corrupt officials, he will be able to get popular support. Instead, we have seen that the leadership is just not willing to take the bull by the horns. Gujral, for example, had the option of taking a strong stand and dismissing the Bihar government, but he has chosen to dilly-dally. Before him, Gowda had the option of dismissing ministers whose names figured in various scams but he chose to hide behind Court orders. When the leadership is rotten, who is to lead by example.

Mr Rohit:—I think, Ms Swati is right when she says that the problem can be solved by only the government. We have to see, for instance, why corruption has arisen in the first place. It has grown because of outdated laws and needless controls. By following laws that require permission for small things, the government is encouraging corruption. Further, the government has to send the message that it is serious. It should remove all the unnecessary controls and also speed up investigations. There are so many pending cases which stretch on without any action being taken. Government action should be swift whenever cases of corruption are reported. Only then will people acquire confidence and come forward to report such things. Unless action is swift, the corrupt will always feel encouraged and have no fear. Unfortunately, swift action has never been taken by any government.

Mr Mohit:—Mr Rohit, you cannot, however, doubt the sincerity of the President and the PM. A special cell has been formed in the PMO and directives have been issued to various departments for streamlining investigations. It can be argued that these are simply bureaucratic responses to a problem which cannot be controlled by bureaucratic methods. That is why, I agree with you that swift action is what is required. One reason that corruption has grown in the country is due to the fact that cases take so long. The courts are guilty to the extent of granting too much time to the corrupt. Rather than indulge in activism in areas outside its jurisdiction, the courts should streamline themselves so that justice is imparted quickly. This will give a lesson to other officers and they will be forced to be honest. Unless all actions are taken simultaneously, fighting corruption will not be an easy task.

Mr Rajneesh:—Mr Mohit's suggestions are very good, but you have left out a very important area and that is of political corruption. If politicians are not clean, every small employee feels it in his right to make money too. But nothing is done to fight political corruption. Even the PM does not have the guts of dismiss corrupt Chief Ministers in spite of clear evidence, nor can he take action when any minister is found corrupt. This has happened in the past as ministers have gone scot free. So, how can we say that the PM is clear about his intentions? Further, how can a common man go on *"Satyagraha"* against a minister? Political corruption can only be fought by the government and any leader who does that will endear himself to the people.

Mr John:—We have had a very good discussion and a number of ideas have been put forward. Most of us feel that the proposal of the PM is not serious enough because the common man is not empowered to do anything. Even his complaints are not heeded. So, how can he launch a *"Satyagraha"*? Mahatma Gandhi's method was successful in forcing a reluctant foreign power to leave the country as they were rendered, helpless. A *"Satyagraha"* will make our present government helpless too, if all citizens start non-cooperation with it. Whose purpose will that solve? Certainly not the nation's. It is the government which should be serious. At the same time, needless controls should be removed. Archaic laws must be replaced so that people are free to do what they want. When power of the government servants is reduced, they will not be in a position to demand bribes. As far as political corruption is concerned, the PM should be strong to take action. In any case, the PM should be decisive and take firm action to show the world what a strong PM can do. Giving impractical suggestions, like a national movement to fight corruption is hardly mature or sensible.

DO PUBLIC FIGURES HAVE RIGHT TO PRIVACY?

No. 1 :—Good afternoon friends! In today's topic of group discussion we will throw light on public figures and their right to private life. It is true that a famous face will always attract curiosity and draw a large number of crowd everywhere. Magazines, journals, electronic and print media and how can we leave behind newspapers of all language that vie with each other to publish their interviews and first-right/exclusive pictures for undisclosed amount of money.

No. 2:—Did you say undisclosed amount of money for a picture?

No. 1:—Yes. Although offering money for pictures is a new concept in India but in abroad it is a very common matter. For example in March' 07 the much publicized and extra lavish wedding pictures of the marriage of British model and socialite Elizabeth Hurley with billionaire Arun Nayyar was sold to the life style Magazine 'Hellol' in exchange of undisclosed amount of money. Basically what I mean is when one is famous, one tends to cash in one's name and fame. Almost all the celebrities hire private bodyguards to protect themselves from unwanted intrusion into their private lives. The trouble with people like late Princess Diana, Britney Spears was and is their activities which are quite high profile. For instance in the case of Princess Diana, her marriage to Prince Charles was the main attraction where as Britney Spears' highly promisciuous attitude attracts a natural curiosity among the masses. But, personally I think the Indian media is more conservative in their attitude towards the public figures as compared to their foreign counter-parts.

No. 2 :—Do you mean public figures do not have the right to live normally?

No. 1:—If they have something to say, they can always call a press conference, why follow them around like scavengers? There should be a code of ethics for the media so that it does not become a nuisance. The idea about our media being different is not correct, too. Since Indian Newspapers also publish such pictures. Take a look at the international pages of any newspaper and you will find useless pictures many a times. These pictures are easy to get from foreign wire agencies and are used without even thinking. Indian newspapers are also guilty because they too have published pictures of Lady Diana. So you cannot say that things are different here than they are elsewhere.

No. 5 :—People all over the World were shocked at the way Princess Diana died in a car crash in Paris, in the most tragic of circumstances. News reports say that her car was pursued by several photographers, at a speed above 100 km per hour, which could have unnerved the driver and caused the crash. It was a sad and untimely end for a woman loved around the globe. The Press had pursued her at every stage, even publishing her pictures while she was bathing or relaxing with friends and, in a way, they had a direct hand in her death. The greed of the photographers was obvious from the fact that some of them took the pictures of a trapped Diana, as she was dying in the car and offered them for sale to newspapers. It did bring to light a most inhuman attitude—rather than helping a person in distress, the photographers just wanted to take pictures and make money out of the accident. In fact, they had to be shooed away from the accident site by the police. The episode raises many grim questions-first, is it justified to pursue celebrities at every step for a mere photograph? Second, don't the celebrities have a right to be themselves? And third, what about the ethics of the Press, which is meant to inform, educate and serve the public interest, but many of the pictures published by them do neither? Answers to these questions are very important.

No. 3:—No. 5, you have initiated the debate very nicely. But before we condemn the Press outright, let us look at the activities of the celebrities. Why go any further? Mallika Sherawat, for instance, used the Press to build up her own image and nobody can deny that the media has also contributed to her aura. Other personalities have done the same. Madonna, for instance, has posed for outrageous pictures to promote her music. Closer home, actresses have frequently dropped clothes for film magazines in order to promote their careers. When the celebrities themselves give up their private self, is it not natural that the media will start pursuing them for more spicy pictures? I think that celebrities love the media attention they get. Is it not like a hunter chasing a victim? The media, on its part, is just fulfilling its purpose of providing information about the celebrities and people do like to read about them and see their pictures.

No. 4:— No. 3 is correct but only up to a point. True, people like to read about famous people but surely not how they spend their private time. What possible public interest is served by publishing pictures of a lady in a swim suit or when she is relaxing? The media has created an artificial market for such pictures. For example, you may buy a paper just out of curiosity to see what is inside but that does not mean that there is a demand for that kind of pictures. The argument that celebrities use the media sometimes, and should not mind when the media pursues them, is also bogus. Celebrities use the media because it allows itself to be misused. And even if someone has misused media to some extent, it does not mean that the entire life of the celebrity should be mortgaged to the photographers. Imagine what a human being would be going through just for being famous. He cannot go to a private holiday just to be with family and friends, without lenses peering from a distance. Before Diana, Jacquiline Kennedy was also pursued and some photographers even went underwater to take pictures of her swimming. This is ridiculous. How would you like to be pursued thus? If we put ourselves in the situation, we might understand the torture that one goes through and the price that one has to pay just for being famous.

No. 5:—I think No. 2 is right. But coming back to the point whether public figures should have the right to privacy, I would say that celebrities are after all human beings and have the right to live life, like everybody else. Why should anyone restrict anybody else's life merely to satisfy the prurient needs of others? Imagine the bad effects that constant pursuing would have on their children. They cannot live like normal people and must always be careful. I think it is very cruel when somebody is forced to live a restricted life. It must be quite unnerving for anyone to be chased at all times, plus the fact that one cannot show natural emotions for fear of being photographed by someone. I certainly think, that no human being should be without the right to public life. Imagine living in a glass house and knowing that, all one's emotions and activities are being watched by the people at all times!

No. 3 :—Why should they put a limit on themselves? Let us remember that the photographers are merely doing their jobs. They are always called upon to cover important events. They rush to accident or war sites to get pictures and inform the world about the truth. We can not complain about that but the driver was also drunk. So who is to blame? Let us remember that a photographer is a mere chronicler. He does not and should not alter events. He is also satisfying the curiosity of the people and that is why newspapers pay high prices for the pictures. An average person surely wants to know about the activities about his favourite hero, including all the personal details. Famous people are role models, so the pictures do satisfy a need however vulgar or base it may seem.

No. 4:—I disagree with No. 3. If you are arguing that all human needs should be met, you will then say that pornographic pictures should be printed in the papers as well. What is the limit to which we will go then? Publishing personal details is all very well, but pictures do violate the privacy of a person. The camera lens is, after all, an extension of the eye and its implacable gaze can twist human destiny. Someone mentioned about Madonna and the Indian actresses who get themselves photographed in outrageous poses and that they do not have a right to complain about photographers. I would say that everyone has a public face and a private face. There are many things that we say or do publically, but surely that does not mean that our private lives should be restricted because of that. Actors have to do many things because it is their profession and show business does require a little boldness. If the newspapers use those pictures, it is because they will profit from them. So it is a matter of mutual benefit. If one voluntarily poses for pictures, that should not mean that he has no right to a private life. If that happened to everybody, most of our leaders, politicians and businessmen would lose their jobs because the compulsions of their jobs require that they speak many things publically which they may not practise in private lives. The public may have curiosity, but it does not mean that all curiosity must be satisfied. The media would do well to apply a one line formula in such cases: does it serve the public interest? If it doesn't, it should refrain from paying photographers for taking pictures of celebrities in compromising situations or personal moods.

No. 1:—Many aspects of the question have been discussed and the question that is recurring is, *"why should access to celebrities be limited only to what they want published? Do the people not have a right to know about those whom they admire?"* The answers to these questions are tough, but

I feel that they have been answered, first, celebrities, are human beings too and must have their share of privacy. Second, though the public may want many things, there have to be limits to their curiosity. We cannot force a person into a life of seclusion merely because a person is famous. As the Press ponders about its role in the west, we in India too must assess whether blind following of media practises is a good thing.

All:— Thank You.

THE MASS MEDIA ARE
THE TOOLS OF SOCIETAL DECAY

Ms Monalisa:— Good morning, friends! In my view, the mass media have proved to be a boon for our society. We are more educated, aware of the issues of the world and enlightened, thanks to the mass media. I cannot imagine a home without TV, a youth who has never watched a Bollywood flick or an elder who does not read a newspaper. Our society is developing due to finely tuned messages of the mass media. The press is free in our country. It has helped the masses raise vital issues of national importance through TV debates, guest columns of newspapers and articles of magazines. The editors of reputed newspapers and magazines have also apprised the masses about the burning social, economic and political issues from time to time. TV is a powerful audio-visual media. It informs, educates and entertains various components of our society; so do cinema, books, magazines and newspapers. Hence, I conclude that the mass media are not the tools of our societal decay. Rather, they are the chief modes for effecting deep-rooted societal growth. Thank you!

Mr Rizwan:—Good morning, friends! Perhaps, Ms Monalisa has looked at only one side of the treacherous coin of the mass media. The Net is full of pornographic web sites. Our cinema portrays women in a filthy manner. Our newspapers are full of gossips, rumours and false news. The quality of TV software is dubious but no one dare challenge media barons like Subhash Chandra (Zee TV Network) or Rupert Murdoch (Star TV Network). Our children sit before the idiot box and imbibe negative cultural values of the West. Sex is free in America and this trend is stealthily setting in here too. Materialism and individualism are deemed two vital ingredients to succeed in life. Our old culture does not approve of such values, which have been imposed on us by the mass media of today. I vehemently support the topic. I suggest that the government, NGOs and social service groups take necessary actions to check the ill effects of the mass media. Thank you!

Ms Joseph:— Good morning, friends! you may like it or not but the mass media have arrived in India to stay. I am sure Mr Rizwan must be viewing movies on Star Plus and popular soap operas on Zee TV. However, he is also critcising the CEOs of these two networks. The mass media have given us the power of information: Entertainment is only one of its major functions. The age of media coverage has proved to be a boon to students, the youth, housewives and old alike. True, we have imbibed some western moral values. However, what is the harm in imbibing them, if they are able to develop our society? If the western individuals are efficient and go-getters, we should also follow their footsteps. The mass media tell us where the world is at present. They give us minute-by-minute information about economy, politics, sports, education and many more fields. They keep us abreast with the latest data in the field of sciences, IT, space research etc. Hence, our society has become ambitious and hard working because it wants to emulate other advanced societies of the world. In my view, there is no ill effect of this trend. Societies must change and the mass media are the most effective tools for bringing change.

Mr Dandekar:— Good morning, ladies and gentlemen! The mass media of today are the stooges of the western corporate firms. They have brought "Pizza Culture" into our society, which was hitherto a heaven of naturalism. Our moral values have changed or decayed because our original value system was much better than that of the West. Even the westerners admit this fact that our culture and moral principles are the best in the world. The mass media have drastically altered our moral values and that is why societal decay has been effected. The mass media shamelessly promote free sex, individualism, materialism, stealthy professional tactics and cleanage of families. We do not support such manoeuvres of the present mass media. Thank you!

Mr Ali:— Good morning, friends! I am indeed pleased by the views of those who have spoken so far. I would tend to align my thoughts and views with those who have opposed the topic. The mass media are not the tools of societal decay. The society of any type or having any traditional feature must be capable of accepting or rejecting the negative values that are bombarded on it through the mass media. Our soceity has a history that dates back to 5,000 years! How can the mass media lead us to our moral decay? Our culture is unique, resilient and strong enough to withstand the invasions of all the types. During the past, such invasions were done through intensions by foreigners. Today, such invasions are from the sky; Cable TV, Internet, Cellular Phone etc are the prominent examples of the invasions of the latter type. Our society has remained a singular entity despite its multi-cultural hues. If the foreign invaders could not tear apart over aeons old socio-cultural canvass, then, friends, be sure that the currently popular mass media would also not be able to do so. We were Indians to the core and shall remain so despite the media blitzkreig. The mass media cannot affect our value system, though they may have been able to make a few dents on our cultural veneer due to their electronic charisma. Thank you!

Mr Rizwan:— Mr Ali, the topic is not about the resilience of our society or culture. Rather, it is about the efficiency of the mass media as the tools of societal decay.

Mr Ali:— I have stated the same thing, my friend. I want to point out that they are not the tools of societal decay.

Mr Rizwan:— But you have said that such tools would not be able to change our socio-cultural tablic.

Mr Ali:— True! I have said almost the same thing.

Mr Rizwan:— That means you admit that the mass media are affecting us.

Mr Ali:— The mass media are trying to effect change in our society but they would not be able to effect deep-rooted change. I want to point out that our society has not degraded so much (due to the media invasions) that we should be ashmed of it. Let me put it in another way—the mass media are trying to act as the tools for our societal decay but they would not be able to effect deep-rooted changes in our culture and moral values. The resilience and perseverance of our complex social system is well-known.

Ms Monalisa:— We have understood what you want to state, Mr Ali. Mr Rizwan was stating that you have slightly altered the topic. you are not allowed to do so. The topic is—the mass media are the tools of societal decay. Do you agree with the topic, or do you want to oppose it?

Mr Ali:— I believe that the mass media are the tools of societal decay.

Ms Monalisa:— Here you are! You stated earlier that the mass media are not the tools of societal decay. After my intervention and careful cogitation over the views of Mr Rizwan, you have finally admitted that the mass media are really the tools of societal decay.

Mr Ali:— I am sorry, Ms Monalisa. However, what I wanted to state was that the mass media would not be able to tear our strong socio-cultural fabric. Am I right?

Ms Monalisa:— Your views have been well taken, Mr Ali. We only wanted to bring you to the focal point of discussion. Although I oppose the topic, yet I agree that your views carry a lot of weight.

Mr Ali:— Thank you for giving me the right direction, friends!

All:— You are welcome, Mr Ali.

Mr Dandekar:— Now that Mr Ali has agreed that the mass media are the agents of our societal decay, we should arrive at a consensus view. Time is running out.

All:— Thank you!

IT SECTOR NO LONGER A GREEN PASTURE

Mr. Premdasa : The IT sector is no longer a green pasture. I fully support the topic. It is not possible to continue the tempo of growth of this sector. The IT bubble burst in the late nineties. It has not grown, after its recovery, to become a big lucrative bubble again. I would suggest that young boys and girls join some other sectors now. Unemployment rates are high in India and the USA in this sector.

Ms. Aarti : This is not a debatable issue that the IT sector has staged a comeback. Look at the BPO sector. This sector has become a wage earner for millions of Indians. It is very much a part of the IT revolution. I want to oppose the topic and contend that the view of Mr. Premdasa is wrong.

Mr. Anees : I agree with Mr. Premdasa. Many people have changed their jobs. They were IT specialists earlier. They are not able to get jobs now. There is a glut in the IT market across the globe.

Ms. Sharmila : I agree with the views of Ms. Aarti. The IT sector is a wage earner for millions of families; India is a hot IT destination. We cannot underscore the importance of system analysts, programmes and other IT professionals. They have a bright future ahead of them. However, unemployment rates are very high in every industry. We cannot pinpoint the IT sector for the anomalies in our system. Despite the fact that the IT sector has received many setbacks since 1998, it is one of the best green pastures the world over. The Chinese are depending upon us. Germany needs our IT professionals. The situation is not as bad in the USA as we imagine it to be. In sum, the IT sector is still going strong and we should invest money and manpower in this crucial industry.

Mr. Anees : There are many other green pastures where the Indians can try their luck. Engineering and manufacturing are two lucrative options. Our industry is growing at the rate of nearly 7.0 per cent per annum. The GDP growth rate is 7.5 per cent. So, engineers and production staff can make hay while the sun shines.

Mr. Premdasa : The import-export business is also doing well. Our youngsters can become exporters. They can also import a variety of goods and sell them in India. Why should we over emphasise the need to join the IT sector? In the BPO sector, the problem of late-night duty is a major hurdle. Women cannot do night duty. I think our youths should choose engineering, production, international trade or basic sciences. Education is also a good field; so is the tourism business.

Ms. Aarti : I do not agree with you, Mr. Premdasa. An IT specialist need not be an engineer. In order to join an engineering or manufacturing firm, you must have a technical qualification.

Mr. Premdasa : Ms. Aarti, conditions are worse even in the IT sector. Novices do not get jobs in any sector. One has to do very well to remain in his office and that is true for all the sectors. We are talking about the number of jobs available in the IT sector and the growth prospects associated with each job. Not much is left in this sector. Only a few top-notch jobs are available for hard-core professionals. I hope you would agree with me on this account. Information is free in the new millennium. The managers of information have already developed state-of-the-art software, hardware and peripheral devices. The market prices of hardware and software have gone down. A PC, which cost Rs. 40,000 in 1999, costs only Rs. 19,000 (or less) in 2005. Too many people are chasing too few jobs, hence the chaos in the IT sector. Know that IT-based firms do not need people; they need machines. Hence, there is no need to make a beeline in front of the offices of IT firms.

Ms. Sharmila : Friends, the group has concluded that the IT sector, despite the fact that it has staged a comeback, is no longer a green pasture. Even after taking a U-turn, it has not been able to support millions of IT professionals in India and abroad. There are some signs of recovery, as far as job markets are concerned. But we must note that this sector may not offer lucrative opportunities to all the youths. Hence, some of them must shift to related or different sectors to keep their kitchen fire burning. IT is an unstable industry. A large number of employees cannot be supported by any firm of the world. This fact is more relevant in the Indian context.

Mr. Premdasa : I was coming to that point in my consensus statement, Ms. Sharmila. Friends, the BPO sector has a lot of potential especially in India. That is because BPO firms of India charge less for providing IT-based services. However, we should note that this field is not a cakewalk for women. They have to be extra cautions while choosing BPO jobs. In sum, the IT sector has a lot of potential but it cannot give lucrative jobs to all the young people. Some of them should opt for other professions. Some of these new fields are quite lucrative. If the manpower load of the IT sector is reduced, it would again become a green pasture. Sinusoidal variations are a part of every kind of industry. The IT industry is no exception to this general rule. We do not rule it out as a major career maker in the markets of India.

SATELLITE CHANNELS ARE
▌CREATING CULTURAL CORROSION▐

Ms Manisha: Good morning friends, the topic given to us is quite a debatable one and I would like to request any of my colleagues who would like to have a go.

Ms Rupali: Well, I favour the topic and I'm very sure that most of my friends will agrees to me that the invasion of satellite channels is proving to be quite detrimental to our society. Honestly speaking, the one section of the society which can be said to be hit badly is the younger generation. Sex and violence seems to occupy the majority of the programmes. For the upwardly mobile, satellite channels seem to open more avenues regarding crime. Sometimes it becomes quite embarrasing to watch these programmes with the family members as most of them are based on extra-marital affairs. In fact the advent of satellite channels have done more harm than good.

Mr Gaurav: I completely agree with the previous speaker about whatever he has said and I'm of the opinion that these channels should be banned. We simply cannot accept all that is shown an these channels. Even some of the advertisements shown are in very bad taste. In other words, these channels have taken the viewers for granted and they care two hoots for their taste. Thank You.

Ms Naina: My friends, both my speakers who spoke before have just said about one side of the coin. As we all know everything has its pros and cons. Satellite channel made its entry into India during the Gulf War in 1990 when CNN telecast the war and most of the people started realising the holocaust of the war and the importance of satellite channel. This was the prelude to satellite channels and today all the top satellite companies are in India to woo the Indian viewers, though our indigenous Doordarshan is still the market leader with vast network and accessibility. I do accept that some of the satellite channels are not showing decent programmes and some of them are quite hackneyed, but in no way they are causing any cultural erosion, as our culture is very strong and has survived many attacks during the last 5000 years. On the contrary, these channels are making individuals aware of more things than before. Viewers have become knowledgeable and have started participating in programmes. Satellite channels have nabbed criminals, brought about a social awareness and taken us to hitherto unknown parts of the world. Moreover the quality of programmes on these channels have helped Doordarshan to polish its own programmes and become viewer friendly. Thank You.

Mr Jitendra: I fully agree with my previous speaker and I would like to add few more points. The invasion of satellite channels have given a new dimension to the entertainment industry. The job opportunities are also there for taking. What once seemed impossible has now turned into reality. Channels like Discovery and National Geography have taken human boundaries to unimaginable extents. They have broadened the horizons of human mind. As far as the programmes are concerned, it is upto the viewers— what to reject and what to view. Moreover, programmes are devised for entertainment and nothing more. As far as the extra-marital affairs are concerned, the channels show whatever is happening in the society. They serve as mirror of society, so we should not be biased. Thank you.

Ms Manisha: Well friends, it has turned out to be an excellent and healthy discussion. As far as my views are concerned with due regards to Ms Naina and Mr Jitendra, we cannot help overlooking the fact that satellite channels have eroded the Indian culture to a great extent. It can be seen from the fact that designer deresses have come on the scene and the dress style has quite trendy. The crime based serials which aim to prevent crimes, are in reality promoting crimes. Our generation has started becoming "zombie" socialising is a passe. A research has shown that an average viewing time by school and college going students is 3 hour. Moreover, with so many channels coming in, one feels lost and develops the habit of channel surfing. No doubt that in USA, TV is referred to as an "Idiot Box." It literally turns its viewers into bumbling iditos. Thank you.

Ms Sushma: As far as I'm concerned, nothing is as entertaining as these satellite channels. I view quite a good number of knowledgeable programme, especially the talk shows are a class apart. You come to know the views of various persons. Cricket is simply superb; people prefer watching cricket on television, rather than in the stadium. To conclude I can only say that satellite channels is a revolution; life has never been the same. Thank you.

Mr Prabhat: Since I do not watch satellite channels as I have no cable connection, I cannot throw much light on this matter. I still believe that Doordarshan is the best. "Be Indian, Watch India."

Ms Sangita: Hello friends, in my opinion watching television is itself a wastage of time and energy, except for the news. However, I feel that satellite channels will one-day break down our old traditions and systems and the day is not far enough when these multi-nationals are going to sponsor our "National Anthem." This is the age of sponsorship. Thank you.

SHOULD WE PUNISH NATIONS WITH WEAPONS OF MASS DESTRUCTION

Mr Khandekar: Good morning, ladies and gentlemen! My name is Ashutosh Khandekar. If you all wish, I could suggest the name of Ms Neena Saha to initiate this group discussion.

All: She is welcome.

Ms Saha: Thank you friends and a very good morning! My name is Neena. Weapons of mass destruction can be of three types — biological, chemical and nuclear. Biological weapons include Anthrax (bacterium), Small Pox (virus), Botulinum (toxin), Ricin (toxin) etc. Chemical weapons include Tabun (nerve agent), VX (nerve agent), Phosgene (choking agent), Mustard (blister agent) etc. Nuclear weapons include Fusion Bomb, Fission Bomb and Bomb. My contention is that Syria, Iraq, Taiwan, Libya, the USA, Russia and other nations possess such weapons. We must move a resolution in the UN Security Council to punish these countries. Thank you.

Ms Norgay: Good morning friends! My name is Norah Norgay. Ms Saha has rightly pointed out that weapons of mass destruction are in the possession of these nations. However, she has forgotten to mention the names of India and Pakistan. She may have omitted these names and many other due to lack of time. Most of the powerful nations have such weapons. The only difference lies in the type and quantity. I don't think we can punish the USA for having a nuclear command. We can only persuade her leaders to do away with such weapons. Nuclear weapons as well as biological and chemical ones are the products of advanced science laboratories. If these laboratories were closed, the world would automatically return to a saner path. Instead of punishing those nations, whom we call culprits, we should persuade them to protect the life forms on earth.

Mr Singh: Good morning friends! My name is Zoravar Singh. Ms Norgay has not asked for punishing India because she is an Indian. We should think beyond the national perspective in the parlance of such weapons. By punishing these nations, I mean that we should tell them to destroy such weapons in the interest of the mankind. And what is more, these nations should also bear the costs of cleaning the remains of such weapons or the utilities that make these banes on our society. We are not going to hang these nations by the neck. We are only asking them to save this world and pay, in financial terms, for the clean-up operations.

Ms Jamal: Good morning friends. My name is Kudsia Jamal or simply, Kudsia. I don't think punishing Iraq would eliminate all the weapons of mass destruction from that trouble-torn nation. All of you have not noted a vital fact—such weapons can be procured or manufactured with ease. Those nations that have these weapons should be persuaded in the UN to eschew these messengers of death. Those nations that are in the process of procuring these weapons should be warned or convinced about the dangers could accompany these. We cannot punish any nation in the sense that we cannot destroy her altogether. In order to do so, the UN-sponsored forces may also need such weapons! We must eliminate all the evil with sanity and not through violent means.

Mr Khandekar: No nation is ready to do away with these weapons. And what's more, other nations are also trying to amass these weapons to balance the strategic equations in their respective regions. If you call it 'punishment', let it be. Even our own country is not prepared to do away with Prithvi, Nag and Brahmos. How can we persuade Pakistan to do away her nuclear command? Realities are different from dreams.

Ms Norgay: Do you think India should be punished?

Mr Khandekar: Punishment, in one form or the other, shall be meted out to our nation too. The only factor is time.

Mr Singh: In this context, my suggestion should be taken by the group as a positive step. We can tell the erring nations to destroy such weapons and pay for clean-up/dumping operations. Kudsia has talked about the interference of the UN in persuading the erring nations. I agree with her too.

Mr Singh: Please allow me to say a few words. We should define a dividing line between punishment and (moral) persuasion. Those nations that do not stop the manufacture and use of such weapons ought to be punished. Will Mr Khandekar define what should be the punishment for such nations?

Mr Khandekar: It could be a judicious mixture of suspension from the UN, economic sanctions, funds blockage and limited wars.

Ms Norgay: But this is a negative view. Further, the Indians have a reason to possess nuclear weapons. They also do not sign the CTBT because Pakistan was at a point of time, prepared to press the nuclear trigger. Similarly, all other nations would also have an alibi to possess such weapons. And the UN or any consortium of nations cannot punish such nations because these would form a clique to oppose those who wish to punish them. Another World War could ensue due to this conflict.

Ms Saha: I and Mr Khandekar seem to be in favour of strict punishment. All others do not want such harsh steps to be taken. Let Kudsia sum up the debate, please.

Ms Jamal: Thank you, Neena! The group has concluded that those nations that have such weapons of mass destruction ought to be warned. If these nations do not destroy such weapons (or contribute to UN-sponsored clean-up operations), then these should be subjected to political boycotts, suspension from the UN and economic sanctions. A full-fledged conflict is the last option. Those nations that are trying to acquire these weapons should also be dealt with through this strategy. But such terrorist organisations as have (or are trying to possess) these weapons should be dealt with an iron hand. On the other level, we should move slowly, beginning from the soft-level talks up to the harsh-level decisive wars. In the case of terrorist organisations, harsh decisions ought to be taken first. Thank you.

All: Thank you!

INDIA NEEDS A LARGE NUMBER OF SMALL FIRMS

Mr. Ballani : Our country is a democratic icon. It has more than 120 crore people. Its peoples are working hard. Nearly 30 per cent or these peoples are living below the poverty line. These persons must be made capable to work out a living on their own. This can be done only if we make a large number of small firms. These firms should work under the gamut of SSIs. We do not need MSIs and LSIs because they create a small number of very rich people. We want the wealth to be evenly distributed in India. Hence, I support the topic.

Mr. Koirala : What about Reliance? What about the Tatas? If we follow your advice, their future seems to be very bleak. They are the gems of India. The ONGC and IOC are Fortune 500 firms. Do you want to tell us that we should break these firms up to make small firms? Please clarify your stand.

Mr. Ballani : I want to clarify my stand by starting that I am not against Reliance or the Tatas. I only want a large number of small firms. The number of small firms should be adequately large so that the economic and other resources are spread among the masses. I want to empower the masses.

Ms. Dhawan : Mr. Ballani is right but I would prefer to disagree with him. Firstly, Mr. Ballani has a narrow vision. He does not know that an SSI has no standing in the world markets. In this era of globalisation, a large number of our firms must go global. An SSI cannot achieve the QC, production and delivery norms of an international level.

Foreign markets cannot be served without creating a few large corporate firms.

Secondly, the owner of a small firm is not aware of the management practices. This firm is normally a one-man show. Its employees do not earn much; nor do they grow in career terms. We need such firms as would provide adequate growth opportunities to employees. A large firm is managed on professional lines. It has better chances to develop its human resource. A small firm is not ask to develop this resource. It cannot take care of the interests of its employees.

Mr. Chatterjee : I would disagree with Mr. Koirala and Ms. Dhawan. They do not want the masses to prosper. Rather, they want a few firms to grow. We want a large number of people to start enterprises, work hard and create wealth. Currently, the firms of today are becoming big sharks. They are amassing wealth and resources. Their employees are mere cogs in machines. This is not fair. We want the common man to prosper.

Ms. Zuari : Mr. Chatterjee, you are not trying to understand the fact that a large corporate firm is more important then a small firm. A large firm would cater to larger market riches. Its market penetration would be more vis-a-vis its small cousins. It can employ a large number of people. It can also help them get job satisfaction. One of my friends has also touched upon the concept of international trade. This is a right concept. A large firm can export goods with ease, not a small fry. All international firms or MNCs are large corporate empires. We can quote the examples of GE, Palmolive, GM, Mitsubishi, Soni, Toyota, Hyundai and LG in this context.

Mr. Koirala : Thank you for supporting us, Ms. Zuari.

Mr. Koirala : You would not like the small firms to grow. Would you?

Mr. Ballani : I never said that. I want all firms to grow. If, however, they remain small yet prosperous, there is no harm in remaining small. The larger the firm, the more is the level of complications inside and outside the firm.

Mr. Chatterjee : I am with you. A small firm can be managed with ease.

Ms. Zuari : What about corporate image? What about export markets? What about the quality of work life and the quality of home life? In small firms, such factors are skillfully ignored. In large firms, employees are treated as human beings.

Mr. Chatterjee : But they remain employees nevertheless. An owner of a small firm is the master of his destiny. He creates wealth by working hard. True, he faces acute shortage of resources. But he remains independent. He takes decisions himself.

Mr. Koirala : I think a large firm is a well-managed entity. You do not know the tenets of management, Mr. Ballani. A small firm is well managed only from the viewpoint of his owner, for he knows he is the chief beneficiary of its operations. Its employees, vendors and markets suffer because of its poor management practices and policies.

Mr. Ballani: Even a small firm can adopt good management practices. Our enterprises must start from somewhere. They can start earning first. Later, they can adopt good management practices.

Mr. Koirala : What are trying to tell us? Should the firm be started first and managed later? Don't you think that is a ridiculous idea in this era that is terming with management thoughts? Today, a firm is managed on a professional basis, else it fails to deliver results. A large firm cannot survive and grow unless it incorporates sound management practices in its operations.

Ms. Zuari : I support the views of Mr. Koirala.

Mr. Chatterjee : But I support the views of Mr. Ballani. He is trying to state that a large number of small firms would help the masses develop a good economic base. The base of a large firm is not so large enough to feed the hungry millions. We are not against large firms. We are only trying to state, in the Indian context, that a large number of small firms would help us eliminate poverty at the grassroot levels.

Mr. Ballani : Let Mr. Chatterjee conclude now.

Mr. Chatterjee : The group has finally concluded that we should let a large number of small firms operate across the length and breath of

India. This would make the Indian masses more independent and financially strong. But large firms should also be allowed to grow. They use latest management practices and technologies to serve their markets. Small firms may not be able to serve their markets well. Their human resources is also not developed, or it is not allowed to develop. Further, if a small firm of India wants to grow—today every firm must grow, lest it should perish—then it should be given resources, technologies and manpower to do so. If an SSI firm becomes an MSI firm, its markets, employees and owners prosper. If it beocmes an LSI—and it is very difficult to do so—then it can become a star corporate player of India.

Mr. Koirala : Large firms can support, not oppose, small firms. Large firms have more resources and highly trained manpower. These firms can help small firms become major market players of India. This action of large firms would help the small firms develop and become MSIs or LSIs in the long run.

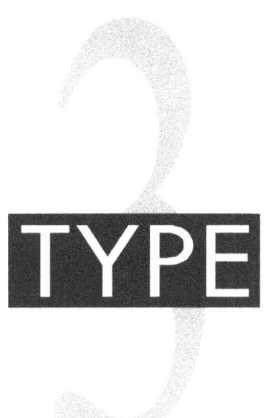

TYPE 3

THE AIM OF CINEMA—
ENTERTAINMENT NOT EDUCATION

Ms Shalini:—Gentlemen, I request your kind attention please. The subject given for our discussion, namely *"The Aim of Cinema is Entertainment not Education"* is an easy and interesting one. I am positive that some of us would agree with the proposition while the others may not. I feel, we could make the discussion more interesting if we convert it into a debate.

Mr Pankaj:—(Interrupt Ms Shalini) Hey, Ms Shalini, just a minute. If you want to make it a debate then we have to have a chairman. It won't be fair if we elect one of us as chairman and give him some special importance. You see, we all have to compete here as perfect equals. Therefore, we have to request the examiner to come back here and ask him to act as chairman. I doubt, whether he would agree. But if Ms Shalini wants this to be a debate, there appears to be no other way out.

Mr Shyam :—Oh! Shut up, Mr Pankaj, you are talking absolute rubbish. How can we ask the examiner to take part in the discussion? He is not an applicant for this job like us. As for Ms Shalini, she is asking for the moon. Why must we have a debate? The subject is damn interesting. I have lost count of the cinemas, I have seen. I can talk for hours about it. I did not miss even a single movie shown during the film festival. I wish, I could tell you chaps what lovely scene, all completely open, I saw in some of the adult movies.

Ms Shalini and Mr Pankaj:—(Interrupt Mr Shyam at the same time) Hey, hey, stop it. You have not understood the subject. No, no.

Mr Shyam:—What the hell do you mean?

Ms Shalini:—Mr Pankaj, would you answer Mr Shyam or would you kindly leave it to me?

Mr Pankaj:—You started the whole thing. Now you can have the pleasure of answering Mr Shyam. But I protest and object to the remarks made by Mr Shyam. He is using unparliamentary language.

Mr Shyam :—Oh! Come on. You are not a Victorian Spinster. Be a man. If you are dumb, let me say so.

Mr Pankaj:—I wouldn't argue with unprincipled and vulgar individuals.

Ms Shalini :—Please, Mr Pankaj leave it to me. I shall answer Mr Shyam. Well, gentlemen, I feel, perhaps I have not fully clarified what exactly I meant when I said we could have an interesting discussion. Okay! Now these who wish to oppose it. Can speak alternately. One will counter the arguments advanced by the other. Thus, we will get more ideas and also the discussion will be interesting.

Mr Shyam :—If you want this session to be really interesting, you have only to listen to me explaining the sexy scenes, I saw in foreign films during the film festival.

Ms Shalini:—Please, Mr Shyam that we shall do after this excercise is over. Now we are all expected to give our ideas. Of course, when your turn comes, you can say whatever you want.

Mr Shyam:—You chaps don't know what you are missing.

Amit:—Please, Mr Shyam, we have already spent a lot of time. I suggest we start with Mr Ganguly and end up with you. Let us each speak for two minutes during the first round. Come on, Mr. Ganguly. Please give your views.

Mr Ganguly :—No, I don't want to be the first speaker. Ms Shalini, started first. Let her speak first.

Mr Amit:—All right, Mr Sachin is it okay with you or would you like to be the first speaker?

Mr Sachin:—(Appears undecided)

Mr Pankaj:—I say, let Ms Shalini start. Meanwhile Mr Ganguly and Mr Sachin will gather their ideas.

Mr Sachin:—Yes, yes.

Mr Amit:—Very good, Ms Shalini, now please speak on the subject for two minutes. I request all others to listen and not interrupt when a particular person is giving his views.

Ms Shalini:—Gentlemen! I fully agree that cinema is meant for entertainment and not for education. People flock to see the films only to get some entertainment and joy, and forget their worries and chores for a while. Whether one is a student, an office-goer or a housewife, all want to escape from the mundane routine of their daily life. Therefore, they want some recreation and change. Some may go for a walk, some to the beach and some to a temple. But it is not certain that one could entirely forget one's worries and get the required mental diversion and entertainment at these places. But if they see a good film, they have this relaxation and happiness. The aim of the cinema should, therefore, be to entertain. People can go to schools and colleges for education. I am sure none of us would have bunked and gone for a movie in our college and university days if we know that the film is only going to educate us and entertain us. This itself is the best proof to show that films are meant to entertain. Thank you.

Mr Amit :—Friends! You have heard the strong arguments advanced by Ms Shalini that our films are meant only for entertainment. While I agree with him to a great extent. I wish to submit that this medium could serve both purposes—entertaining as well as educating—at one and the same time. In fact, it is rare when a film does not educate its audience in one way or the other. Take any film you have seen. I am positive it has given you some ideas. It has put some thoughts in your mind. It has made you think and wonder. How do our film heroes and heroines get their images and popularity? It is because they have influenced the minds of the audience who see their movies. We say violence has increase of because of the violence or violent scenes displayed in films. Robinhood commits robbery, but he distributes the looted money among the poor and needy. But, unconsciously, the idea that doing an unlawful act for a noble purpose is not that wrong or sinful, may enter the mind of audience. Here, the audience has been educated, though in a negative manner. Education does not mean only reading books, attending lectures and writing examinations. Education means knowledge and the spreading of new ideas. Films more than any other medium, I include TV when I talk of the film—they plant new ideas in the minds of its viewers. That these ideas are good or bad is a different matter. Cinema has the inherent capacity to educate while it does the major job of entertaining. Well, I have already exceeded my time limit and beg you to forgive me for the same. Now you can give your views on what I have said when you speak. Thank you.

Mr Sumeet:—My friends, I find it difficult now as to what I should do.

Mr Shyam:—What do you mean? You have to talk and say something. If you can't, say sorry and shut up.

Mr Sumeet:—My..........(Looks confused and looks helplessly at Mr Amit.)

Mr Amit:—Come on, Mr Shyam. We had agreed that we won't interrupt a speaker when he is on his feet. Besides, I am afraid that, perhaps, you had not followed what our friend was aiming at. Please give him a chance. Now, Please proceed, Mr Sumeet.

Mr Sumeet:—My difficulty or dilemma is whom to support between Mr Amit and Ms Shalini. In my opinion, both are correct. But I see films only for entertainment. However, I agree that one can get a lot of ideas from films. Now I don't want to annoy Mr Shyam any more. That is all.

Mr Pankaj:—Well, friends! I do not agree with the view that films are meant only for entertainment.

Me Shyam:—Oh! Well! What rubbish ideas. You must go to the Himalayas or the African jungles, man. You are not fit for civilised society.

Mr Pankaj:—I refuse to talk if Mr Shyam is going to interfere in this manner.

Mr Deepak:—He was not interferring when Mr Amit spoke.

Mr Shyam:—Because he spoke some sense and his talk was interesting. But Mr Pankaj gave absurd statements.

Mr Pankaj:—I gave my views. That is all.

Mr Shyam:—Your ideas are totally outdated.

Mr Amit:—Mr Shyam, I suggest you give your views, including criticisms of others, when your turn comes. If you keep interrupting this, not only others but you yourself won't get a chance to speak. Now, Mr Pankaj, please continue.

Mr Pankaj:—I am sorry. I did want to present a convincing case or the view that our films should educate us. By now my mood is changed because of Mr Shyam.

Mr Deepak:—Well, gentlemen, initially I thought of speaking in favour of the view that films are meant only to entertain us. But I find my neighbour Mr Shyam is going to do that in big way. You all must know that cinema is used primarily to educate people in Russia and China as Mr Amit said, education means knowledge and ideas. Russia used the medium cinema to provide ideas and knowledge to the people. Even radio and other mass media are used primarily for this purpose. We also know that in Nazi Germany, films, radio and other mass media were used to brainwash the people. Thus, cinema can be used to educate. What type of education it can give is a different matter. It can even give sex education besides sex exhibition over which Mr Shyam has fallen head over heels in love. But no such nonsense in Russia, China and Vietnam. There, cinema is used to educate the people with their national and party goals. You cannot deny that in these countries the premium is on education and not on entertainment, well. Thank you, I have made my contribution.

Mr Shyam:—I hate, I mean, I totally and completely disagree with what Mr Deepak has said. He is perhaps a Communist or a naxalite. It is only in dictatorial or communist countries, like Russia or China, that the cinema is misused like this. If the people are given a free choice they would like to see only sexy and revealing pictures. I ask you. The more sexy the pictures, the greater the exposures, the bigger the crowd. People in France produce blue films for entertainment. For education, we have schools and colleges. The picture will flop at the box-office if there is no sex, no fight and no entertainment. I challenge you to bet your money, Mr Deepak, and produce a picture purely to educate? I ask you.

Mr Deepak:—I am not a film producer. Please do not be personal. Talk about the subject and not about individuals. If you do not agree with my views that is your business. But I have every right to express my views.

Mr Amit:—Well, Mr Shyam, your two minutes are over. Now come on Mr Ganguly.

Mr Ganguly:—(Shakes his head to say he does not want to speak)

Mr Amit:—Well, What about you Mr Sachin? It is your turn now.

Mr Sachin:—Personally, I like films that provide entertainment. In this respect. I support Ms Shalini. That is all.

Ms Shalini has the following leadership skills
(a) Courage to initiate
(b) Original idea—Creative idea
(c) Handling unruly people like Mr. Shyam. She does not lose her compose inspite of Mr. Shyam's misbehaviour. She pacifies Mr. Pankaj as well as Shyam. She doesn't shy away from doing so.
(d) Organising skills
(e) Consensus building approach and striking good rapport with other group members. She shares good rapport with Mr. Pankaj, Ganguly and Amit.
(f) She is a good decision maker as she takes a stand and supports it with conviction though her arguments are not very strong.

Her interpersonal skills and ability to exhort others in the group make her an asset to the organisation.

Mr. Shyam is ill mannered, rude, vulgar and subversive.   *—Rejected*

Mr. Pankaj lacks in interpersonal skills. He is an escapist—instead of confronting opposition tactfully, he passes it on to Ms. Shalini. He doesn't have a stable mind as he gets jittery on Shyam's interruptions. Ultimately he refuses to speak at all. Such people are unable to work in a team. So rejected. He is too sensitive to be a team member.   *—Rejected*

Mr. Amit is instrumental in resolving the impasse. He shows leadership quality. He speaks politely to other group members. He sticks to time stipulation. He comes up with original ideas. He has a balanced approach towards the issue. He devises a middle path—a more rational path between the two extremes. He has taken a stand and supports it with lucid arguments. He has a harmonious personality. He shows the ability to resolve conflicting claims.   *—Selected*

Mr. Sumeet has a confused personality. He appears to be nervous and lacks self-confidence. Not a suitable candidate.

Mr. Deepak does not have a stand. He just enumerates facts. It is clear, as he confesses, that his speech is mere rhetoric without conviction. He enjoys taking dig at Mr. Shyam. This shows his casual attitude towards everything, irrespective of its seriousness. Knowledge with conviction and a definite stand is infructuous. So Mr. Deepak is not a strong contender. He speaks just once—when his turn comes. He remained an on-looker when Ms. Shalini and few others were trying rein in Mr. Shyam. Thus, he lacks initiative to participate in a group work. He is a man sitting on the fences.

Mr. Ganguly doesn't speak at all. He is a misfit in a team.
—*Rejected.*

SHOULD NRIS BE GIVEN SOPS

No. 2: Hello friends! We have been allotted the topic "Should NRIs be Given Sops" for discussion. With your kind permission, I would like to start the deliberations and give my views on the same.

No. 1: No! Ladies first! Let us start from the lady sitting at the other end of the group.

All: Yes! Please go ahead.

No. 5: Thank you ladies and gentlemen! The Pravasi Bhartiya Divas was celebrated recently, in New Delhi. The government has offered many sops to 20 million NRIs who are, in fact, Indians to the core. It has offered dual citizenship to the People of Indian Origin (PIO) who are living/working abroad. It has also offered a compulsory insurance scheme to those Indian workers who migrate to the Gulf. Further, a Bill may be passed by the Parliament to create a welfare fund for the overseas Indian workers. Finally, seats would be reserved in academic institutions for the children of the Indian expatriates in the Gulf. This list of sops is likely to be expanded. The government wants these NRIs to invest in India and support her poor masses through various philanthropic schemes. It is quite justified in doing so. If Bill Gates can dole out ₹ 2000 crore for the non-resident Indians why can't the Indians themselves do that? After all, the NRIs are also Indians; and they are proud of this fact. So, I support the topic.

No. 4: Hello friends! No. 5 has rightly pointed out that the NRIs are likely to invest in India. Moreover, they are also likely to support the Indian viewpoints at the major global fora. That is because they are

Indians. But why grant them dual citizenship and allow them to visit India at will without any visa restrictions? When all the Indians get equal treatment by the State, why should 20 million odd people be singled out for princely treatments. The visa officer, commission or consulate in the foreign country would lose millions of Dollars, if the NRIs were to be given this status. Further, the NRIs would also be allowed to invest in properties (in India). What about those Indians who are not NRIs? They would not be able to buy these properties due to financial constraints and the NRIs would buy such properties with the help of their Pounds, Dinars and Dollars. The already rich NRIs would become richer. Our natives would become poorer. That is because of the NRIs are going to take care of their own interests by conducting business transactions with India.

No. 3: Hello friends! I have a friend who is a Keralite, just like me. He is working in Qatar. He is earning valuable foreign exchange for India. If he gets dual citizenship, he would visit India quite often and be able to meet his kith and kin. And he would also start an enterprise, which can give jobs to at least 10 persons. So, what is the harm in accepting the NRIs? They would help their brothers and sisters (in India), develop the economy and create a better society.

No. 1: Please don't quote examples from your family or friendship circles. You should maintain the decorum of the discussion.

No. 3: I don't think I have stated something irrelevant or offensive.

No. 2: Please do not interrupt, No. 1. No. 3 has not stated anything wrong. Now, it is the turn of No. 6.

No. 6: Hello friends! I don't like a hostile attitude towards the NRIs. They bring in foreign exchange, technology, modern thoughts and business opportunities from their respective countries of residence. We can use these to develop ourselves on social and economic fronts. If they look for some warranty, respect and facilities, then we should not object. My contention is—if we can love foreigners, why can't we love our own people? So, I would support the idea of giving sops to such people and request you to align your views with those of mine.

No. 1: Hello friends! I support the views of No. 6. The NRIs can help us become prosperous and efficient. They can invest in our business firms and industries. All such investments would develop our economy. We must not use the word 'sops.' Instead we should use the phrase "facilities that are smitten of love and warmth." We should realise that we need support from the NRIs at the social, political and economic fora of the world. So, I am in favour of giving good facilities to the NRIs.

No. 7: Thank you No. 1! We are moving towards the end of this discussion. I think that the interests of our nation as well as those of the Indians (NRIs) must be protected. I am not supporting or opposing the topic.

No. 4: No! You must either support or oppose the topic.

No. 7: All right! I would then, oppose it. The reason is that NRIs, who have been living abroad for the past many decades, cannot understand how we work in India. We have to welcome them but not make them privileged citizens of our country. That is because they already are privileged. So, if they are given these sops, they would become Not Required Indians pretty soon.

No. 3: And how would that happen?

No. 7: The native Indians would oppose such moves.

No. 1: That is a Utopian concept. We need them.

No. 7: Because they are rich?

No. 1: No! Because they are Indians.

No. 7: It is difficult to talk to you.

No. 2: Please, No. 1 and No. 7. 'Do not spoil the decorum of the discussion'.

No. 4: No. 2. I would appreciate if you could wind up the debate and give the consensus of the group.

No. 2: Thank you, No. 4! The group has arrived at the conclusion that there is no harm in giving extra facilities to the NRIs and Persons of Indian Origin (PIO). But the documents and formalities should be the same for all the NRIs. They should either be given PIO cards or dual citizenship. They are investing in India for our benefit. They also protect our interests at the global fora and in the respective countries of their residence. Further, FDI investors and foreign businessmen (of other origins) should also be given certain facilities (so that they do not feel that they are being discriminated against). All the NRIs should be given fair treatment by the bureaucracy. Red tape and corruption should be eliminated at least from such offices which deal with these privileged diaspora from abroad. They are a part of India and can help her become an advanced nation of the world. Thank you!

All: Thank you!

CORRUPTION IS A POLITICAL NECESSITY

Mr. Dandekar : Good evening, friends! My name is Anurag Dandekar. I want to support the topic, which is— corruption is a political necessity. Nowadays, every business organisation uses corrupt means to earn money. Politics is also a business in the new era. Hence, corruption is prevalent in the political corridors of the world. We should not be surprised by the scandals and scams of the world. Rather, we should be happy to learn that they are finally unearthed. Nothing remains a secret in this age of Information Boom.

Ms. Desai : Good evening, friends! My name is Anushka Desai. My friend, Anurag, is sarcastic about the topic. That is why he has supported it. I do not know what prompted him to support it. Our leaders, social workers and NGOs are trying to cleanse the political and social systems. We are born with limitations. But it does not mean that we should become corrupt to the core. The character of a nation is decided by how much honest its citizens are. If our leaders, especially political stalwarts, are corrupt, how would the masses trust them? Already, there is a lot of chaos in our political, social and economic systems. We can remove this chaos by becoming a politically honest nation. If a businessman approaches a politician with a bundle of currency notes, the latter must refuse to take it. The politician in question should set an example before his colleagues and the masses. Thank you!

Mr. Singh : Good evening, ladies and gentleman! My name is Parwinder Singh. I would like to align my views with those of Mr. Dandekar. It is not possible to cleanse our political system. Corruption is rampant in all political circles. Tell me, which party is sans corruption nowadays? You cannot name a single politician who is not involved in one scam or the other. There have been nearly 100 minor or major scams and many more would come up soon. The Volcker Report says that nearly 2000 firms of the world were involved in the Oil for Food Programme of Iraq. Saddam himself was a corrupt politician. Similarly, there are many skeletons in the Indian cupboard too. We all know how 'clean' our political leaders are. The country would become a hotbed of chaos, both political and economic. We have to keep on chugging along till we find better alternatives. It is hoped that when all politicians would have their fill, our nation would become a decent place to live in. Till that time arrives, it is better to wait. Good times will come later. Thank you!

Ms. Paruthi : Probably, our friend, Mr. Singh, has ignored the sermon given by Ms. Desai. A nation can prosper if it is corrupt but it can never raise its head in pride. We do not want to live in prepetual shame. We are ashamed of the fact that our politicians are corrupt. We must reverse this trend, lest it should be too late to mend the ways of the political juntas of our country. Today, we have taken it for granted that our leaders are or will be corrupt. But little do we realise that their corrupt practices are harming the nation. If a leader is corrupt, his followers take no time in becoming corrupt. Let us go back to the glorious era in which our political leaders were our gods. Today, a leader is respected because of his gunpower and manpower, not because of his political astuteness. He has to feed an army of supporters. He has to grease the palms of many businessmen who support him during the election days. We must break this vicious cycle. That is because we want to create an honest and sensitive society. We do not want to create political criminals and hooligans. Thank you!

Mr. Jamieson : Good evening, ladies and gentleman! My name is Donald Jamieson. We have to think about the problem from a pragmatic angle. Corruption is the oldest disease of the world. Every political party has some corrupt leaders. They are the ones who arrange money for election campaigns, vote bank purchasing and development of cadres. If a political party has to survive, it must arrange money. It does not have any factory or land to lean on for this purpose. How will it arrange the money? Naturally, from its supporters and business empires. When it comes to power, it needs to reciprocate and give back money or other favours to these investors. Hence, someone has rightly stated that politics is also a kind of business. Corruption is an essential part of business. Hence, corruption is a part of politics as well. I know that this is a bad phenomenon, as one of my opponents has pointed out. But what can be done to resolve the problem? There are no alternatives. Only a corrupt man would join politics.

Ms. Paruthi : We ourselves must cleanse the system. Wealth earned through illicit means tears the intestines of man and kills him in one go.

Mr. Singh : Ms. Paruthi, there is no need to give these morality—based statements. Look at the scenario of the present. Corrupt politicians alone can survive in today's competitive political playgrounds. The position of power almost always carries the corruption tag. Even the PMs, Presidents and governors of many countries have been proved to be corrupt. You know very well that our own former PM was involved in many a scam.

Ms. Paruthi : If our PMs were involved in scams of various kinds and hues, we should not be proud of this fact. We must eliminate corrupt politicians from our system. Why are we hell bent upon supporting them?

Mr. Jamieson : That is because this corrupt system cannot be changed. Only a bloody revolution can change it.

Ms. Desai : We are a democratic nation. We have seen many a revolution. But we are not prepared for a bloody revolution. We must change the system peacefully.

Ms. Paruthi : The group has agreed on the point that corruption is rampant in the political circuits of India. This is a necessary evil today. But tomorrow it must be eliminated at all costs. If a politician is corrupt, either fire him or defeat him in the elections. The political leaders must become honest and virtuous to the core. If need be, they can be given more money, powers and facilities so that they may not indulge in corrupt practices. Thank you!

All : Thank you Mr. Paruthi!

FOR RAPID RURAL DEVELOPMENT–IS EDUCATION MORE IMPORTANT THAN INDUSTRIALISATION?

Mr Manoj: (Springs upon his feet the moment the examiner's back is turned), Gentlemen, I request your kind attention please. The subject given for discussion, namely, rural development can be very fast and more effective through education and literacy than by other means like setting up industries in villages, is an interesting, fairly easy and much in the news topic, of course, it can create a good deal of heated arguments and controversy, I am positive that some will strongly support education while others would vehemently opt for rural industry. I feel we could turn it into an excellent debate.

Mr Sujeet:—(Interrupts Mr Manoj) Hey, Mr Manoj, just a minute. How can we have a debate? We have no chairman or presiding officer. You see the chairman has to be neutral. He cannot be one of us. Therefore, we have to call back the examiner and make him the chairman.

Mr Amit:—Oh, shut up, Mr Sujeet, you are talking absolute rubbish. How can an examiner take part in the test? You have gone nuts. And, Mr Manoj What the hell is wrong with you? Why should there be any arguments? It will be so damn interesting to talk about family planning which is the core of all development. There is an 'A' certificate film on it. My God, what a kick you can get from this film, you know. Let us all talk about family planning, men. If you ask me, all the rural industry we have is only family production (He laughs at the big joke he had cracked).

Mr Manoj and Mr Sujeet:—(Interrupting Mr Amit at the same time) Hey, hey, you have got it all wrong.

Mr Amit:—Stupid. Both of you are fool.

Mr Manoj:—(Observing that Mr Sujeet is itching to retort Mr Amit) Mr Sujeet, would you like to answer Mr Amit or would you kindly allow me to do it?

Mr Sujeet:—You started the whole thing. Now you can have the pleasure of answering Mr Amit. But I protest and object to his unparliamentary language.

Mr Amit:—Oh, come on, Mr Sujeet. Do not be a prude. You are not a Sissy of a Victorian spinster, are you?

Mr Sujeet:—I refuse to argue with vulgar people, who use filthy language. It is below my dignity.

Mr Manoj :—Please, Mr Sujeet, kindly leave it to me. Well, friends and Mr Amit? Perhaps, I have not fully clarified what I meant, when I spoke about an interesting debate. We don't need a chairman and all those formalities. I only meant we will have independent ideas and different views on this controversial subject. It could resemble a good debate and prove very interesting.

Mr Amit:—If you want something interesting and also exciting. I suggest you, people listen to what I have to tell you about the techniques of family planning. By the way, family planning can solve the unemployment problem also. Of course, I can also describe about the film I mentioned. You know who is the heroine and how many rape scenes are there?

Mr Manoj : — Please, Mr Amit, I dare say you will have a lot of exciting things to say about films, family planning techniques, etc. 'But right now, we have to deal with our subject properly.

Mr Amit : — You chaps do not know what you would be missing.

Mr Ranjeet : — (Intervenes and lends support to Mr Manoj) Please, Mr Amit. I suggest, let us complete the excercise first as suggested by Mr Manoj. Let us start with Mr Shashi, then go on to Mr Ravi, Mr Manoj and so on and end up with you Mr Amit. We can speak for two minutes each during the first round and may be a minute or so in the second round. Now, come on.

Mr Shashi:—No, no please. I do not want to be the first speaker. Mr Manoj started first. Let him continue and be the first speaker. Then yourself. I shall see if there is anything to add when my turn comes.

Mr Ranjeet : —All right. Now Mr Ravi can you start the discussion?

Mr Ravi :— (Appears undecided) you see, Mr Shashi wanted that Mr Manoj should be the first speaker.

Mr Ranjeet :—You do not want to speak now, Mr Ravi?

Mr Ravi :—I will do what you say. I only wanted to remember what Mr Shashi recommended.

Mr Sujeet :—I say, let Mr Manoj start. Meanwhile, Mr Shashi and Mr Ravi can gather their ideas.

Mr Shashi :—Yes, yes.

Mr Ranjeet :—Very good, Mr Manoj, now please speak on the subject for two minutes. I request all others to listen and not interrupt the speaker. It will lead to delays. Each can give his criticism, counter-points, etc, when his turn comes or during the second round.

Mr Manoj:—Gentlemen, I tender my apologies. Perhaps, I could have continued with my speech uninterrupted if I had made myself clearer to you all. Anyway, things have gone round a full circle and we are now back to square one. I must thank you for officially choosing me to be the opening speaker. Our subject wants us to choose between education and creation of employment opportunities for rapid rural development. I belong to a village and lived there till I completed my high school. I came to the city only for my college education. In the cities, most of us look for employment only after we have completed our school. But in the villages, only a few can afford education, even at the elementary level. Poverty and suffering are far more acute there than in the cities. The land is owned by a few and the majority are landless labourers. I do not deny that the need or importance of rural development is linked to education and family planning. But for a hungry man, food is God. He wants a job so that he can feed himself and his family. Because of poverty, people become old too soon and more hands are needed to support those who can no longer work. Hence, the opposition to family planning in the rural sector. Rural industry can provide employment to the village folk. Hence, it should get the preference.

Mr Ranjeet:—Friends, as you all know only too well, India lives in her villages. In other, words, nearly 68 per cent of our people live in the villages. At the time of independence, our population was less than half of what it is today. Then 90 to 95 per cent population lived in the villages with the growth of industrialisation the population moved from the land and villages to the factories and cities. Within 66 years, India has become one of the most industrialised nations among the developing countries. Our economic growth rate has been steady and by no means unsubstantial. But the benefits of our economic growth are nullified because of population explosion. Population growth outplaces the economic growth. If family planning had been successful, more people from the villages would have moved to the cities and only a small percentage of the total population would stay in the rural areas to till the lands. This is the case with all western countries, including Russia. Secondly, rural industry is limited in market scope. It will not be benefitted by mass production and high technology, If you start a large industry, say a steel factory in a village, soon there would be a steel city. The concept of rural industry will have to be re-examined for its validity. No matter what you earn, you will continue to be poor unless you contain population growth. The opposition to and inhibitions regarding family planning can be overcome by education. Therefore, top priority in the villages should be accorded to family planning and education.

Mr Vijay:—Well, I find it rather difficult as to what I should do.

Mr Amit:—What do you mean? You have to say something. If you cannot do that you can say sorry and shut up.

(Now, Mr Vijay, confused, turns to Mr Ranjeet for help and support).

Mr Ranjeet:—(Intervening in a friendly way) Oh, come on, Mr Amit, we had agreed that we would not interrupt anyone, while he is addressing the group. It is only fair that everyone should be given full encouragement to express his views freely and frankly. Please do proceed, Mr Vijay.

Mr Vijay:—My problem is, who I should support between Mr Manoj and Mr Ranjeet. I think that both are right. Besides, I have seen some villages, but I have not really lived there. I do not want to upset anyone. I would like to stay neutral.

Mr Sujeet:—Gentlemen, in my view the subject given to us for discussion needs to be looked into afresh. With regard to rural uplift, I feel the scope cannot be limited to family planning, education or employment alone. There are many other factors. We all understand something about family planning.

Mr Amit:—(Interrupting Mr Sujeet abruptly in the middle of his speech) Well, well, well. Did you say that you understand family planning? How interesting. I would like to see your understanding. Tell us how do you practise it? What do you favour prevention or cure?

Mr Sujeet:—Now, this is unfair and I lodge my protest. How can I talk if Mr Amit is going to interfere like this when I am speaking?

Mr Amit:—Hey, stop it. Do not cry like a child. I thought we can put some life into the discussion by highlighting the latest and, of course, foolproof methods of family planning.

Mr Sumeet :—(Intervening for the first time) No, Mr Amit, Mr Ranjeet has already asked you not to interrupt but give your ideas, criticisms, views when it is your turn. If you wished to speak first, you could have said so and volunteered. If you want, I will forgo my chance and you can use up my time also. Not only that, I can promise you on behalf of the group that we shall have a special sitting with you after this excercise is over so that you can tell us all you wish about the extremely interesting experiences of yours in the field of family planning. Now please observe silence and let Mr Sujeet continue.

Mr Ranjeet:—I fully endorse what Mr Sumeet has said. I am sorry Mr Amit that you are not honouring the common agreement that no one should be interrupted while he is on his feet. (Turning to Mr Sumeet) Thank you, Mr Sumeet, for your offer to forgo your chance and give extra time to Mr Amit. But that would not be necessary since you have mentioned about a separate setting. Besides, the group is interested to know your views on the subject.

Mr Manoj:—Yes, yes, certainly.

Mr Sumeet:—Okay, now, Mr Vijay, Please continue Mr Sujeet. Sorry, I have really forgotten and the trend is broken.

Mr Ranjeet:—You were talking about the scope of the subject and mentioned that we understand what family planning generally means.

Mr Sujeet:—Yes, yes, thank you. But the trend is gone. You see, I really do not know precisely what rural industry implies. Is it cottage industry, mini or small scale industry? Will each village have some industry? Then what about the skill, training, etc, can attend to agriculture during the season? On the other hand, how can you keep the mill or factory closed for half the year? Do you see the problem? Then we need education, electricity, health, housing, roads, communication facilities, etc. These are as important as family planning and industry.

Mr Sumeet:—Friends, let me first clear the deck with regard to the queries raised by Mr Sujeet. I feel there is nothing wrong with the proposition. Nobody denies that our villages need many inputs for rapid development. No one doubts that we need education, health, roads, communication, drinking water and many others besides family planning and rural industry for the development of the people in the villages. But the subject singles out two items, namely, family planning with education and rural industry, and wants us to discuss as to which of these two should get priority. In other words, we are to assess their respective importance from all aspects and make a forced choice as to which should be accorded priority over the other in terms of funds, time and efforts. In order to decide the priority and importance of these two, we must first think about our goal or overall objective. The aim is to improve the standard of living of the people our villages and help them lead a meaningful and full life. Now, even with family planning if we were to attain as it is today. Since, the majority today is below the poverty line, even with zero growth we would still need industry and employment opportunities to increase the income of villagers. It is evident that the available land, despite the Green Revolution, will not eradicate poverty and unemployment in the villages. People have to be shifted from land to industry. Since the cities are overcrowded, there is no point adding more industries to them. It is better, therefore, to locate new industries in rural and remote areas. It will then be a whole-time job for many living in the rural areas. They can be trained and taught the skill. Industry would not be seasonal. Even agriculture need not be seasonal. We can have crop rotation and ground water irrigation along with mechanised farming. Once there is significant economic growth and improvement in the standard of living, family planning would automatically follow. Therefore, it is obvious that rural industry should get top priority. Thank you.

Mr Amit:—Okay, folks, I have already told you about my choice. I am all heart and soul, body and mind, now and forever for family planning. The "industry wallas" are mad. They are short-sighted and prejudiced. I do not buy all that crap Mr Sumeet was trying hard to sell. It is a white lie if anyone were to tell that we have not had good economic growth. The point is that population growth is outstripping economic growth. Poverty breeds population. Even Mr Sumeet admitted that rich people have small families. In America, many have no families. Despite their free sex life, there is zero or negative population growth there because of ready, easy and safe family planning facilities. You must use all mass media—cinema, drama, television, radio, etc, to propagate family planning techniques. There should be compulsory sex education. I told you about the film on family planning. You all must see it, at least once. I can say with experience that you will never stop with just seeing the film once. You will see it again and again. I would therefore say "*family planning zindabad*".

Mr Shashi:—(Remains silent and does not speak)

Mr Ranjeet:—Come on, Mr Shashi. We are all waiting to hear your views.

Mr Shashi:—You see, nothing special to add. I agree.

Mr Manoj:—Agree with whom?

Mr Shashi:—Well, with all. Nothing more. You can ask Mr Ravi to speak.

Mr Ravi:—Personally, I would like to go by the majority of the people. Ours is a democratic society and we must abide by the majority verdict. People do not want family planning. They want employment, food, clothes and shelter. The emergency brought home this lesson. Since people want employment, we must give it to them.

TO STAY UNITED AND BECOME A SUPER POWER—DOES INDIA NEED A VERY STRONG AND STABLE CENTRAL GOVERNMENT WITH FULL POWERS OVER THE STATE GOVERNMENTS?

Mr Bharat —Dear friends, I have something important to tell you all. Can I request your kind attention for few seconds please?

Mr David —Well, Mr Bharat you mean, "Friends, Romans and countrymen. Lend me your ears." Is that what you want?

Mr Bharat—Thank you Mr David (Pauses for a second and smiles at Mr David) Yes, you are right. Dear friends, I could see our friend, Mr David, is an authority on Shakespeare. He has put my humble request in the picturesque and poetic words of the famous play right. However, to save time I shall be direct and make my announcement in simple words.

Mr Ramesh:—Yes, yes, we are more interested to hear what you have to tell us. Please, let us not interrupt him. Come on Mr Bharat What is the announcement you were going to make?

Ms David:—One second please, Mr Bharat. If you don't mind. I object to the insinuation of Mr Ramesh. He implies that I am interrupting you. On the other hand, you have appreciated my apt comments. If you ask me, honestly it is Mr Ramesh who is interrupting.

Mr Ramesh:—I know, Mr David is interested in hearing his own voice. Now he has started again. I say, he just won't allow others to say even a word edgeways. I know, because I happen to be his neighbour and it has been my ordeal to endure him. He has been boring me from the very beginning.

Mr Hari:—Hey, you Mr David and Mr Ramesh. Will you both shut up and pipe down? If you chaps want to quarrel and fight, get the hell out of here, go outside and fight it out to your heart's content. Okay?

Mr David:—Who the hell are you to tell us to shut up and get out? Do you know what a Group Discussion means? For your information everyone here has the full right to say what he wants.

Mr Hari:—My foot, I have the right not to hear you.

Mr Bharat:—Please friends, I appeal to you all. Kindly listen to me. In particular I appeal and request Mr David, Ramesh and Hari to cooperate and kindly hear me out.

Mr Hari :—Don't you see Mr Bharat that I want to help you. Mr David thinks too much of himself and if you allow me, I will just put him in his place. If nothing works, I will give him a sound thrashing, I don't mind even if, I don't get selected and the examiner throws me out. Mr David must learn his lesson.

Mr Chetan:—Please let us all calm down. No need for quarrels and misunderstandings. Let us first listen to Mr Bharat. Please go ahead Mr Bharat.

Mr Bharat:—Friends, we have to complete this excercise in less than half an hour. If I am right, we must have already lost a lot of time in our preliminary deliberations. Now, I suggest we start in the earnest without further waste of time and talk on the subject one by one. Each one can talk for two minutes in the first round. We can start with Mr Arpit and go clockwise, closing the round with Mr Hari. That means each will speak on his turn only and there won's be any interruptions and arguments. If you wish to comment, counter or disagree with any speaker you must do so when your turn comes or during the second round.

Mr Chetan:—I am sure you have a reason for stressing non-interruption. You see, in a Group Discussion one should react naturally without inhibitions. One should be able to express his views as they come to his mind.

Mr Bharat:—You are right Mr Chetan, but you will agree that once interruption starts, there will be no end to it. All will talk simultaneously and soon it will be chaos, confusion and fiasco. The one who should speak as per his turn will not be allowed to express his views freely. Hence, we must cooperate and remain disciplined. It may sound difficult but we have to excercise self-restraint.

Mr David:—To enforce discipline, it is better that we have a chairman or presiding officer. Otherwise person like Mr Hari will start bullying us.

Mr Hari:—Mr Bharat, I also think we need a Chairman to make sure that Mr David does not talk out of turn and keeps his mouth shut. If necessary I am ready to put my hand on his mouth and choke him.

Mr David:—By talking big and frightening others, if you think you can get elected as chairman. You are mistaken. We are interested in brains and not brawn.

Mr Bharat:—Please, please, my friends, we are again going off the mark. The time is running out. Come on Mr Arpit. Let us have your views on the subject.

Mr Arpit:—You see, I am sorry, I don't know much about the subject. I am a science student. I mean zoology was my optional. I prefer to speak later and not be the opening speaker.

Mr Chetan:—You see, how right David was in suggesting that we first elect a chairman. I am sure you will agree to my proposal that we choose Mr Bharat as chairman.

Mr David, Mr Ramesh and Mr Arpit:—Yes, yes, we agree.

Mr Hari:—Why you fellows, Mr Frank and Mr Gopal. Why don't you fellows say yes?

Mr Frank and Mr Gopal:—Yes, yes,

Mr Bharat :—Mr Hari, you said you didn't want to be the last speaker, would you then like to be the first speaker?

Mr Hari :—No, thanks. But I also don't want that big mouth Mr David to speak first either. He would be yapping the whole day.

Mr Bharat:—No, Mr Hari. It is not fair. If you accept me as chairman you must co-operate and help me achieve our task successfully. No reference to personalities. We must all talk about the subject and remain objective.

Mr Hari:—All right, all right. Please yourself. I will give you all the co-operation, just as you want. But don't regret and blame me later.

Mr Bharat:—Well, as neither Mr Arpit nor Mr Hari wants to be the first speaker, I think we can start with Mr Chetan and proceed clockwise. I will then be the last speaker and it is perfectly okay with me. Come on Mr Chetan please go ahead and speak on the subject.

Mr Chetan:—Friends, as you all know, ours is a country of diverse people, speaking different languages, observing different customs, following different practices and enjoying different cultures. We seek unity in diversity. In a country having such differences it is advantageous to have authority decentralised so that each group can progress with certain amount of freedom. On the other hand, if authority is to be centralised at one place, the interests of the minorities are likely to suffer. The majority interest will over-ride and prevail over the minority interests. Secondly, we have large territory divided by natural geographical features. The distance and the isolation resulting from natural boundaries also demand more regional autonomy. Further, nearly 68 per cent of

India's teeming millions reside in villages. Communication is not easy. Keeping these factors in view, Mahatma Gandhi favoured decentralisation of power with simple village economy and Panchayati Raj. This means devolution of power to the villages. At present, power is concentrated at the Centre and the States share some with the Centre. No real power has been given to districts and villages. The States are now clamouring for greater autonomy and power. But State autonomy by itself may do more harm than good. I therefore, feel more power should be given to villages and local bodies.

Mr David:—Gentlemen, I must say, I got confused. I mean the subject is confusing and it has got me confused, you get what I mean. I am afraid you don't follow me. Now let me explain. The subject implies autonomy to the States will harm national unity and integration. I say that devolution of more power to the districts and villages is more important. Now of the States do not have autonomy, that is power, how the districts and villages can get them. If there is no porridge in the pot, how can you serve it on the plate. Do you understand me? If you can't, I give up. I can't make it any more simpler. Now you see why there is confusion. Since the argument is not rational, no point in discussing it. We will only get more confused.

Mr Hari:—Hey, stop talking rot man. You can't criticise your colleagues like this. I agree you are confused. Now keep quiet and don't confuse others.

Mr David:—See, gentlemen, I appeal to you-honourable members to be the judges. We solemnly agreed that there would be no interruptions. But Mr Hari has broken the pious oath. I demand justice at your hands.

Mr Ramesh:—Honourable members of the group. The father of the Nation has categorically advocated village autonomy and village rule. The States and the Centre are to have minimum of authority. Similarly, Loknayak Jayaprakash Narayan declared that the Centre should concern itself only with external affairs and defence and leave the rest to Gram Panchayats. I wonder whether any one in his right mind can challenge the considered views of Bapuji and Jayaprakash Narayan. It will be blasphemy. These great leaders knew what they were talking about and our duty is to follow their leadership. I for one, pledge myself to walk on the path charted by them and not to deviate. Thank you.

Mr Frank:—Friends, the Constitution of India envisages a federal set-up with a unitary bias. The federal outline is only an appearance and has no meat. The makers of the Constitution, having witnessed the partition of the sub-continent, did not want to give room to divisive forces in India. The Centre was vested with the residuary powers and all the financial resources. The shape and size of the States or provinces could also be changed at the pleasure of the Centre. Subsequent experience has shown that the framers of the Constitution have done the right thing. If India had been made a true federation with full autonomy to the constituent States, by now we could be having several independent countries in the land which was once India, i.e., *Bharat*. I therefore, do not favour autonomy either to the States or districts or villages; we must have a strong Centre.

Mr Gopal:—Friends, I fully endorse the views expressed by our friend who spoke before me. There is a lot in what everyone has said. In a crucial subject like ours there is bound to be difference of opinion. We should regard it as a healthy sign and welcome frank opinions. I thank you all for educating me. Since I have no disagreement at all, there is really nothing more to be said by me. Thank you.

Hari:—Friends, I want to be blunt and I am calling a spade a spade. I don't care whether you agree with me or disagree with me. That is your problem. I know for sure what I say is right, and that is what counts. Now, all this talk of decentralisation, greater State autonomy, devolution of autonomy to districts and villages, etc, are rubbish, woolly and worthless ideas. If you give away the powers to all and Sundry, each one will be at the throat of the other and before you can say Jack Robinson, we shall be slaves once more, as we had been for centuries. Let us stop this nonsense here and now. I tell you, soon there will be nothing to distribute, decentralise or devolve. You all better face the truth and accept the realities. The way different States and politicians are struggling to peel off. It is sheer madness and blind stupidity to think of giving autonomy to States, districts, villages and hemlets. It is sheer disaster. Now, you do what you like. And don't tell me that I have not warned you.

Mr Arpit:—Friends, I want to do my duty and say a few words as is required of me. Left to myself, I would have preferred to remain silent. You see, I already told you that Constitution and politics are Greek and Latin to me. Science is my forte and zoology my favourite and I can speak to you for hours in those areas. All I could see is that this subject seems extremely controversial and my friend Mr Hari seems to be highly excited. I am always for moderation and stability. I suggest, let things stay the way they are now and let attention be paid to other matters like education, eradication of illiteracy, creation of employment opportunities, economic growth and so on. Thank you for your kind indulgence.

Mr Bharat:—Friends, the founding fathers of our Constitution wanted a strong and United India with democratic institutions and we are all for it. But with the advent of non-congress governments at the Centre, different interpretation is given to the concept of democracy and autonomy. The regional parties seem to feel that there cannot be democracy without autonomy. But the happenings in Mizoram, Assam, West Bengal, J&K, Punjab and Tamil Nadu and so on, seem to undermine the unity of the country. Under the present circumstances, greater autonomy to the States, which have linguistic or religious emphasis and bias, is not advisable. We do not have a long history or tradition to fall back to preserve our nationhood. The alternative is to give more authority and financial resources and powers to the districts and villages. In other words, we give powers directly to the people in the villages bypassing the politicians at the provincial or State capitals. There is no conflict or contradiction in this approach and I regard it as an imaginative solution. We should give it an honest try and I am confident it would solve many problems facing the country and bring her strength and success.

INDIAN PRESS—IS IT FREE?

Mr Ajay:—Please, my friends! May I request your kind attention for a few seconds. I shall be very thankful for your co-operation.

Mr Deepak:—I suppose, Mr Ajay, you want your friends to lend their ears to you.

Mr Ajay:—Yes, that is right. I see that you are an ardent student of Shakespeare. Well, I request you all to lend me your hearts besides your ears.

Mr Nitin:—What a pity? There is not a single lady candidate in the group. Otherwise, you can ask for the hearts both inside and outside. I would make a bid even for their gentle lips.

Mr Deepak:—I can guess what you will get. There won't be a question of lend or lease. They all will let fly their shoes and chappals at you. If there is a judo expert, you will also get some hefty kicks. How about that?

Mr Nitin:—May be some girls slapped you or threw rotten eggs on your face. But when I talk to the girls, I get what I want.

Mr Deepak:—I challenge you. Let us take a bet.

Mr Nitin :—How much are you willing to bet? I am ready for anything and as far as I am concerned, sky is the limit.

Mr Ajay:—Please, Mr Nitin and Mr Deepak. You will agree that both of you have become rather personal and emotional. Please smile and let us forget about our travails and concentrate on our task.

Mr Vijay:—You are right Mr Ajay and I agree with you hundred per cent. Now please proceed with what you wanted to say about our task.

Mr Ajay:—Thank you Mr Vijay. Well, friends! Since, we have only limited time to complete our Group Discussion. I suggest we start with Mr Nitin and go clockwise, that is Mr Dinesh, Mr Deepak and so on upto Mr Sunil. Each would take not more than two minutes to give his views, ideas or comments on the subject given for discussion. After one round is over, we can have another round provided there is time. By the way, we all must agree that none will interrupt or interfere in anyway when one is talking. Otherwise there will be delays.

Mr Vijay:—What happens if I disagree with what Mr Deepak or say Mr Virendra says?

Mr Ajay:—Yes, sorry, I forgot to clarify that. Well, you can mention that during your turn in the first round or in the second round according to the opportunity you get. But we must be firm that we won't interrupt when one is on his feet.

Mr Deepak:—All right. Let us start, come on.

Mr Nitin:—You are to bell the cat.

Mr Nitin:—No, no, wait. I have a better idea.

Mr Deepak:—I know, I know. You will come out with some silly suggestion as you did a while ago. You better forget about your better idea and do what you have been told. Get going with the task and speak on the subject.

Mr Nitin:—Will you shut up. Mr Deepak? I have every right to express my views. It is for the group to accept or reject it. I told the group that I have a better idea and it is high time you realised that I mean what I say. I am not an idiot like you.

Mr Ajay:—Please, gentlemen. Why quarrel over nothing? Now, Mr Nitin, if you have a better suggestion, the group will surely accept it. Let us hear what is in your mind.

Mr Nitin :—I totally disagree with the suggestion of Mr Ajay. It is completely wrong. That is very important.

Mr Vijay:—Okay, okay, Mr Nitin. Tell us what you want? What is the alternative you are suggesting?

Mr Nitin:—Why don't you give some excercise to your own brain? Why don't you suggest an alternative yourself?

Mr Vijay:—My dear chap, how does that question arise? It is you who is not agreeing to the suggestion of Mr Ajay. The rest of us agree with his plan. Am I right gentlemen?

Mr Deepak, Mr Pankaj and Mr Sunil:—Yes, yes.

Mr Vijay:—All right. Now, all those who disagree with Mr Ajay. Please raise your hands. There you are Mr Nitin. If you have a better idea, then speak it out. As you can see, the time is running out.

Mr Nitin:—Oh! Rubbish. You have already made sure that no one will accept my plan. Why should I waste my breath now? I refuse to say anything.

Mr Ajay:—Now, come on Mr Nitin. Please, for my sake, I already told you that I am ready to accept your plan if it is a better one. When I am myself ready. I am sure others will also agree.

Mr Deepak:—I say, we are wasting time, Mr Nitin. I guarantee that he has nothing in his mind at all. He is just bluffing for the heck of it.

Mr Nitin :—Shut up. I challenged you before but you backed out. What is the bet?

Mr Deepak:—Do you think we are all gamblers assembled here to bet. Sorry, we have a task to perform and your betting can wait. Friends, you could see that Mr Nitin is obstinate and proving obstructive. If you order me. I am ready to start the ball rolling. Now let us ignore Mr Nitin.

Mr Ajay:—I am sorry, Mr Deepak, we are a simple group and must work in unison. No, question of ignoring anybody please. I appeal to you, Mr Nitin, Please do let us have your idea, no matter how you feel about it.

Mr Nitin:—No, no, no. It is of no use. If they don't want to have the better idea, let them not have it. I also don't want to speak first. Now you can go ahead as per your plan. I don't care who speaks first or last and what happens.

Mr Ajay : — Now, come on Mr Dinesh. Please give your views on the subject.

Mr Dinesh :—Sorry, you see, I think the subject deals with newspapers. It is rather unfortunate that don't read them much. At the most, I give a casual look to the film magazines now and then. I wish they had given a better topic. This is very dry. You know, I never believe in the newspapers. It is all propaganda and brainwashing. I suppose, they have all the freedom they want and more if you ask me. Otherwise, how do they write all rubbish and cock and bull stories.

Mr Deepak:—Friends, the subject given by the examiner for Discussion by our group reads. *"Indian Press Is not All That Free"*. In my opinion the proposition is not correct. During emergency, we had censorship and the press was gagged. But now all those restrictions have gone. If you go by what Mr Dinesh said just now, the press does enjoy the freedom to write or publish what it chooses, good or bad, true or false, weighty or trash.

Mr Vijay:—Gentlemen, I would say that the Indian Press is entirely free if we go by the letter of the law. But the moot question is, whether the press in India is truly or really free. You could hear all political leaders, whether in power or in the opposition, accusing the press to be partial, one sided and even blind. In their view, the press is biased. In other words, the reporting in our press is not objective and impartial. It is more so with the editorials and articles appearing in the press. They are coloured and motivated. If something compels the press not to be objective an impartial, then one cannot easily or lightly dismiss the feeling that the press is not really free. There could be vested interests. Big money may play its part. There is always political horse trading, changes of foreign influence have also been levelled. I request those who would be speaking after me to consider these aspects and give their views. Now I will stop as the allotted time is over. Thank you.

Mr Pankaj : — Friends, in my humble view, the Press in India is no doubt free, but it is abusing the freedom. In a democracy like ours where freedom of speech and expression, which automatically covers the press, is guaranteed as fundamental right. The press must at least have its code. But the press in our country does not respect or believe in any such code, self-restraint or self-discipline. Since they want blindly to support one political party or the other and also want to increase the circulation, they totally abuse the freedom. Not only the tabloids and the yellow journals and party mouthpieces resort to sensationalism and partiality, but even the established newspapers follow the same path. (With a laugh) I would say we have only yellow and blue journalism in India. By Blue I mean obscene and pornographic writings. Thus, there is too much freedom and the need of the hour is some restrictions and discipline. We want decency and honesty and not the licence that the press has got today.

Mr Ajay : — We all agree that in accordance with our Constitution and going by the letter of the law, the press is free in India. It is also true that some journals, periodicals and newspapers abuse the freedom, some totally and others to some degree. But if the public and the government so desire, there are legal remedies to stop such abuse. Now let us turn to the moot question of press really or truly being free. As you are aware, the dailies, weeklies, etc, are owned or managed by some well-to-do and influential people. Those who control the purse of the Press often, dictate, what it should print. In other words, editors, writers and reporters, are forced or induced to touch the line of the management or the owners. In India, most of the newspaper chains are owned by big industrial or business houses. They virtually enjoy monopoly situation. Thus, truth is blacked out and the papers become the mouthpiece of the owners or the management. Next comes the influence of the advertisements. These days no newspaper or periodical can survive without advertisements. The industrial houses, as also the Union and State governments, who release the advertisements, have big impact on the press. Another area of pressure or influence is the newsprint quota allocation. The cost of newsprint has shot up phenomenally and it is difficult to get it. These are important constraints on the freedom of the press. Finally, the press has also to compete with other agents of mass media like the TV, radio and cinema, which have greater impact on the vast illiterate rural masses in India. Despite these constraints, I would say press in India is fairly free. A lot depends on the editors, reporters and journalists. If they play their assigned roles properly, the Indian press can always remain really free.

Mr Virendra:—Thank you, Mr Ajay. I congratulate you and must say that I learnt so much from what you said just now. I wonder whether anyone can add anything more to what has been so brilliantly presented by you already. If I say something, it will be only a repetition and I see no sense in carrying coal to newcastle. Thank you once again.

Mr Sunil :—Gentlemen, I for one, firmly believe that the press in India is really, truly and totally free. Before I proceed further, we must be clear in our mind as to what precisely, we mean by real and true freedom. As you all know, every right also carries a duty with it. Thus, the freedom of the press also carries with it, certain duties and responsibilities. Thus, national security, unity, harmony, peace, individual privacy, good foreign relations demand certain contraint and self-discipline on the part of the newspapers. These cannot be regarded as impediments to real freedom. In fact, without such self-disciplined code of conduct, the freedom will degenerate into lawlessness and get lost. Secondly, free competition, whether with other newspapers and periodicals or even with radio, TV, etc, promotes than hinders the press freedom. If one newspaper rather agency suppresses or twists or ignores some important news or facts, its rivals can highlight them. Such competition exists in India and hence, I will assert our press is absolutely free.

Mr Nitin :—(Remains silent and all are waiting)

Mr Ajay :—Come on, Mr Nitin. We are waiting to hear your views. Please let us have the benefit of your ideas.

Mr Nitin :—Sorry, I told you already that I am no longer interested and I will have nothing to do with your plans. I don't want to force myself or anybody. If I choose, I can blow all your arguments to pieces. But I don't want to demean myself by entering into a controversy. You are welcome to say what you like and come to any conclusion. You wish, I don't care a hoot. It is nothing.

SHOULD POLITICIANS RETIRE AT THE AGE OF SIXTY

Mr Amar: Thank you for allowing me to start this group discussion, friends. The topic is—"Should politicians retire at the age of sixty?" My answer is: Yes! Every government official retires at the age of 58 to 60 years. Every (private) businessman gives charge of his business to his children (or managers) when he grows up to cross the sixties. Then, why should we not have a system of political retirement? If politicians retire early, they would pave the way for the entry of young blood in their political groups. These young people would be more innovative and energetic. They would serve their country with zeal. The elders would not be able to travel through the length and breadth of the country and comprehend the problems of the masses. Hence, politicians must retire at the age of sixty years. Thank you.

Ms Shweta: I do not agree with the views of Mr Amar. Why should a politician retire at the age of sixty years if he can deliver results even after this age? He is not a government official. He joins a political party and works hard to build an image of himself or of his party. This naturally takes a lot of time and energy. When there is time to become an MLA, MP or CM, you tell him to call it a day. That is not fair. Mr Amar has pointed out that businessmen retire during the sixties. Can he give examples in the context. No businessman retires; Mr. Ratan Tata is the only exception in this context. Businessmen continue to guide their business empire through their children or managers even when they are in their late seventies. If some one can perform, let him. Why should we put restrictions on the tenure of politicians? Thank you.

Mr Vedpal: I would prefer to align my views with those of Mr Amar. Every politician should give opportunities to the posterity. If he could not deliver till the age of sixty years, how would he deliver beyond that age? This also confirms the efficacy and efficiency criteria of politics for every political system. For example if a politician is able and mass-oriented, he would deliver by the end of his fifties. Rather, he would be forced to deliver, given that he would know that the time of his retirement is about to arrive. Mr. HKS Surjeet had retired at the age of 89 years. Did his party get any advantage because of his late retirement? I don't think that it did. The communists as well as other parties could not infuse fresh ideas into the minds of party cadres simply because old stalwart of their party were trying to pursue hackneyed policies. Had new politicians arrived at the centre stage of communist parties, these parties could have made governments in many states much earlier. Occasionally, the communists were a part of the UPA, they were not the *de facto* ruling party. With passage of time, the thinking and adjustment abilites of person take a beating. Today's politics is all about making compromises. Hence, old leaders cannot adjust according to the dynamic situations. Thank you.

Mr Rajesh: I think Ms Shweta has the right set of views that can be depended upon. The present era is forcing every one to deliver. Mr. Vajpayee could not deliver and hence, he as well as his party is out of reckoning. But Mr. Vajpayee is still the most respected icon of the right-wing groups. Why had he retired? Mr. Advani could not become the PM. He could have become one had he wished so in the last general elections. Mr. Advani is in his eighties. Should we tell him to hang his boots? He is the single most respected leader, after AB Vajpayee, who can keep the constituents of the NDA together. His age should not be detrimental to the process of election of the future PM of India. Hence, the proposition of retirement of politicians after the age of sixty years is not based on the foundation of rationale. Thank you.

Ms Rekha: It is not in the interest of the country to retire seasoned politicians. If the second-generation politicians of a political group are not prepared to take the responsibility of managing the affairs of the group, their elders must remain at the helm of affairs. When the younger politicians become mature enough to control party cadres or to rule the country, the elders can hang their boots. Their experience can be utilised by the young Turks of their party to consolidate its position in the centre as well as in states.

Mr Kamaldeep: Bill Clinton retired at the right time and age. On the other hand, Mr. Advani is being promoted as "neither tired nor retired." He is not allowing young leaders to take charge. That is bad for the BJP. Senior leaders must put in their papers and pave the way for the accession of young, energetic and innovative leaders. That is how good parties ought to function. Today, change is the only constant. Hence, young leaders would effect change. Old leaders would continue to tread the old path. I do not agree with Ms Rekha. I want all politicians above sixty years of age to call it a day.

Mr Anuj: Friends! We have had a good debate. It is my turn to speak now. I would like to align my views with neither of the factions that have been created during this brief period. I think we should adopt according to the situation. If a political party wants the retirement age to be fixed at 60 years, let it do so. Other parties need not follow that norm. Hence, I do not support or oppose this topic.

Mr Kamaldeep: You can either support or oppose the topic. You cannot stand on the borderlines.

Mr Anuj: You cannot force me to decide. You can never put words in my mouth.

Mr Rajesh: Mr Anuj, he is right. You can either support or oppose the proposition.

Mr Anuj: I would prefer to stay neutral.

Mr Vedpal: All right! Round one is over. Now, we have to evolve a consensus after discussing the issue among ourselves. What is your opinion, friends?

All: We are with you.

Mr Anuj: Very good! Shall we request Mr Amar to sum up and evolve a final consensus statement?

All: Yes, sure.

Mr Amar: Thank you, friends! Some members of the group agree that politicians should retire at the age of sixty years. Some others do not agree with them on that account. My opinion is that the age of retirement should be fixed at sixty years but at the same time, highly efficient veterans should be allowed to continue. Do you like this idea?

Ms Rekha: I do not agree with you. How can a political party decide whether its veteran leaders have delivered results or not?

Mr Vedpal: It is very simple. Their track records of the past can be scanned. Their achievements and failures can be highlighted while extending their tenure. If they have done well in the past, they should be allowed to continue.

Mr Kamaldeep: Age is a major factor in this context. Mr. Vajpayee and Mr. Surjeet were too old to continue. With passage of time, the physical and mental abilities of every person takes a beating. Even if a person is a seasoned astute politician, he may not be able to deliver concrete results after he crosses his sixtieth birthday. His party can bite dust at the hustings that way.

Mr Amar: He can guide his juniors. His experience can be utilised to the best advantage of the party. Why don't you understand that he knows more about politics than his young juniors.

Mr Kamaldeep: We cannot accept your theory.

Ms Rekha: Mr Amar, please incorporate the views of Mr Kamaldeep.

Mr Amar: The group has decided that politicians should voluntarily retire from active politics at the age of sixty years. If their health permits, they can guide their juniors from behind the curtain. They can also occupy important positions in the party, provided they are physically and mentally fit to do so. However, retirement at the age of sixty years should become a norm in all countries. New, young leaders should be told to manage the party affairs. They must not bypass the directives and philosophies of their retired seniors in any case. Thank you!

UNSTABLE DEMOCRACIES IN OUR NEIGHBOURHOOD CAN HARM US

Mr Gautam:—Good afternoon, ladies and gentlemen! The topic for today's discussion is: Unstable democracies in our neighbourhood can harm us. Well, I don't agree with this statement. India is an independent country. Her people are wise enough to ward off any threat from the neighbouring countries. If Nepal has become an unstable nation, India has not been affected by it. Pakistan has remained more or less unstable since 1947. But her state of affairs could not stop us from developing and becoming a major regional power. Hence, we are least affected if our neighbours remain unstable or undemocratic. Thank You!

Ms Reena:—My friend, Mr Gautam should note the facts carefully. Unstable neighbours can harm our social, political and economic systems. Inter-country trade is affected. People are unable to meet their friends and relatives. Border villages become high alert zones becuase of threats of armed conflicts with insurgents or even military forces of unstable neighbours. It happens sometimes that the leader of an unstable nation orders his army to attack a neighbouring country to divert the attention of the masses of his country from the burning national issues. Hence all the neighbours of India must become stable, peaceful and prosperous. We must not forget that India is striving for a developing Regional Forum in the Indian subcontinent on the lines of other regional trading block, eg., ASEAN. We want a progressive regaional organisation in the form of SAARC. For this our neighbour must be stable. Thank you!

Mr Fransis:—In my view, an unstable neighbour cannot harm any interest—political, economic or social conditions of a country like India. Let me give you an example. The USA is located in the North American subcontinent. The nascent democracies of Central America and South America never gave their people any kind of economic and political stability. Never were the Americans affected by this chaotic state of affairs in central and South America. Chile, Uruguay, Argentina, Brazil and Mexico remained unstable at one point of time or another. But the USA has a resilient democratic system that is powerful enough to withstand shocks of her neighbours. Thank you.

Ms Ela:—I agree with Mr Fransis. India is a large democracy. It is powerful enough to face the challenges posed by her neighbours. However, we should always be prepared to counter the threats of terrorists, armies, smugglers and other anti-social, elements of unstable neighbours. They can disrupt normal life in India, as they have been doing in the past. Hence, I am supporting both the viewpoints-Ayes and Nays. Thank You.

Mr Madhav:—I have heard the views of my friends who have spoken so far. I would like to align my thoughts with those of Ms Reena. Unstable neighbours have always proved to be harmful to our country. Mr Fransis has stated that the USA is more or less aloof from the political developments of Central and South America. I do not agree with him. An unstable region would certainly affect all the component nations of that region. This effect may be visible after long period, though. This is a small world. A flutter in Kochi can cause a furore in Karachi. How can Mr Fransis and Ms Ela conclude that unstable neighbours would not affect us? There are ethnic problems. There is the Shia-Sunni divide. There is the Kashmir imbroglio. And finally, there is the problem of insurgency of Maoists in Nepal. If Sri Lanka is peaceful today, don't assume that she would remain peaceful forever. If the LTTE takes to arms, this small island down south would again simmer with the heat of mortars and gunfire. And India would be affected due to this heat. The LTTE cadres are Tamilians. If the LTTE is suppressed in Jaffna, the direct impact of this suppression would be felt (almost immediately) in the entire state of Tamil Nadu. Hence, the concept of "aloof secluded regional superpower" is nothing but an immature thought of my friends, Mr Fransis and Ms Ela. Thank you.

Mr Zamir:—Friends! In my view Mr Fransis and Ms Ela should agree with other members of the group. Mr Gautam has also aligned his viewpoint with theirs. All these friends are ignoring the fact that the acts of terrorism, sabotage, bombing and smuggling all being carried out in India at the behest of the masters of her unstable neighbours. If these countries become politically stable, India would also remain stable. Our cultures are almost similar and our religions are the same. Hence, we can affect them and can be affected by them. I agree with Ms Reena and

Mr Madhav. They have already said enough about the topic. I need not repeat their versions. Thank you.

Mr Rajeev:—I agree with Mr Zamir and also with Ms Reena and Mr Madhav. India can remain stable only if her neighbours remain stable in political and social terms.

Mr Fransis:—Mr Rajeev, do not try to form a clique to get your opinion accepted. We cannot change our stand.

Ms Ela:—I support Mr Fransis. India shall remain a democracy even if her neighbours are unstable. How can we take a guarantee of Bangladesh? She has never remained a stable country since independence. Terrorists are operating training camps in that country. But these camps could not dissrupt the functioning of economic, social and political forces in India.

Mr Rajeev:—The group concludes that unstable neighbours of India can harm her political, social and economic interests. Although we are a stable democracy, we must remain vigilant about the machinations that might have been planned across our borders. I hope all of you agree with me on that account.

All:—Yes, we do!

Mr Rajeev:—Thank you for your co-operation.

POLITICS, BUSINESS AND BUREAUCRACY FORM A FATAL TRIANGLE

Mr Purva:— Good afternoon, ladies and gentlemen. My name is Raman Kumar Purva. I would like to start the proceedings with your kind permission. May I start now?

Ms Goyal:— Mr Purva, there has to be a system in this discussion session. Please get the permission from all of those who are present here.

Mr. Purva:— That is what I am trying to do.

Mr Gonzalez:— I think we can start from one corner of the table. Mr Purva is a nice person to listen to. However, he is in the middle of this horse-shoe-shaped row of candidates. We can start from Mr Paruthi and move in a clockwise direction. Finally, I would present my views. I hope all of you agree.

All:— We agree.

Mr. Purva: — Mr. Paruthi can start now.

Mr Paruthi:— Good afternoon, friends! My name is Jinesh Kumar Paruthi. In my view, politics, business and bureaucracy form a fatal triangle. Every businessman wants to earn profits. He contacts the bureaucrats of our country to get loans, coal quotas, gas quotas, contracts, raw materials, export orders, electric power, plant, land in industrial estates etc. The bureaucrat is a starved individual. He milks the businessmen. The latter also promotes a politician or his party during elections. When the politician comes to power, he helps the businessmen through various bureaucratic channels and procedures. Together, these three utilise the lacunae of the system and generate wealth for themselves. This procedure has been going on in our country since independence. I am sure, corruption must have been prevalent even during the days of the British Raj. However, I do not have any data related to that era.

I would not have censured this nexus, had it not harmed the interests of our masses. This nexus has given birth to several heinous scandals and scams. Starting from the securities scam, which hit our economy during the nineties, we have come a long way. Today, the Tehelka expose, fodder scam, Telgi Stamp scam, Judeo tape case and the bribery case of Mr Ajit Jogi are stealing the limelight. The masses have become immune to these scams simply because they have realised how corrupt our system is. I fully support the topic. Thank you!

Ms Goyal:— Good afternoon, friends! My name is Anukriti Goyal. I do not agree with the views of Mr Paruthi. The bureaucrats are not corrupt. Rather, they are forced to act as pawns of politicians. The businessman is also not corrupt. He has to start, operate and continue his business. He tries to remove the bottlenecks through clumsy and agonising bureaucratic procedures. However, his time and money are wasted. So, he uses money to circumvent the problems that his business faces from time to time. He recovers all these costs by charging extra prices from his customers. Now a days, business cannot be conducted by incurring losses. So, the viewpoint of the businessmen is also correct.

Let us come to the politician now. He is a part of the corrupt system. This system uses the businessmen and bureaucrats to its advantage. The politician uses the corrupt system to mint money. The businessman pays to the politician unwillingly. The bureaucrat works for the politician because the latter is a democratically elected representative of the masses. The politician defines the laws. He controls the law-enforcing agencies. He rules through the bureaucrats. If businessmen or bureaucrats do not conform to his directives, he withdraws his support to him. Hence, the businessman loses his business and the bureaucrat is transferred to a place where he finds himself to be misfit. Or, the bureaucrat is demoted or even told to quit. Hence, the politician is solely responsible for the decay of the system. There is no triangle of these three elements. Rather, we have a corrupt apex at the top of a pyramid. Below this apex, the bureaucrat and politician serve the apex (the politician). The bottom of the pyramid comprises the masses. The hunger for money was generated in the politicians of today during the fag end of the sixties. I admit that some bureaucrats are also corrupt. But who made them so? Naturally the orders flow from the apex of the pyramid. The hunger for money lured the bureaucrats as well. These two elements (the politician and the bureaucrat) started milking the businessmen, who, ironically, were required to develop the nation in economic terms. Hence, the real culprit is the politician. There are many good bureaucrats in our country. We can be proud of them. Some of them are TN Seshan, GK Khairnar, KC Pant and many more. Thank you!

Mr Purva:— Good afternoon, friends! I have already given my introduction.

Ms Sheikh:— Celebrities do not need any introduction.

(All laugh for a few seconds).

Mr Purva:— I appreciate the views of Ms Sheikh. She is a witty person. In my view, the politician alone is not responsible for the decay process that has started in our country. Businessmen and bureaucrats are also responsible for creating this precarious situation. Hence, the concept of a lethal triangle is very much in place. If politicians alone were corrupt, bureaucrats and businessmen could have exposed them. However, instead of uncovering their wily machinations, they colluded with them. And why they did so, can be easily imagined. Government jobs do not yield high incomes even for the bureaucrats in high offices. Further, some of them become fond of leading high-quality life. They emulate the living norms of the West. These norms cannot be adopted unless they earn extra money. Hence, they use businessmen to earn extra money. Businessmen, in turn, use politicians and bureaucrats to serve their own base ends. Hence, this vicious cycle continues. Corruption was prevalent at the grass root levels during the sixties and seventies. However, it is sad to note that it is a chief feature of the top brass of bureaucrats now a days. The primary reason is the same—they want to earn money through the operations of businessmen; and the businessmen need protection of the politician as well as the bureaucratic support of the officials of the government. Nobody can break this evil nexus. I would like to support the topic. Thank you!

Ms Sheikh:— Good evening, friends! My name is Asifa Jahan Sheikh. I have been carefully listening to the views of my friends, Mr Purva, Mr Paruthi and Ms Goyal. In my view, corruption starts from the grassroot level itself. We want to pay bribe and that is why bribe is accepted. If we refuse to pay the bribe, no one dare take it from us. If the task is such that its execution could be obstructed, we pay the bribe (so that it could be done with ease). Here lies the crux of the issue. If we have to get something done and we are not sure about its legitimacy, we shall pay bribe. I can give you an example in this context. If a person knows how to drive, he would get a driving licence. If he doesn't, he would pay bribe to get this driving licence made through touts. The problem lies in the ability of the person. If he wants to learn driving, he should learn it in a driving school. The government also gives him a learner's licence and allows him to learn driving for six months. However, he has to appear in a written test to get this learner's licence. Later, he would be required to appear in another test in which, his driving skills would be tested by the police. He bypasses all these formalities and gets his driving licence made without even moving his finger. So, the individual is corrupt, not the system. Procedures are defined and rules do exist in all the departments of the State. However, people want to bypass such rules and procedures. They want to save time. So, they spend money. This money feeds the corrupt system. Ultimately, this money reaches the politicians. Hence, the businessman, who goes as an individual, meets the bureaucrat. The latter goes to the politician. Thus, the system becomes more corrupt every day. This system can be changed only if we stop offering bribe. If we do so, we would have to depend upon our own strength and merits. This can be done only if we are competent. This competence can be developed if we are educated, hard working and honest to the core. Hence, we should not blame the politician, bureaucrat or businessman because all of us are the parts of a corrupt band of brothers. Hence, the issue has not been able to draw my support. Politicians, bureaucrats and business persons belong to our society, which is highly corrupt and immoral. Thank you!

Mr Gonzalez:— Good evening, friends! My name is Roger Gonzalez. All of you have given nice views. In my view, the politician-bureaucrat-businessman triangle has proved to be a bane for our socio-economic processes. I need not repeat the views given by my friends who have supported the topic. My only contention, in this context, is that politicians, bureaucrats and businessmen are the important elements of any society. I admit that our masses can be corrupt. But can our political leaders afford to be so? Or, can our bureaucrats be caught taking bribe? The case of Mr RPS Siddhu is very much prominent in this context. He gave jobs to hundreds through the PPSC and stashed away millions in his bank lockers. Finally, a businessmen can be given some leeway because he has to get things done to continue his business operations. But why should he become corrupt? If the bureaucrats and political leaders are keen to develop our economy, they can help businessmen in all possible ways without taking a penny from them. The civic life and the administrative systems in the West are sans corruption, red tapism and sleaze. Why cannot we effect changes in our corrupt system? Politicians can prove to be agents of change. However, they have become the agents of decay, if you carefully review the latest scandals and scams. I have given my views. Now, let Mr Purva give the consensus view and wind up.

Mr Purva:— Thank you, Mr Gonzalez. The group has concluded that politicians, bureaucrats and businessmen are squarely responsible for creating an evil nexus that is destroying the political, moral and economic roots of our nation. Corruption is the most lethal output of this nexus. The masses promote corruption because they have to get things done in time or at low costs. However, these three elements of our society should never be swayed by the glitter of money, favour and materialistic assets. As they are hell-bent upon perpetuating this evil system, the masses should take the initiative to decimate it. However, the masses would have to learn a few lessons on morality and honesty before they attempt to annihilate this gargantuan anti-India triangle. Thank you.

All:— Thank you!

A NEW VISION FOR THE UN IS NOT A PRAGMATIC IDEA

Mr. Savarkar : Good morning friends! My name is Rajat Savarkar. The UNO is a maid of Uncle Sam. It is running all of its vital organs by providing funds to them. It is not going to make the UNO a democratic and world-oriented organisation. Hence, the new vision given by the Secretary General, Ban Ki-Moon, is not a very pragmatic concept. Many countries, including India have supported the concept of democratisation of the UNO. But these are Utopian dreams, given that the USA and UK are ruling the corridors of the UNO.

Ms. Sandhu : Good morning, ladies and gentlemen! My name is Satinder Kaur Sandhu. If we do not give a new vision for the UNO, how will this organisation adopt it? Many countries have advocated the concept of democratisation of this organisaton. True, the USA and other nations of the West would not accept it. They are the de facto controllers of the UNO. They would not like to release it from their clutches. But some one has to take an initiative to liberate the UNO. A new vision is the first step towards the democratisation of this world body. Hence, I oppose the topic. Thank you!

Mr. Nabi : Good morning, ladies and gentlemen! My name is Abdullah Nabi. The UNO is a puppet of the USA and its close allies. Even the Russians and Chinese cannot liberate it from their clutches. They are grappling with their own problems. The new vision given by the UN Secretary-General at the recently concluded UN General Assembly is only an eyewash. The USA can attack Iran at any point of time. It has forced North Korea to shed its nuclear weapons programme. It has signed a nuclear pact with India and the latter would be required to abide by its clauses. Around the world, the supremacy of the USA is reflected in the operations of various UN organs. From this position of unlimited power, the USA would not like to retreat at any cost. The status quo shall be maintained, as far as the control of the USA over the UNO is concerned. Thank you!

Ms. Watson : Good morning, friends! My name is Cynthia Watson. I do not agree with the view of Mr. Nabi. This status quo can be changed; and we will change it soon. The new vision of the UN Secretary-General would help the UNO restructure itself. Democratisation is but one part of this long-term process. We would have chopped off the useless organs of the UNO and make it more human friendly and mass oriented. Poor nations have no say in the UNO. They must be allowed to speak up for themselves. The other two superpowers—Russia and China—must come forward to make it a balanced global organisation. It is not an exclusive property of the United States and its allies. I would suggest that the UNO purchase a new place, outside the USA, and make its headquarters at that place. Today, the UNO is in the pocket of the US Administration. We shall accept this status quo. If the world is to be made a peaceful place to live in, the UNO must be democratised. Thank you!

Mr. Bendre : I disagree with you, Ms. Watson. The UNSC has not admitted India in its realm. The USA is opposing our entry into this organisation. Japan, a small country and a larger donor to the UN funds, has been picked up by the USA as the new member of this (permanent) council. Sooner or later, Japan will become a full-fledged member of the UNSC. How can you oppose this decision of the USA? Poor and developing nations do not have any chance to get themselves heard. I fully support the thoughts of Mr. Savarkar. If the UNO is democratised, the USA would oppose the move. This will open up Pandora's box. Thus, the entire world would face chaos, given that the USA would not like to release the UNO from its powerful clutches.

Ms. Watson : I feel that the UNO can be made a better organisation by adopting the new vision. Dr. Kofi Annan has set the ball rolling. What we need is to give some impetus to this process. This small vision would become a revolution. Finally, the UNO would be restructured. It would become a democratic entity. We never knew that India would become free one day. But we worked hard to liberate it from the British rule. The same example can be applied in practice to the UNO as well. Note that change is the only constant in life.

Ms. Sandhu : The group has concluded that the UNO is a pawn in the hands of the USA and its close allies. Its liberation is a necessity of the poor nations of the world. Global economic and political scenarios are being dominated by the West. This status quo must change at the earliest possible date.

Ms. Sandhu : I admit that the existing status quo cannot be changed so easily. But changing it in the long run should not be an impossible task to accomplish. After all, there are 193 countries in the UNO. Not all of them would like the organisation to work under the thumb of Uncle Sam. Your contention—that the new vision for the UN is not a pragmatic idea—is a myopic view of the things. The new vision may not help us today. But it will certainly become a potential agent of change in the times to come. We should not rule out the possibility of the UNO becoming a more useful organisation for the poor and developing nations of the world. Let us try to make it more democratic and friendly towards weaker nations of the world. I hope all of you would agree with me on that account.

WILL LIMITED NUCLEAR WAR EVER REMAIN LIMITED?

Mr Shambhu:— The examiner said *"Limited Nuclear War"* but did not clarify what it means. In what sense is it limited?

Mr Ashutosh:— Why don't you ask the examiner himself? He asked us repeatdly whether anyone had any doubts.

Mr Shambhu:— Others may hear and even the examiner can overhear us. Now, coming back to my doubt, you have not answered my question.

Mr Ashutosh:— Well, *"limited"* means limited. You can make your own assumptions. I don't think you should worry about it.

Mr Shambhu:— I think you are joking, or, may be you also do not know the answer.

Mr Ashutosh:— You are welcome to draw conclusions.

Mr Ashish:— What is the secret you two seem to be sharing between each other?

Mr Ashutosh:— Your neighbour, Mr Shambhu has some problem. May be you could solve it.

Mr Ashish:— That is easy. Mr Shambhu, take it for granted that your problem is already solved. That is my responsibility. But first of all, let us start the GD session. We must complete it within the given time frame.

Mr Ashutosh:— That is a right attitude. Let us start right away.

Mr Rajan:— Friends, may I request for your kind attention please? Kindly bear with me for a moment. I have a small announcement to make and what I have to say concerns all of us and our task.

Mr Rupak:— Mr Rajan, we are all ready and too eager to hear what you have to say. Please go ahead.

Mr Rajan:— Gentlemen, we have just half an hour to complete out group discussion. I am afraid we have already spent more than five minutes on sweet nothings and small talks etc. We can't lose any more time. Let us, therefore, get down to the brass tacks.

Mr Ashutosh:— Mr Rajan, before you proceed further, I want you to sort out the problem posed by Mr Shambhu.

Mr Shambhu:— No, please. I asked Mr Ashutosh but I am pretty clear.

Mr Ashish:— Well, I had already told Mr Shambhu that I could solve all his problems, including his doubts.

Mr Rajan:— Mr Ashutosh, Mr Shambhu and Mr Ashish, please do not speak in subtle terms. We are losing more time as you are not coming to the real issue.

Mr Rupak:— That is right, Mr Shambhu. If you have any problem, please tell us straightway.

Mr Shambhu:— No! Please proceed.

Mr Ashutosh:— I think he is hesitating. If I am right he was not too clear as to what exactly the term *"Limited Nuclear War"* means. The term 'limit' could refer to the size of the nuclear bomb or its capacity to destroy.

Mr Rajan:— Thank you, Mr Ashutosh. Don't worry, Mr Shambhu. We shall be discussing this very point, besides many other aspects, during our GD session. Now, if you all agree, we can start. It would be a good idea to start with a volunteer. Then, we can proceed one after another.

Mr Rupak:— Excuse me, Mr Rajan. Would you like to say something about the time limit? I mean, how much time each candidate can take?

Mr Rajan:— Yes, it is important. What is your suggestion?

Mr Rupak:— I think, we should have two rounds and each one should get minmum two chances to speak. During the first round, two minutes per head should be the maximum. In the second round, if could be half to one minute.

Mr Rajan:— Okay, I am sure, all will stick to the time limit. Now who wishes to speak first? If there is no volunteer, we can request Mr Rupak to open the discussion.

Mr Ashish:— All right, I shall volunteer.

Mr Shambhu:— I want to speak last.

Mr Rajan:— Fine, that suits us well. Mr Ashish will set the ball rolling. Then, we move on to Mr Ashwani, Mr Rupak, Mr Anil and so on, and finally come to Mr Shambhu to complete the round. Please go ahead.

Mr Ashish:— Friends, the proposition given as the subject of our discussion states that *"limited nuclear wars can never remain limited"*. As you all know, the Soviet Union was one of the two Super Powers because of its nuclear capability to retaliate and inflict unacceptable nuclear damage on its opponents. America was the other Super Power. Today, the mightly Soviet Union is no longer in a position to dictate its terms. It has disintegrated into twenty independent republics and the Russian Federation, the largest of such independent republics controls the nuclear button. Already, there is strong disagreement between Ukraine and Russia. Thus, there could be limited nuclear wars among these Soviet republics. Such nuclear proliferation will lead to nuclear wars and ultimetely, all nuclear powers, including the USA, will get affected. The remaining sole Super Power, cannot control or stop such limited nuclear wars. Hence, all nuclear wars should be banned and all existing nuclear weapons should be destroyed. We must have a nuclear free world.

Mr Ashwini: — Gentlemen, the destruction of the two Japanese cities, Nagasaki and Hiroshima, with their entire civilisation, by the dropping of two atomic bombs, makes us think of a nuclear war in the future. The destructive capacity of nuclear bombs has since increased by thousands or millions of times. A few hydrogen bombs are now sufficient to obliterate an entire country. One should, therefore, be prepared to protect the country against such danger. To have peace, we have to be prepared for war. If a country has the capacity to survive a surprise nuclear attack and then, retaliate to such an extent where the damage can be unacceptable to the attacker, then it will serve as a deterrent. Of course, it means a nuclear armament race. But it cannnot be avoided. It is a necessary evil. Even when you think of a limited nuclear war, you must be prepared and have the capacity to fight it. Even mistakes and misunderstandings can lead to a nuclear war. We should be prepared for anything on the nuclear front. Hence, I agree with Mr Ashish that we should give due consideration to the doctrine of a nuclear free world.

Mr Rupak: — Friends, the *"limited nuclear war doctrine"* enunciated by America, envisages a surprise attack by the USA on select strategic and nuclear targets of the enemy. For instance, with a first attack on Iran's top political leadership or on Syria's nuclear war-heads, the US experts feel, the USA can minimise or even escape nuclear attacks on its bases and forces. In other words, the initial or pre-emptive surprise American attack will be limited. The aim is to destroy the political leadership and also the retaliatory capacity of the enemy. If America can achieve this, then, it can be said to enjoy relative nuclear monopoly in the armament race. But despite the demise of the Soviet Union as a Super Power, its nuclear arsenal is still there. Further, there will also be nuclear proliferation. Big powers like China, France and the UK also have nuclear weapons. Under these circumstances, limited nuclear war can not remain *"limited"*. It will spread and engulf the world. Hence, all nuclear weapons and wars should be banned. But America will not agree to it. Today it is the only Super Power. Hence, it should use the concept of nuclear deterrence and stop nuclear proliferation and nuclear threats. It should nip the nuclear danger in the bud.

Mr Anil:— Gentlemen, I mean friends. It is difficult to decide, to whom I should support – Mr Ashish and Mr Ashwini have taken one side and Mr Rupak has taken the opposite side. To me, both appear to be correct. Therefore, I cannot but remain neutral. I like to stay non-aligned. I should listen to others, particularly to Mr Rajan, before I make up my mind. I would like to support majority opinion when this GD session is over. But I agree in general that nuclear war is bad and dangerous, no matter whether it is total or limited.

Mr Rajan:— Friends, the most valid question is whether a limited nuclear war can remain limited. Mr Ashutosh wanted to know what exactly the term *'limited'* signifies. As one of the speakers said, the limit could be in terms of targets or area of attack or limit of damage. But how far and how long any of these can remain limited? There is bound to be escalation of any nuclear conflict. The loser will always like to fight to the finish, using all that he could muster or command. If one side is ready to come to terms as a result of a limited nuclear war, the result can at best be a temporary truce. He will only make a tactical retreat for the time being in order to attack later with greater strength and force. Secondly, it does not make sense to observe that America can destroy war leadership and retaliatory capacity of its enemies by resorting to a surprise limited nuclear attack. It is gross underestimation of the enemy. These days, the nuclear missiles can be launched from satellites and submarines, besides the ground stations. We have already seen that the present hydrogen bombs, are far more destructive than the old atomic bombs. Hence, even a few bombs can cause grave damage to America. Besides, the other nations have to pay a heavy price. Nor the nuclear war could be limited to a particular target. The loser will always think of the more vulnerable targets of the enemy for this attack. Hence, escalation is inevitable. Therefore, limited nuclear war is still dangerous.

Mr Ashok:— Gentlemen, I suppose, Mr Rupak and Mr Rajan are right. Nevertheless, there is no harm to see if the nuclear war can be limited where it cannot be altogether avoided or eliminated. Let us assume that the Super Powers will not wage a nuclear war because of mutual nuclear deterrences. Then other irresponsible small countries like Pakistan or Libya may resort to a nuclear attack if they succeed in acquiring the so-called Islamic bomb. Such an eventuality can be avoided by a pre-emptive limited nuclear attack on them by any of the super power through mutual agreement among them or even under the aegis of the UN. There is no question of war escalation since the Super Powers will resort to such limited attack only after prior agreement or UN authorisation. Secondly, it may also be possible to use nuclear weapons in a technical manner. The damage will be limited to selected targets. Thirdly, the WMD and nuclear weapons can be found in Iran, Libya, Syria or North Korea. The USA should use the UN to find them out and tell these nations to destroy them (if they are found). In fact, Libya has stated that it has done away with WMD and nuclear weapons.

Mr Ashutosh:— Comrades, from what I heard, I could see that limited nuclear war will not suit India. Let us not worry about the Super Powers, but think of our own interests. We should not limit our own interests. We should not limit our options. We must develop nuclear capacity and grow into a Super Power. Hence, we should not agree to limited nuclear war.

Mr Shambhu:— In my view, the nuclear war, if triggered, can never remain limited. India must prepare for it. She has already taken measures to counter such attacks.

Mr Rupak:— This GD session has come to an end.

All :— Thank you!

LOKPAL BILL

Mr Janak: Good evening, friends! My name is Janak Vashishth. May I have your attention, please.

Ms Kamini: Oh! you are trying to impress every one through standard dialogues. This scheme will not work.

Ms Maria: Your attention please, friends!

Mr Rajat: What is it? Why don't you let us plan this GD session.

Ms Maria: That is what we are trying to do in this group. I think we can start from the lady sitting in the end.

Ms Gloria: We can start from the other end too.

Mr Janak: Miss, why are you opposing this lady?

Ms Maria: I wanted that lady to start the discussion because she was sitting in the left corner. From that corner, we would move towards the right one. But if you want to start the session, you are welcome.

All: No, you decide the turns.

Ms Maria: All right, let that lady start. Then, we will continue from the left to the right corner.

Ms Afshan: Thank you, friends! Good evening to all of you!

All: Good evening!

Ms Afshan: My name is Afshan Razameer. I have the privilege of speaking on a topic which has been haunted by our parliamentarians and governments for past 43 years for unknown but obvious reasons. The government has finally introduced the controversial Lokpal Bill in the Lok Sabha. Though the Bill is dated August 1, 2011 but it is introduced in Lok Sabha on August 4, 2011. The Bill is aimed for establishing the institution of Lok Pal to inquire into the allegations of corruption against the public functionaries in high places. The Lok Pal will have own investigation and prosecution wings. The Lok Pal will have powers to search and seizure, and also certain powers of a civil court as also to attach property acquired by corrupt means. I must state that this is a welcome move by the government to eradicate the evil of corruption from India.

Mr. Janak: Good evening, ladies and gentlemen. My name is Janak Vashishth. I don't think that this introduction of Lokpal Bill is a welcome move by the government at all. I also don't think that a "Lokpal" can eradicate the evil of corruption from India. After all a Lokpal will be chosen one from the masses of India, he is not going to come down from the heavens like a "Super Human". Indian masses are habitual of corruption and by choosing any one from them will never eradicate the evil of corruption. Thank You.

Ms Maria: Good evening, friends! My name is Maria D'costa. I would like to take "few clues from the statement of Mr. Janak. He has stated that a Lokpal can not eradicate corruption and most of the people here are corrupt and to deal with them we need someone "Super Human", so we must prey to God to eradicate corruption and send a Lokpal from the heavens. Only God can help us now and save this country. Thank You.

Ms Kamini: Good evening, ladies and gentlemen! My name is Kamini Malhotra. I don't think that we need a "Super Human" of "Godly" figure to deal with and eradicate corruption from India. It is also not correct to say that all of us Indians are corrupt or habitual of corruption. It is true that some of us are over-ambitious and adopt quick means of making money by indulging in corrupt practices but not all the finger of a hand are equal. If there are thieves in the society, there are saints also. We must have a Lokpal with good integrity and character to deal with corruption at high places but still I don't understand why the government has taken 43 years to reach this conclusion about Lokpal Bill. Thank You.

Mr Rajat: Ms. Kamini, it's not the matter of discussion that how many years the government has taken to introduce the bill but the matter is the Lokpal Bill itself.

Ms Kamini: What exactly is the Lokpal Bill?

Mr Rajat: The Lokpal Bill provides for establishment of the Lokpal for inquiring into complaints of corruption against certain public servants.

The members of the Lokpal shall be appointed by the President. The Lokpal shall consist of one chairperson and upto eight other members. The chairperson shall be a present or former judge of the Supreme Court. The Lokpal can enquire into offences related to corruption committed by the former PM, current and former Ministers, MPs and group A officers and above. It also includes any director, manager, secretary or other officer of a society or organisation of trust financed or aided by the government or receiving public donations.

Ms Gloria: Good evening, ladies and gentlemen my name is Gloria Donaldson. Ms. Afshan and Mr. Rajat have told a lot about the Lokpal Bill but I am confused that if the Lokpal has to conduct so many enquiries and to do so much work, how will he function. One single person as Lokpal with just eight others members cannot handle so much work judiciously. I doubt, he can deliver the goods and eradicate corruption fully.

Ms Afshan: No, Ms Gloria it is not the case. The Lokpal will be competent enough and well equipped. The Lokpal will be constituted of two wings. The Investigation wing and the Prosecution wing. Further, their will be special courts to hear cases referred to them by the Lokpal. The Lokpal will recommend the number of such courts.

Ms Kamini: It is all right that Lokpal will be a powerful person with sound integrity but I still have doubt over his functioning. I mean, how will he come to know that someone is indulged in corrupt practices?

Mr Rajat: Let me throw some light over the functioning of Lokpal. A complaint against the specified officials can be made to the Lokpal for actions committed prior to seven years of the date of complaint. The Lokpal can ask the investigation wing to conduct enquiry into such allegations. If the enquiry concludes that an offence was committed. The Lokpal may recommend disciplinary action to the competent authority. It can also file a case before the special court through its prosecution wing.

Ms Maria: But all this process will take many years to complete as in courts.

Ms Afshan: No, Ms. Maria, the Competent Authority will be bound to initiate disciplinary proceedings and inform the Lokpal of the action proposed or taken within 30 days of receipt of the recommendation. The Bill also removes the requirement of sanction for intiating investigation and prosecution.

Ms Kamini: But the preliminary Investigation by Lokpal may take more time.

Mr Rajat: No, Ms. Kamini the Preliminary Investigation or enquiry has to be completed within a maximum period of three months. The following enquiry by the Lokpal is to be completed within a maximum period of one year. The trial before the special court is to be completed within a maximum timeframe of two years.

Ms Maria: What if a person files a false complaint before Lokpal? Will it not waste his precious official time and resources in investigating such false cases?

Ms Afshan: Let me explain the remedy provided for this problem. The penalty for filing false and frivolous complaint is imprisonment for a minimum of two years to a maximum five years and a fine of ₹ 25,000 upto ₹ 2 Lakhs.

Ms Kamini: What if a Lokpal does not peform his duty well. He will be so powerful official, how will he be controlled or removed from office?

Mr Rajat: The Lokpal may be removed by an order of the President on the basis of the reports of the Supreme Court on a reference by the President. A reference to the Supreme Court may be made by the President himself/herself or on the basis of a petition signed by 100 members of the Parliament or on the basis of a satisfactory petition made by a citizen. This also makes clear that in a democracy a citizen is supreme power.

Ms Maria: All right, we have understood the Lokpal Bill, its scope, powers and functioning but I donot understand one thing that if this Bill is so good and in the welfare of Indian people then why people like Anna Hazare and opposition parties are not happy with its introduction?

Ms Afshan: Anna Hazare is a great leader who has been demanding this Bill for long. In fact he initiated a mass movement and sat on a hunger-strike for many days in the New Delhi's Jantar Mantar and

Ramlila Maidan and also jailed to demand the Lokpal Bill. It was under his pressure that in a historic gesture, the Lok Sabha and the Rajya Sabha unanimously resolved to endorse his three key ideas in the draft Lokpal Bill. According to Team Anna, the present Bill is a weaker one and demanding that their own draft of the Bill should also be circulated to the Parliamentarians to let them decide what should be the way to enact law to curb corruption. They have announced another hunger-strike and a mass-movement if a stronger Lokpal Bill is not passed in the Parliament.

Ms Kamini: One thing I do not understand that if Lokpal is in the benefit of Indian People then why the government is so reluctant in its enactment and not making it srong and powerful enough to curb corruption. Why they are so relactant that it took them 43 years and nine attempts to clear an institution of Lokpal?

Mr Rajat: Ms Kamini, you are right here that an institution like Lokpal should have been made 43 years back with his full strength and powers right in the first attempt itself. In my view. This could not happen for so many years and in so many attempts because of the weak political will of the various governments that ruled this country during that period. It may also be the reason that corruption has become such deep-rooted and chronic phenomenon in this country that it may stop, hold or delay the introduction of such a Bill which may hamper its growth and attack its origin and perpetrators.

Mr Janak: In my view, the introduction of Lokpal Bill is a futile exercise by the government and a waste of time of the Parliament in a discussion over it. I think people like Anna Hazare and opposition parties protest for it for the sake of being in limelight and headlines of newspapers. If at all a Lokpal Bill is passed and a Lokpal is made, in a very short time he will also indulge in corrupt practices and will become a part of the same corruption-riddled rotten system.

Ms Kamini: Is it the consensus view?

Mr Janak: Yes, I have delivered the consensus view.

Mr Rajat: That it is not the consensus, Mr. Janak

Ms Gloria: Mr. Janak, you should have incorporated the views of all the participants. You have simply repeated your views. Now let Ms. Afshan wind up the proceedings.

Ms Afshan: Thank you ladies and gentlemen for all your valuable views. The group has concluded that Lokpal Bill is indeed in the benefit of Indian people. The indian system is rotting with deep-rooted corruption at all levels and badly needs a remedy like Lokpal Bill with its full strength and power to curb corruption at the earliest and weed it out from this country forever.

Mr Rajat: Thank you, ladies and gentleman with this consensus decision which was delivered by Ms. Afshan on behalf of the group, I wind up today's GD Session. I thank you all for your active participation.

All: Thank You, Mr. Rajat.

DANGEROUS DEBT TRAP-ULTIMATE OUTCOME OF EVER INCREASING FOREIGN AID

Mr Shiv Shankar:—Friends, may I request your kind attention please, I appeal to you all to remain silent for a few seconds so that everyone could hear me. Please lend me your ears as I have something important to say to all of you. As you all know, the examiner told us that we must complete our task within the time limit of half an hour. Since he has left, we have been making small talk with our neighbours, but the minutes have been ticking away. May be, we have lost 4 or 5 minutes already. My submission is that unless we start the discussion immediately and proceed in a planned manner, we may not be able to complete the task. If you all agree, we can start straightaway. No point wasting any more time. Mr Amar and Mr Mayank, please pardon me for interrupting you. Kindly extend your co-operation and stop talking in asides and address the group as a whole. Another request. Let all of us maintain perfect silence when one is addressing the group. Let each speak in his turn. There will be no confusion and the exercise will be completed in time.

Mr Amar:—What is all this about? For your information, we had begun discussing the subject since the moment the examiner left. We have not wasted any time. In fact, you are the one, who is interrupting and holding up progress. What do you say, Mr Mayank? Don't you agree with me?

Mr Shiv Shankar:—I am sorry and I beg your pardon Mr Amar. I am afraid, I have not made myself clear perhaps. In this Group Discussion task, each one in the group must speak to others in the group collectively as a whole. I mean, he must share his ideas with all and should not limit it to his neighbours or a few only. The group as a whole must learn the views of every member.

Mr Amar:—What do you mean? I saw everybody talking and discussing with neighbours or friends. And I also did the same. Why blame me then? Anyway, what do you want me to do now? What is your arrangement? You say the time is limited. If everyone is to give a lecture, where is the time, I ask you. Who is going to be the first speaker anyway?

Mr Robin:—A volunteer. I want to be the first speaker.

Mr Anshul:—Why should Robin be first, may I ask? Why not me? I am a student of Economics and I feel, I can do justice to the subject. May be. Others don't have to speak at all. I can cover all aspect.

Mr Robin:—What do you think, we are all here for? Only to listen to you? Besides, you studied Economics in your college and the subject now we have to talk about are not one and the same.

Mr Anshul:—Hey Mr Robin, you better keep mum. Otherwise you will be exhibiting your ignorance more. If foreign trade is not Economics, what else is it, I ask you? You make me laugh really.

Mr Robin:—Now, who is displaying his ignorance? I am not that dull to get confused between foreign trade and foreign aid. We certainly do not want a lecture from you on it. I never imagined you could be that stupid.

Mr Anshul:—Mr Robin, you are quite rude and insulting. I won't tolerate it. I like to use my hands rather than words when I want to teach somebody a good lesson.

Mr Robin:—I accept the challenge. Don't think my hands will be idle. I can take care of myself.

Mr Shiv Shankar:—Come on Mr Robin and Mr Anshul. Both of you are getting emotional and personal. Let us perform our task as friends. I assure you that everyone will get an equal chance to express his ideas. It does not matter who speaks first and who at last. For that matter, I am ready to be the last speaker.

Mr Shiv Shankar:—Mr Jitendra, will you please set the ball rolling. Let us have your ideas. Come on. Be quick.

Mr Jitendra:—You see well, I mean, I would like to have some time to think. It is better for others to speak in the meantime. You see I did not volunteer. Only Mr Anshul and Mr Robin wanted to speak first. You can decide on one of them. Anyone. It is all the same to me.

Mr Shiv Shankar:—All right Mr Jitendra please don't worry. You can speak last if you wish. Let us begin with Mr Anshul. After him, it would be Mr Robin. Now Mr Anshul, please take the floor. Let us hear your views, please.

Mr Anshul:—My dear friends. I am indeed surprised that when the world has almost shrunk to the size of your palm and when we have so many international fora, UN agencies, regional co-operation and bilateral agreements in the sphere of economic advancement and growth and when addition to the North-South dialogue, we are also having South-South dialogue to share the world's wealth. We are confronted with the topic that implies our country should learn to do without foreign aid. It is unimaginable and it really staggers me. Can you ever imagine such a thing? Today every country in the world, whether big or small, be it a Super Power like the USA or Russia or an economic giant like Germany or Japan or even a collective community of developed nations like the EU, has to necessarily resort to import and export for economic isolation, totally divorced from other countries is not only outmoded, but it is dead and gone like a dodo. We have either to export or perish. We can not live without foreign exchange. In order to export, we need some input for import too. Therefore, I can only laugh at this proposition. This is against all known, established and accepted economic doctrines and concepts. Even the great Adam Smith, the father of Modern Economics will assert such.

Mr Amar:—I say old man! I mean you, Mr Anshul. I think, you better collect yourself, please, I dare say that you are absolutely off the track. We all know the economic theories and principles formulated by Adam Smith. For that matter I can secure for hours, or on the supply managed economics propounded by Prof Galbraith. But, should we talk about it now? It is relevant at all?

Mr Anshul:—You, you shut up Mr Amar. I know damn well what I am talking about. I challenge you for a debate on any economic concept. Do you know about macro and micro-economics? Have you heard about them?

Mr Amar:—I say, this is too much. I just can't stand this fellow. Please Mr Shiv Shankar, I beseech you. Please stop him.

Mr Shiv Shankar:—Please, gentlemen. Let us not get emotional and personal. By the way, Mr Anshul, the two minutes time is up. Do you still wish to continue?

Mr Ansul:—Sorry, I can not carry on if people are going to interrupt me rudely and disturb the train of my thoughts. I am sorry. I can not continue, at least for the present. But if Mr Amar throws a challenge, I am still ready to face it.

Mr Shiv Shankar:—Please, we have already decided that we would keep the discussion above personal level. No quarrels please. Let us also stick to the time schedule. Come on Mr Robin.

Mr Robin:—Gentlemen, the subject given to us for discussion implies that "*dependence on foreign aid will lead to debt trap*". And I, for one, am in total agreement with the proposition. Although I listened to our learned friend Mr Anshul with rapt attention, I fail to understand why he poohpoohs the whole subject. The main or the only reason he had advanced, so far as I could make out, is that world has become small, and interdependence among nations is inevitable. This, I beg to disagree strongly. For his information and for the benefit of others also, may I submit that China carried on for over 30 years all by itself, keeping aloof both from the West and the East.

Mr Anshul:—No, you are wrong. China got the USSR aid. Now it is getting American Aid.

Mr Robin:—No, you are misquoting me Mr Anshul. I said for 30 years. Today everybody knows that China has become a camp follower of Uncle Sam. In the beginning China had outwardly close ties with Russia. But even then they were rivals. Besides, Russia was hardly in a position to give any aid worth talking about in these days. Anyhow, let us now come back to India. That is our main topic of interest. I would recommend India should follow the Gandhian path. If Gandhi were to be with us today, I swear, he would have gone on a fast unto death to stop India from begging for loans and aid. As an independent nation we must have self-respect more than anything else.

Mr Anshul:—What about defence? Where will you get the military hardware?

Mr Robin:—Stop interrupting Mr Anshul, will you? You spoke all rubbish during your turn and now you are using up my time. Well Mr Shiv Shankar, I lodge a strong protest. Following Gandhiji, I will now observe silence as a protest against injustice. I refuse to say even one more word.

Mr Amar:—Friends, we have to make our country economically, militarily and politically strong. Economic dependence automatically leads to exploitation and external domination. The Nehruvian economic model was, therefore, consciously chosen to make India an industrialised and economically powerful nation. Since we simulaneously adopted democratic Socialism as our political philosophy and goal, the economic progress had been painfully slow. Now, we can not achieve industrial growth fashioned on the Nehruvian model without foreign aid. Initially India banked on Soviet aid. But this was not found adequate. In the sixties and early seventies, food was our major worry and we had to seek US aid. Later on the oil crisis came and we were forced to take more loans to import oil. Luckily our green revolution became a phenomenal success. We have also taken giant strides in the industrial sector and oil exploration. All these would not have been possible without going in for foreign aid and loans. But we could have put the aid and loan funds to better use. We should not continue to lean on foreign loans forever. We have just started giving aid to least developed countries. We must make serious efforts to free ourselves from foreign aid in near future since the industrially advanced countries have started using aid loans to employ pressure to bring about foreign and local policy changes. This interferes with our sovereignty.

Mr Shiv Shankar:—Come on, Mr Mayank. It is your turn now and we are all waiting to hear your views.

Mr Mayank:—Smiles, but does not talk.

Mr Shiv Shankar:—Of course, Mr Mayank. You can tell us what ever you feel. Do not worry about any criticism. You know this is just a friendly exchange of ideas. You can say what you feel like.

Mr Mayank:—Yes, yes. I mean, I agree, no, no. I agree with Mr Amar and not with others. Sorry, I agree with you also Mr Shiv Shankar. That is all. Now you can ask Mr Nitin to speak.

Mr Nitin :—Friends, as you all know, the Super Powers had been giving free aid, both military and economic only to their allies. Thus, the USA gave massive aid to Germany, Japan, South Korea, NATO countries, Middle-East treaty organisation countries and SEATO National. Similarly, USSR extended aid to Warsaw Pact countries. The military aid had been selective. The loans for all, including the non-aligned, were extended by international forums like the World Bank, IMF, IDA, etc. There were also bilateral aids, where equipment or machinery were supplied on loan basis. The loans have to be repaid and they also carry interest. This aid and loan to India has been shrinking after the USA patched up with China. Besides, India has been championing the cause of non-alignment and total nuclear disarmament. India did not sign the NPT. It also did not subscribe to Missile Control Regime. Without foreign help, India conducted nuclear explosion and established nuclear power units. India has also launched an IRBM Missile, 'Agni' on its own. America and its allies like the UK were annoyed and the USA was threatening to apply its infamous Super 301 provision against us. India has also raised internal loans. Repayment of loan instalments and interest is posing the danger of debt trap. Hence, as far as possible, we should do without loans and aid. We have the capacity to do this and we must act now with firmness and resolve.

Mr Ved Prakash:—Friends, I fully endorse the views expressed by Mr Nitin. I am afraid, I can not add much to what he had already said. He spoke of some changes in the US attitude, but in reality, it means nothing. Believe me, I am ready to take a bet and I assure you that the Americans will never give you aid without strings. However, if someone is clever enough to get aid without strings, or if there are countries which are foolish enough to give aid like charity, I don't see any harm in accepting the same and make hay while the Sun shines. We can accept both military and economic aid and for that matter any aid, they are willing to give. You can say that I am all for aid. Thank you.

Mr Shiv Shankar :—Friends, as you all know, Japan in Asia and Germany in Europe, are rated today as the word's strongest economic powers. Ironically, these two countries lost World War II (1939-45). They suffered the maximum losses in terms of manpower and material. Japan was subjected to atomic bombing and Germany to carpet bombing. Germany was portioned as West Germany and East Germany and Berlin became a divided city. But within a period of four decades, both of them have united and become the topmost economic giants. Right now, besides these two, South Korea, Taiwan, Singapore, and quite a few West European countries have also become economically advanced countries. Now they all could achieve this economic miracle only through large American aid. But they also have to pay the price and become camp followers of America. Rapid industrial growth, economic progress and technological breakthrough is not feasible without foreign aid. Hence, in my view we should go in for selective foreign economic aid. But I fully endorse the view that we should not depend on foreign aid and loans for ever. Like Japan and Germany, we should free ourselves from such dependence at the earliest.

Mr. Shiv Shankar shows leadership skills. Apart from the skills already mentioned elsewhere, he is a good orator, a disciplinarian and self-restraint on his emotions. He is calm and composed. He is able to resolve the initial chaos with his polite countenance. He soothes his group members; sympathises with their troubles (in case of Mr. Jitendra and Mayank); and appears to be a considerate person. He can manage the unruly group very efficiently. He also comes up with relevant and strong ideas on the issue. This shows he is a well informed person and has clear opinions. He has the ability to take a definite stand. He is modest as well. —*Selected*

Mr. Anshul is a jealous and haughty fellow. He is knowledgeable and well read but a subversive element in a group. —*Rejected*

Mr. Robin is also a knowledgeable person but he dissipates his energy in his verbal fight with Mr. Anshul. He is an inefficient person in the face of adversities or incongruities. He is impulsive and cannot be trusted with a serious task because he is too sensitive. He refuses to speak when he is indignant. This shows he can leave a task halfway through when he is in an agitated state. —*Thus, rejected*

Mr. Amar again is a very knowledgeable person but he too is egoistic. He gets offended when he is asked to pay attention. He lacks leadership skills. He is unruly and undisciplined. He wouldn't readily conform to group etiquettes. He says... "I can't stand the fellow..." This shows he is a failure as a team member because he cannot take antagonists in his stride. —*Rejected*

Mr. Mayank doesn't speak at all. —*Rejected*

Mr. Nitin is a good speaker but apart from knowledge and rational approach he shows no other qualities that are necessary for group cohesion. —*Therefore his candidature is under consideration*

Mr. Ved Prakash has no original ideas. He is neither a good speaker nor a group organism. —*Rejected*

IS GLORIFICATION OF VIOLENCE AND CRIMES IN FILMS AND TV A REASON FOR A HIGH CRIME RATE?

Mr Santosh: I watch movies because I love my cinema idols. If somebody here doesn't know about films, I will say that he is not enjoying his life. We should not censure TV and films. They are helping our society grow. For those, who haven't had first hand experiences, I can tell them about film shooting and film stars. I advise them to watch TV and cinema.

Mr Indrakant:— Mr Santosh, I am afraid you got it all wrong. Our discussion is not going to be exclusively on films. This is an extremely controversial topic. I don't know whether you have been scanning parliamentary debates and newspaper write-ups and also, judicial rulings on this subject. In fact, I can talk for hours on this subject.

Mr Santosh:— Mr Indrakant, will you shut up and listen to me carefully? Before you talk any further, I want to make two things clear. First of all, I warn you that I do not like anyone to oppose me and cross my path. That tenet is true for everybody here. I want that to be very clearly understood. Let no one blame me later.

Mr Indrakant:— Hey, all I said was ...

Mr Santosh:— I told you not to interrupt me. Now, you are just doing that. Next time you do that and you will find me really nasty (Mr Ravi gently pats reassuringly on the arm of Mr Indrakant).

Mr Santosh:— The second thing you said or implied was that I had not read the newspapers and what not. I demand an instant and unconditional apology from you for insulting me like that. For your information, we get more than half a dozen newspapers daily at our house. I read more magazines, books and periodicals, than you do.

Mr Indrakant tries to get up and wants to tender apology demanded by Mr Santosh. However, Mr Ravi pulls his hand down and indicates to him to remain silent and seated.

Mr Ravi:— Well friends! Please permit me to intervene and say a few words at this juncture. You see, I am in the unenviable position of having been sandwiched between these two stalwarts. Mr Santosh is on my right and Mr Indrakant on my left. Therefore, my first and foremost request, to my two beloved friends is to spare me from this ordeal.

Mr Lalit:— Thank you, Mr Ravi. We were really worried that an unpleasant fight might break out at any time between our two friends. However, you have broken the ice and transformed the entire atmosphere. I am so glad by your positive attitude. By the way, time is running out. Why don't you go ahead with your views to start the discussion on the subject?

Mr Kameshwar:— I agree with you, Mr Lalit.

Mr Ravi:— Well, Mr Santosh, since you set the ball rolling, you may perhaps like to start the discussion. Please give your opinion on the topic now.

Mr Santosh:— Mr Indrakant interfered, so the trend of my thoughts was broken. Anyway, I don't want to talk first. I suggest you start with Mr Lalit and he should not shirk his responsibility.

Mr Lalit:— Thanks for the honour being given to me. It will be my pleasure to initiate the discussion on the subject. Nevertheless, if some one else is keen he should get the preference to speak.

Mr Ravi:— Okay, let us see. Are there any volunteers to speak first please? All right Mr Lalit, you can set the ball rolling. By the way, let us go in an ascending order of roll numbers. After Mr Lalit, it will be the turn of Mr Kameshwar. Then, Mr Devendra will speak and so on, till we finish off the first round with Mr Sharmendra. Go ahead Mr Lalit.

Mr Lalit:— Friends, the topic implies that our films are to be blamed for the growing lawlessness and violence in the country. I can't say that I am a cinema addict but I do watch a film or two now and then. I must say that our films contain, a lot of sex and violence. Further, crime is glorified in our movies. *"Criminals"* are made heroes and the police is ridiculed. One gets the impression that sex, violence and crime have been deliberately injected into a story that really does not need them. The idea seems to be to attract viewers. Thus sex and violence get commercially exploited. If people are exposed to sex and violence at the times, they may be psychologically conditioned to accept them as facts of life. Imitating their films heroes, heroines or even villains, the viewers may also indulge in violence, sex and crimes. This may result in a serious law and order problem. Many blame the exploitation of sex and violence by our films as the causative factor for the rising number of crimes in our country. Now my time of two minutes is over. I will request Mr Kameshwar to come forward and present his views. Thank you.

Mr Kameshwar:— Gentlemen, at the outset, I wish to make my stand clear. I do not agree with the proposition. First of all, what exactly do you consider as exploitation by films? The word is a cliche and politicians, journalists and self-styled leaders of people with nil or negligible followers keep talking about exploitation by films. Movies like *Vaastav*, *Company* and *Road* have shown the sleaze of the underworld. *Raaz* was a horror movie. The values and norms change from place to place. Today, we have the so-called 'A' certificate films. In what way it stops anyone from viewing that film? In fact, many producers want the 'A' certificate to promote their films and the censor is taken for a ride. Then, there are the so-called art films. In my view, the causes for increase in violence crimes and sex are to be found in other social and economic factors but not films. I am not able to discuss at length as the allotted two minutes are over. Thank you.

Mr Devendra:— Friends, Mr Kameshwar has tried to act like a lawyer, attempting to give a leak proof definition of the word 'exploitation'. But I am sure, barring Mr Kameshwar, none of us has any doubt as to what exactly the proposition signifies. In the context of our subject. I understand that exploitation of sex, crime and violence in films implies too much of sex scenes, rape scenes, fights, shoot-outs and so on primarily to appeal to the base instincts of the audience. Well, there are noble and baser instincts in every human being. If the story or theme involves, in the natural and normal course, some sex or violence, it cannot be termed 'exploitation'. On the other hand, if sex and violence are deliberately thrust into the film solely to attract audience, then it would amount to exploitation. Therefore, I do not want to be swayed by the legal arguments of Mr Kameshwar. The question is whether excess of sex and violence in films should be permitted or not. I do not say that they should not find a place in films. I know you will support the proposition. Where sexual content is needed, it should be added to the movie. But it should be added in a decent manner. The same should be the case for violence and crimes of various types.

Mr Santosh:— Well, all I can say is that I am rather disappointed. I am totally disappointed with Mr Lalit, Mr Kameshwar and Mr Devendra. I don't understand what they are fighting about. The Indian films are useless portrayals of sex, violence and crime. Well, you have to see the sex oozing from a movie to believe my words. And our friends have not seen original, uncensored foreign films. American, French, Italian, Spanish or German. I do not want to talk about the films of Denmark and Sweden. Sex and violence are depicted with shameless elan in the movie of the west. Our movies are still far better than theirs.

Mr Ravi:— Friends, our subject does not amplify how films alone are to be blamed for the growing violence and crimes in the country. It simply asserts that films are to be blamed. However, you will agree that sex and violence have their rightful places in films. Only their exploitation should not be permitted. Now, next comes the question as to what exploitation means. Can exploitation be clearly defined or accurately quantified and measured? To me, exploitation would imply abuse and misuse. It would mean cheating others and taking them for a ride. It would mean deliberately misleading people and deceiving them. In our cinema, it would mean the abuse of sex and violence in films to earn money. Exploitation also means lack of honesty and sincerity. Obviously, such exploitation of sex and violence would cause decay of our moral values. Of course, I do not go along with Mr Santosh and say there is no sex or violence at all in Indian films. We have copied many bad things of the West. Now, would banning such films help us achieve the objective? Further, poverty and employment also contribute to crimes and violence. We must initiate measures to reduce poverty and unemployment. We must educate our masses and tell them to become mature to differentiate good cinema from bad one.

Mr Indrakant:— Gentlemen! Perhaps, I think I should not step on the toes of others. I may not agree with some of the views of others but every participant is entitled to give his views, whether they are right or wrong. At one time, even students were not allowed or encouraged to watch films unless these films were based on history, religion and the other good topics. Even a talk about sex was a taboo. Today, time has changed; so have ideas and vlaues. We talk about films. What about actual life? What about corruption, black money, prostitution and the power game? There were crimes even before the advent of cinema and video boom. Are there no fights, violence, rape incidents and sex in our religious stories and the literature? All I say is that these have existed and will continue to exist.

Mr Manikant:— Gentlemen, in my opinion, it is better to see a real sexy and violent film or better still a real violently sex film and then discuss rather than talk about this subject in a practical fashion. The primary object of the film is to provide entertainment and relaxation. If you concede that, then do you think that a picture without violence and sex could be entertaining? Well, you know the answer is in the affirmative. You can get real entertainment. It is sheer hypocrisy to say that pictures should have no sex, violence strong themes etc. We can go to a church for a sermon. Why we forget that sex is natural and a part of human life. Are the Hiroshima and Nagasaki disasters not the incidents of violence? What about the US-led invasion on Iraq? What about the *"devadasi"* institution? What about the red light areas? What about cabarets? I think we are just wasting time.

Mr Dharmendra:— Friends, I am the last candidate to speak and I find that those who spoke have analysed the subject threadbare from every angle. The whole thing has been discussed and I cannot add or say anything new. You can now vote and decide. Thanks.

Mr Ravi:— The group has finally agreed that violence, sex and crimes must not be exaggerated in our movies lest they should affect our youth and children in an adverse manner. Our movies are partially responsible for effecting moral decay of our society. The Censor Board and other State-controlled organisations must take strict actions against such film makers. Moral values of our ancient society must be promoted. A limited content of sex, violence or crimes that is relevant for the plot may be allowed but not in an obscene and degrading manner.

Thank you!

Expert Comments

Mr. Santosh is rude and ill mannered. He does not know group behaviour. Rejected for being a subversive fully.

Mr. Indrakant doesn't have creative ideas. He is meek, humble and submissive. He lacks confidence. —*Not suitable for team jobs*

Mr. Ravi, though he doesn't initiate, rises as a leader. He watches the way the group is behaving and then intervenes wisely. He manifests all the qualities of a good leader—he is a good organiser, a good co-ordinator and a good orator. He tackles Mr. Santosh, the bully, very efficiently. On his turn he gives a well informed speech. He shows his balanced approach towards the issue. Moreover, he takes up the task of concluding the

session. He lays out the group consensus after harmonising the disparate ideas of all his group members.
—*He will be an asset to the organisation*

Mr. Devendra rejoices in taking a dig at his colleague Mr. Kameshwar. His speech is largely incoherent. Perhaps he has not grasped the topic properly. He wastes most of his time on bashing his colleague. —*Rejected*

Mr. Manikant does not show leadership skills, nor does he show any skill necessary for group cohesion. Moreover, he appears to be a lascivious degenerate person, i.e., he has immoral tendencies. His speech is irrelevant and incoherent. —*Rejected*

Mr. Dharmendra has nothing to speak on the topic.
He remains on the edges. —*Rejected*

CAN DIFFERENT CULTURES BE INTEGRATED TO EVOLVE A GLOBAL CULTURE?

Ms Lalwani :- May I have your attention, friends?
(No one listens to her. There is chaos in the discussion room).

Mr Shaharyar :- (Raising his voice above those of all others). Friends! We are wasting precious time that has been allotted to us. Shall we determine the order and start the proceedings?

Mr Sohi:- My dear, we want to start the proceedings but we would like a lady to start the show.

Mr Shaharyar:- Any special reason for doing so?

Mr Sohi :- I am trying to follow the policy of "Ladies first".

Ms Sadana :- Mr Sohi is right. We can start from Ms Lalwani. Then, we can move in a clockwise direction.

Mr Shaharyar :- Why not in an anticlockwise direction, Ms Sadana?

Ms Sadana :- All right! We can start from Ms Lalwani and move in an anticlockwise direction. After her, Mr Sohi will speak. He will be followed by Mr Shaharyar and Ms Gokhle. I will speak in the end, after Ms Gokhle I hope that would be acceptable to all of you.

All :- That would be fine.

Ms Sadana:- All right! Let Ms Lalwani start the discussion.

Ms Lalwani:- Thank you Ms Sadana. Good morning friends! My name is Suchitra Lalwani. The topic for today's discussion is—Can different cultures be integrated to evolve a global culture? I would like to support the topic by stating that it is very much possible to integrate different world cultures to evolve a new coherent culture. We are human beings. We can be convinced by logic and facts. If the people belonging to different cultures can be convinced about the new concept, they would certainly help in evolving a new global culture. Cultural homogenisation is a pre-requisite for the all-round development of the mankind. We can take the positive teachings of every culture and integrate them into the new one. That way, the masses practising or adhering to a particular culture would not oppose the evolution of a new cultural ethos. That is because they would be happy to learn that key positive features of their culture have been incorporated in the new one. Thank you!

Mr Sohi:- You have given nice views, Ms Lalwani. However, culture is not an edifice like a building. It is a set of values and emotions of the people of a society. It is dynamic and always subtle. It cannot be integrated with any other culture. No society would like to do away with its own culture and adopt a totally new one, simply because it is a part of the new world. Culture is a society-based phenomenon. It is invisible. Our culture has always been hailed as supreme. The West had better alter its culture and align it in tune with ours. Our ancient books like the *Vedas*, ancient scriptures, folk dances, paintings, dressing codes, ornaments and music represent our unique cultural identity. I am very much against aligning our cultural values with those of any other culture to evolve a new culture. Thank you!

Mr Shaharyar :- Mr Sohi has forgotten to take a note of his fine dress. It is a modern Jean. The T-shirt he is wearing has been made by Rohit Bal. The jeans seems to be imported. His personality is western but his mind looks eastwards.

Mr Sohi :- What do you want to state?

Mr Shaharyar :- Our culture has already changed a lot. The folk dancers have been replaced by disco dancers. Sanskrit Shlokas have been replaced by the pop songs of Michael Jackson and Madonna. The pizza burger culture has made deep inroads into our urban culture. In such a condition, if the examiner is giving us an opportunity to evolve a new culture, we should feel pleased. After all, our cultural values would also be incorporated in the new culture. The healthy norms of every culture would be integrated in the new cultural code. Instead of letting our culture decay, we should accept the emergence of a new global culture. Thank you!

Ms Gokhle :- Good morning, friends! My name is Lavanya Gokhle. I do not agree with the views given by Mr Shaharyar. Why should we give up our old cultural values? Let the world define a new culture but we will stick to our own. It is true that our culture has been transformed by the western media. The West wants to effect homogenisation of culture around the world. That is because the films and governments of the West are keen to sell their products, services and concepts around the world. Differences in cultures are the inhibiting factors so far as globalisation of trade and thought processes is the issue. Hence, the West is trying to effect homogenisation of culture. Our society has remained unique, despite the cultural invasions of the West, Middle-East and North. We have accepted good points of other cultures. Hence, our culture is already a melting pot of several cultures. We need not alter the present structure of our culture to align it with a unique global culture. Rather, it should be the other way round; there should be a global culture to support our unique culture. Thank you!

Ms Sadana :- Good morning, friends! My name is Deepshikha Sadana. I have been listening to the views that have been presented by you. I think all of you are giving rational views, though I can find two camps within this small group. First of all, let us find out whether we need a new global culture at all. It is a fact that the diverse cultures of various corners of the globe have led to many wars, battles and clashes of ego. It we unify the cultures of the world and evolve a new culture, we, as the human race, would grow at much faster pace.

The second question arises–can different cultures be integrated to form a new, unique and synergistic whole? My answer is Nay! That is because every culture is different. The east is east and the west is west and never shall the twain meet. Due to diversity of cultures, we cannot integrate them.

Finally, a question emerges before us—can different cultures be integrated to evolve a global culture? I have answered this question and stated that it is not possible. However, it is always possible to create a new global culture to protect the interests of the human kind. The UN was formed to protect the human kind from the ill effects of war. It succeded partly in its pious task, though. In fact, many organs of the UN as well as those of other organisations promote universal brotherhood, peace and harmony. Hence, some organisations are already working to unify the world in cultural terms.

Hence, my contention is that a new cultural ethos can be developed at the international level. This ethos can be a separate entity that would be quite different from the individual cultures. People would conform to the norms of their respective cultures. However, they would also adhere to the norms of a new cultural order at the global level.

Ms Lalwani :- I fully support the views of Ms Sadana. She is thinking in the right direction.

Mr Sohi :- You are supporting because of the gender. Please support the topic on the basis of rationale and pragmatic reasoning.

Ms Lalwani :- I can choose to oppose or support the topic. What is the harm if I support it? Why should you be worried if I give support to Ms Sadana?

Mr Sohi :- I appreciate your views, Mr Lalwani. I also agree with Ms Sadana on many accounts. However, both of you are taking a quantitative view of the cultural transformation of this world. As already stated, culture is not a logical combination like two plus two equals four. We cannot alter our culture overnight. Even if we have to alter it, we would have to ponder over the consequences of doing so. Our culture does not promote the concept of free sex, to quote an example. The West promotes and supports this concept. Our moral values have decayed beyond compare due to the invasion of the media. In the new culture, many of our old values would be given a back-seat. Such values are very dear to us. I can give another example. We value family norms to the core. The societies of the USA and Europe are based on the freedom of the individual. The institution of family is fragile in the West. Britney Spears married her boy friend and then, gave him divorce within hours! Can we accept this kind of culture?

Ms Sadana :- But in the new integrated culture, the negative values and norms are likely to be removed.

Mr Sohi:- You are right. But how would you convince the people of the West, that marriage is the integration of two souls and not bodies? There are many other values, which are deemed old or hackneyed by the westerners but cherished by us. Hence, there cannot be any kind of cultural union of various cultures of the world. The Iraq-US war is also a kind of cultural conflict. On the face of it, we find the Iraqis fighting the US forces. However, below this veneer, we can easily point out the grueling conflict of two cultures. You have also stated that the east and West cannot meet. You have repeated the statement of Rudyard Kipling. Many others cultural scientists also have similar views. The Asian societies are slow, tradition-bound and we-oriented. The western societies are fast, willing to take risks and I-oriented. How can these two poles merge to form a single cultural realm? We cannot land in a Utopia of culture!

Mr Shaharyar :- Mr Sohi, we are already in a new Utopia. The media have changed our values and cultural norms. Some values remain to be changed. You have given the example of free sex. It is being practised even in small cities and townships of India. The institution of family has many lacunae even in our society. Our culture is drawing its sap from materialism now a days. Monetary issues decide our value system. So, why should we not accept the emergence of a new culture? It is just possible that the new cultures may be sans anomalies of the old cultures from which, it is to be formed. We cannot sit in a conference hall to decide the edifice of the new cultural ethos. It would emerge automatically despite our whole-hearted opposition. What I want to state is that we should guide those forces that are working hard to evolve a new cultural spectrum. We should help our social scientists eliminate the negative points of the new emerging culture. Commercialism and materialism are also a part of the new culture. We should inform the masses that too much craving for money is harmful for them. In this context, the tenets of Indian culture can be incorporated into the new culture. These transformations would be effected at a pretty slow pace. People would realise that commercialism is not the be all and end all of life. Then, they would return to the path of devotion, good deeds, celibacy and chastity. At the same time, the good values of other cultures must also be imposed. Finally, a new cultural canvass would be created in this world. It would be based on sound moral principles, love for the mankind and healthy family norms.

Mr Gokhle :- Mr Shaharyar, whatever you are trying to incorporate in the new culture is already a part of our aeon-old culture. Secondly, there is no guarantee that the world would accept our good moral values. The values of all the cultures are different. Whatever is deemed good in one society may be looked down upon in some others. These differences shall always remain. We cannot overcome them. In my view, our culture is supreme. The societies of the world should align their cultural norms with ours. That would help them grow in spiritual and moral terms. Finally, the question of moral decay of our society must also be discussed. As already stated by some of my friends, this decay was effected due to the media invasions from the West. Further, the British Raj was also responsible for changing our values. The British had tried to impose their cultural imperialism on our society. That was a coercive tactic. However, in the parlance of today's media operations the cultural invasion (of the west) is a persuasive tactic. Today, we are being persuaded or motivated to break family norms and indulge in free sex. The mass media are taking us to pleasure zones and we think that these zones are the real synonyms of heaven. Hence, we have to protect our culture against these invasions. Our culture has remained resilient for 5,000 years. It can be retained in future too. Finally, I would like the world to adopt our culture, with a few changes, so that this world becomes a better place to live in. As already stated, the West also admits that our culture is reliable and supreme. Slowly but surely the westerners would adopt it. So, there is no need to integrate other cultures into one culture. All the human kind should accept our culture with some minor modifications.

Mr Shaharyar :- It is very important to arrive at a consensus decision. Although, we are supporting different viewpoints, yet we must present a solution that should include the viewpoints of all those who are present here.

Ms Sadana :- Who would like to present the consensus view?

Ms Lalwani :- The one who is totally impartial.

Ms Sadana :- Can we give this initiative to Mr Sohi?

Mr Sohi :- If all of you agree, I can present the consensus view.

Mr Gokhle :- But we have not arrived at the consensus yet. I am in favour of the culture and value system of India. I am against the topic.

Mr Sohi:- My views are quite similar to those of Mr Gokhle. I can state with confidence that we must return to our old cultural values. We have the best culture and value system in the world.

Mr Shaharyar :- You may agree with me or not but change is inheritable. Today, it is being imposed on us. The media are the agents of cultural change; so are education, entertainment and industrialisation. You should speak in favour of the topic.

Mr Sohi :- No! I am against it. That is final.

Ms Sadana :- Then, how do we conclude? We are running out of time. We must conclude within five minutes.

Ms Lalwani :- We can accept the good points of Mr Sohi and Mr Shaharyar.

Ms Sadana :- And precisely how can we do it?

Ms Lalwani :- If the group agrees, I can present the censensus view.

All :- Please go ahead.

Ms Lalwani :- Thank you, friends! The group has concluded that Indian culture is supreme. The concept of integration of different cultures of the world seems to be a remote possibility. However, the culture and norms of India can be spread in all the nooks and corners of the world. The same may be altered to evolve a new cultural ethos. It is not possible to set up institutions of culture on the pattern of the UNO. That is because culture and values draw their energy from a host of factors, viz, religion, societal processes, political mechanism, education, ambitions of the masses etc. Hence, culture is an amorphous and complex entity. The world must address the issue of cultural decay. The social scientists must define what should be a good norm or value. Accordingly, they should spread the message to help the masses of the world understand these norms. Every society has to evolve a value system on its own. It cannot be imposed on it from any other society. And it should never be; cultural invasions by the western media are the prominent examples in this context.

All the human beings are born equal and they should be treated as equal. Cultural differences should not make them gods or demons. It is not possible to evolve common cultural ethos today but it may be possible to do so after resolving the major issues that the human kind faces as on date.

WILL MORE STATE AUTONOMY LEAD TO INDIA'S DISINTEGRATION?

Mr Raju: —Please pay attention to me. I said silence and it means you stop talking till I finish. I think we have done enough of 'tete-a-tete'. Now, let us get going and start the proceedings. The sooner we finish, the better it is. Then, we can decide about the consensus. Let me then set the ball rolling. I will now initiate the discussion. Frankly, I don't agree with the proposition. May I start the discussion with your kind permission?

Mr Rajneesh: —Mr Raju, hold on. I have not clearly understood what exactly we are supposed to discuss. The subject given to us seems to be a riddle. I suggest somebody explained everything first.

Mr Raju: —What's wrong with you Mr Rajneesh? Don't tell me that you can't comprehend the real meaning of the topic given to us. There is nothing strange or novel about the subject. Everybody else seems to have understood it. You are the only one who has not understood it. Anyway, I have no time to repeat all that the examiner said. You will soon understand what it is all about. When others start discussing the issue, you will get vital clues.

Mr Peeyush: —Mr Rajneesh appears to be a science student and that accounts for his not being very familiar with political science, constitutional matters and similiar other areas of humanities. If I were you, I would have clarified his doubts and briefly outlined the scope of the topic so that he could understnad your arguments with interest and enthusiasm. Perhaps, there may be others like Mr Rajneesh who would like to understand the subject first. Besides, you may also like to clarify the procedure that we are going to follow in this GD session. It is not a lecture, talk or debate. It is a formal discussion and all of us must participate and make their contributions to it.

Mr Raju: —If everyone in the group is going to act like Mr Rajneesh and Mr Peeyush, we will never be able to complete this session and arrive at a consensus. We will only be wasting time by giving explanations and clarifications.

Mr Peeyush: —I am sorry, Mr Raju. Perhaps, I have not made myself clear. Since you wish to be the first speaker, I felt it would be a good idea for you to explain the subject so that Mr Rajneesh or others who are not familiar with the topic could appreciate your views. Later, they can make worthwhile contributions. Next, you would also like to finalise who would speak after you and also the order of speakers thereafter. There is yet another point. We must also fix the time limit for each speaker so that all get equal opportunity to voice their opinions.

Do you agree, friends?

Mr John: —Yes, I entirely agree with Mr Peeyush.

Mr Raju: —What do you mean by saying you agree with Mr Peeyush? I myself cannot follow what Mr Peeyush wants.

Mr John: —If you can't understand what Mr Peeyush has put across, how would you take an active part in this GD session? I suggest you keep quiet and leave it to Mr Peeyush to conduct the discussion.

Mr Raju: —You are a stooge of Mr Peeyush. I would not be swayed by your thoughts or rules.

Mr John: —I think we are wasting time. We ought to come to the real issue. I hope all of you agree with me.

Mr Raju: —That would be the right thing to do.

Mr Peeyush: —Mr John, please leave it to me. After all, Mr Raju was only criticising me. Time is running out. Mr Raju, you go ahead and speak on the subject. If you all agree, each candidate can speak for two minutes at the most during the first round. If anyone wants more time, he can do so during the second round. Let us start with Mr Raju, then proceed with Mr Mohit and so on and complete the first round with Mr Neetesh. All right Mr Raju. Please take the floor.

Mr Raju: —No, thank you. Mr John must tender openly and publically an unconditional apology. Otherwise, I will not talk.

Mr John: —I am sorry, Mr Raju. However, someone else can start the proceedings.

Mr. Peeyush: — Right, Let us start with Mr Manish and end up with Mr Mohit.

Mr Rajneesh: —Just one request please, I don't want to be the second speaker. Rather, I want to speak at last. I suggest you go in an anti-clockwise direction after Mr Manish. In other words, after Mr Manish, it can be Mr Mohit, then Mr Raju and so on till it is my turn to complete the round as the last speaker.

Mr Peeyush: —Very good. Mr Manish, please initiate the discussion.

Mr Manish: —Friends, as desired by Mr Rajneesh and for the benefit of those who are new to this topic, which is related to constitutional aspects and political science, I want to outline briefly the nature and scope of the topic. Let me restate the topic which says *"India will Disintegrate with more State Autonomy"*. According to the Constitution, India is a union of states. It has not been described as federation of Independent states. During the British period, we had provinces and princely states, all subordinate to the Viceroy and the Governor-General ruling from Delhi. Before the advent of the British, India was divided. The invaders conquered and ruled India since there was no unity among those who ruled different regions and parts of the subcontinent. After independence, there was bloodshed and chaos, and the country was divided into two sovereign nations—Pakistan and India. The framers of our Constitution wanted to preserve the unity and integrity of the country while affording scope for the development of regional culture, language etc. Thus, India got a federal pattern with a strong unitary base. For four decades since independence, we have seen a stable government at the centre with a single political party or a coalition of like-minded parties (i.e., the NDA) commanding sizeable majority in the Parliament. In Bihar and Uttar Pradesh, the regional parties came to power in the state elections. We already have regional or opposition party governments in Odisha, Tamil Nadu, West Bengal and Jammu and Kashmir. The 2009 General Elections showed that we cannot have single-party rule in the Lok Sabha. A coalition government will be weak and unstable. It will be unable to keep the state governments under control. What we want, therefore, is a rational approach or outlook.

Mr Mohit: —Gentlemen, I have no disagreement on the facts presented by Mr Manish. However, I cannot subscribe to his interpretation and conclusions. India of today is different from India at the time of Alexander's invasion, Kushan's invasion or Afghan, Turk and Mughal invasions and finally the British conquest. During those days, India was not a nation. Secondly, the masses or the majority of the people were not involved in the wars waged by the local rulers against the foreign invaders and conquerors. The battles were waged or fought by only those warriors who were a small minority. Today, the people of India, which means about 1020 million people, are conscious of their rights and the power they exercise through the ballot. The result of the elections of 2009 have shown that the electorate is mature and cannot be taken for a ride. Most of the regional political parties serve their regions with elan and finesse. Hence, our aim is unity in diversity. This is not possible without greater state autonomy.

Mr Peeyush: —Mr Raju, it is your turn. We are keen to hear your views on the subject.

Mr Raju: —I refuse to speak. I have made it amply clear already. I don't care what you people say or do.

Mr Peeyush: —Mr Raju, kindly reconsider you stand. This is a personal request from me and I am also appealing to you on behalf of the group.

Mr Raju: —I refuse to speak on the issue.

Mr Peeyush: —I do not give up hope. I am sure you will respond to our appeal later. Now, let us move on to Mr Neetesh.

Mr Neetesh: —Well, Mr Peeyush and friends. Thank you for asking me to give my views. I am not a politician, nor do I have any knowledge of political science, Consititution etc. I am interested in my research work in Zoology and prefer to spend my time inside the laboratory. It is up to you people to decide what is right. I will abide by the group consensus.

Mr Prakash: —Friends, in a Parliamentary system of government, there must always be an alternative party to choose in case the electorate is keen to have a change. Since independence, we have had only one-party government for four decades. When there was an opportunity and the Janata Party offered to rule, it was voted to power. But the Janata Party proved that it was not a single or united party but just a coalition of convenience. When the Janata Party disintegrated before its full term could be completed, the people, in disgust, voted the Congress (I) back to power. But the Congress (I) also failed. The JD and its factions also failed. Finally, the NDA took charge in 1999. Many regional parties have come to power. Despite one-party rule for over 45 years, we have not achieved much. I feel that no harm will be done if regional parties assume power in the states. If the coalition does not work in the Centre, the electorate will again choose a strong national party to rule in the Centre.

Mr Peeyush: —Friends, the need of the hour, in my view, is adequate autonomy for our states consistent with the paramount requirements of national unity, security, integration, preservation of security and our survival as a sovereign and independent nation. As one nation and as united people, we can grow to become strong and meet all the challenges. If we do not have a strong and stable government, we cannot overcome these external threats successfully. Some internal problems are also giving us tantrums. First, there was insurgency in the North-Eastern States. The *'Sons of the Soil'* attitude is gaining strength. Secondly, we have terrorism in J & K. There are inter-state rivalries, territorial quarrels and river water disputes. Then, there are problems of linguistic minorities. Everywhere communal and caste conflicts are on the increase, both in terms of number and intensity. Unemployment, illiteracy and inflation continue to bother us. Population is rising. Many states are still backward and need proper allocation of national resources for rapid development.

I have a doubt, whether regional parties wedded to the *'Sons of the Soil'* policy will help to solve these problems. There is no doubt in my mind that the present wave of regionalism in India is a danger signal. Thank you.

Mr John: —Gentlemen, I agree with Mr Peeyush. His analysis of the present Indian situation is correct and I entirely support his conclusion that regionalism is retrograde and dangerous. Those, who are arguing for regionalism, do not know what they are talking about. I don't want to waste my time arguing with them. I differ from our friend, Mr Peeyush. He puts all his faith in democracy. I agree, on the other hand, with Dr Ambedkar, who said that democracy itself is alien to our way of life and it is a mere top dressing on foreign soil. All the problems listed by Mr Peeyush have not been solved because we did not have a strong Centre to implement. We know that linguistic provinces will cut at the root of our unity. But we gave in because of this notion of democracy, fear of losing the elections and what not? If we had a really strong Centre, we would have resolved most of these problems long ago. A strong Centre is needed for India's progress.

Mr Rajneesh: —Gentlemen, thank you all. But I do not know whom I should support and to that extent, I am quite confused. Everyone seems to be right. I support everybody. Thank you once again.

PRESS FREEDOM

Mr. Sunil: May I have your attention, friends!

Mr. Dharamvir: We would not like you to start the proceedings.

Mr. Sunil: I am only trying to end the chaos and start a meaningful dialogue.

Mr Manoj:—Your intention is good. But we must define a system or an order of rotation. Let me discuss this point with others.

(Mr Manoj Starts talking to the candidate sitting to his left)

Mr Sunil:—Mr Dharmvir and Mr Manoj. You will agree that both of you have become personal and we are off the mark. Let us now relax and start the session.

Mr Karndeo:—You are quite right Mr Sunil. Let us not waste time on extraneous matters. Mr Sunil, you wanted to tell us what you had in mind about the session.

Mr Sunil:—Thank you, Mr Karndeo. Well friends, since we have been given only half an hour to complete our GD, I suggest that we start with Mr Manoj and go on in a clockwise order to Mr Sanjay and so on. Finally, Mr Mahesh would get his turn to give his views on the subject. This would be the first round during which each one of us can speak for not more than two minutes. We can manage the time, if there are no interruptions and each one of us is allowed to present his ideas without any disturbance or interference.

Mr Dharamvir:—What happens, if I don't agree with the views expressed by the member or speaker? May be, he says something unpleasant or weird. Let us say he quotes Tennyson but gives the credit to Shakespeare. Should I not intervene and point out the mistake?

Mr Karndeo:—We are not supposed to intervene. We can point out the mistake when our turn comes and we present out own views.

Mr Dharamvir:—But many of you are going to speak after me and not before?

Mr Sumit:—After the first round is completed we shall have a second one when each one of us will get one minute to voice his criticism, rebuttals, after thoughts and whatever.

Finally, after the second round is over, there may be a few minutes left still left for arriving at the consensus.

Mr Karndeo and Mr Ankit:—That is fine.

Mr Manoj:—Wait a minute. I have a better idea.

Mr Dharamvir:—I know you will come out with something silly as you did earlier. We can have your pranks later on. Let us now proceed with the task as advised by Mr Sunil.

Mr Manoj:—Will you shut up Mr Dharamvir? I have every right to express my views. Then, it is for the group to decide where I stand. I told you I have a better idea.

Mr Sunil:—Please, gentlemen. Why quarrel for nothing? Mr Manoj, we would like to hear your views. Please go ahead.

Mr Manoj:—Gentlemen, I totally disagree with what Mr Sunil has suggested. It is completely baseless.

Mr Karndeo:—Tell us what you want. What is the alternative that you would like to suggest?

Mr Manoj:—Why don't you suggest an alternative?

Mr Karndeo:—Those, who do not agree with Mr Sunil's plan, may raise their hands. There you are Mr Manoj! If you have an alternative, please let us have it. Otherwise let us go ahead as we have decided earlier. You can see that no one has raised his hand.

Mr Manoj:—You have already made sure that no one would accept my plan. Therefore, I refuse to talk about it.

Mr Sunil:—I had told you that I will accept your plan if it is a better one.

Mr Dharamvir:—We are wasting time. I guarantee that he has no other solution, leave alone a better one.

Mr Manoj:—I challenged you earlier but you asked out. What is the bet now?

Mr Dharamvir:—We are here for the GD Test and not for a verbal or physical duel. Friends, you can judge that Mr Manoj is stubborn and obstructive. If he does not start the session, I shall recommend that we begin from Mr Sanjay and proceed.

Mr Sunil:—That does not appear to be correct Mr Dharamvir. I appeal to you, Mr Manoj. Please start and give the outline of your plan of action.

Mr Manoj:—It is of no use. If they don't want a better idea, it is up to them. I am not keen to start the discussion. Now, you can start from Mr Sanjay, as suggested by Mr Dharamvir.

Mr Sunil:—Mr Sanjay, please give your views on the subject.

Mr Sanjay:—The subject, in my view, deals with newspapers. I don't read newspapers regularly. I like cinema and my hobby is photography. If you ask me, newspapers make a mountain of a molehill. That is all.

Mr Dharamvir:—The subject of our discussion deals with the Press freedom. I would say that the question should be whether our Press is free or not. I think that the press is free. It was not so during the emergency. What is the guarantee that there will not be such emergencies in the future? I am of the view that freedom of the Press with self-restraint is a must for the survival of not only the Press, but also of democracy in India. The Press councils play useful roles in this context.

Mr Karndeo:—Friends, the Press should observe restraint for its survival and freedom. Assuming that the Press now enjoys full freedom, the question to be debated is whether such freedom should be unrestricted and total, or whether it should be subjected to certain restraints, imposed from inside or outside. If one takes the view that Press is not at all free, the question of any restraint does not arise at all. It would then mean that the Press now is gagged in our country. Some newspapers have resorted to irresponsible reporting and hence the masses are affected. The alternative, is self-restraint. This restraint should come from within and there should be a press code which should be honoured.

Mr Ankit:—Gentlemen, in my view, the Press in India has been given too much freedom, which a few newspapers are abusing. Mr Karndeo referred to a code. There is no code or restraint. We have too much of yellow journalism. In our country, ask any cinema actor or actress and he or she will tell how he is being maligned. This is done to increase circulation, earn money and amass lot of power. The same is the case with the politicians too. Now, the industrialists are also becoming targets for such attacks. The existing laws related to libel etc are so inadequate that newspapers can get away with any kind of objectionable or false article or report. You also know that many magazines are practically pornographic. Hence, I would say that we need restrictions rather than restraint.

Mr Sunil:—Friends, you will all agree with me that at this point of time, the Press in India is quite free and the only limitations are those of ownership by big newspaper chains. There is a keen competition but people are becoming more knowledge conscious. The Press is also quite zealous about its freedom. Sometimes, people are quoted out of context. In other words, it could lead to deliberate misreporting. With new newspapers mushrooming each day, survival becomes a major problem. In this situation, and with all the corruption and political pressures, it is true that self-restraint won't work. Hence, in my view, the Press should evolve a code and leave it to the authorities to enforce it through proper legislation. The courts are there to ensure that the freedom of expression guaranteed by the Constitution as a fundamental right is not taken away from the *hoi polloi* of India.

Mr Vineet:—I agree with what our friends have said so far. I have nothing against anybody. It is good to observe restraint. Mr Sunil has also stated the same point. I have nothing to add now. Thank you!

Mr Mahesh:—There are always some implicit restrictions. The Constitution does provide for reasonable restrictions. What I do to others, others can do to me. But if you allow the government to impose restrictions or even enforce restraints embodied in a code, it can result in abuse and discrimination. Besides, the government already has the patronage of advertisements. Hence, I do not favour government's interference.

Mr Manoj:—I told you earlier and I would have to repeat my views, I don't agree with all this. Everything has been done in a wrong manner, and you did not choose to listen to me. I can prove that all that you have said is totally absurd. But I have decided not to say anything, just to register my protest. You can come to any conclusions you like but I am not a party to it. That is all.

PRIVATE SECTOR WITH ECONOMIC LIBERALISATION—INDIA'S
BEST HOPE FOR RAPID ECONOMIC GROWTH

Mr Rohit:—Friends! May I have your kind attention for a few seconds please? Hello, Mr Shyam and Mr Jonny. May I claim your attention also, please? I have something to tell you all.

Mr Shyam:—I say, what is this? Why are you interfering in our discussion? Why do you want us to listen to you now? This is not a lecture you see we are busy. Myself and Mr Jonny are discussing the subject and we should be left in peace. We do not want to waste anytime listening to lectures and sermons. What do you say, Mr Jonny?

Mr Jonny:—I agree with you all. I was only listening to Mr Shyam. I am ready to listen to others also.

Mr Deepak:—Hello, Mr Shyam. I do not see your point. What precisely is your objection? Why are you getting worked up? Mr Rohit says, he has something to tell us all and he is requesting the group to listen to what he has to say just for a couple of minutes. I, or shall we say, all the rest of us see nothing wrong in that. Can you tell us what is your problem?

Mr Shyam:—Now, now this is too much. Am I a witness, who is being cross-examined or am I supposed to do group discussion? You are welcome to listen to whomsoever you want. That is your problem. But why not leave me alone?

Mr Rahul:—Hey, Mr Shyam. There is something radically wrong. Either you are dull like a donkey or obstinate like a mule. On behalf of the group, Mr Deepak told you that we agree to the request of Mr Rohit and all should listen to him. As soon as Mr Rohit requested us, we all stopped our conversations and talks. But you persisted with your aside with Mr Jonny. Now we see that Mr Jonny has no objection to listen to Mr Rohit. Therefore, why don't you shut your trap and listen to Mr Rohit?

Mr Shyam:—You are nobody to tell me to shut up. I protest and strongly object to your calling me a donkey, mule and what not. I will certainly lodge a written complaint against you with the examiner. Now you better watch your steps.

Mr Rahul:—All right, go to hell or drown yourself. But for heaven's sake, don't be a nuisance to us. Why don't you get lost?

Mr Rohit:—Please, friends, I am a afraid we are moving away from our goal, you see, we have already lost some precious minutes in these avoidable arguments. Now, Mr Shyam please bear with me for a second. My intention is not to interfere with you in any way. It is obvious that

I had not explained myself clearly. Please let us cooperate and make our discussion a success. Just bear with me for a few seconds.

Mr Shyam:—All right, all right.

Mr Rohit:—Friends, as you all would agree, if everyone is talking at one and the same time, there will only be confusion and no one would know who is saying what. That is what has been happening since the examiner left. Are you all with me?

Mr Deepak:—Yes, yes, that is correct.

Mr Rahul:—You are right, Mr Rohit. What do you advise us to do?

Mr Rohit:—I suggest that we take turns and speak one after another. Only one candidate should address the group at one time and give his views on the subject. Let each one also restrict his speech for two minutes only during the first round.

Mr Deepak:—I am ready to do what the group wants from me. I feel it may be a good idea to start with Mr Rahul and proceed clockwise and wind up the first round with Mr Deepak. In case mr Deepak would like to be the second speaker, then we can breed anti-clockwise, starting with Mr Rahul. I have no objection at all to be the last speaker. But we must maintain the order without breaking the calm.

Mr Shyam:—Why must we start with Mr Rahul? He was so rude and he told me to shut up and called me names. I don't agree.

Mr Rahul:—Did I say anything wrong? Isn't it better to call a spade a spade.

Mr Rohit:—Please, let us not quarrel and deviate from our task. I am sure, Mr Rahul won't mind if someone else were to begin the discussion.

Mr Rahul:—No, not at all. In fact, I am not ready and would like a little time for collecting my ideas. But if Mr Shyam keeps talking, all my ideas will evaporate.

Mr Ranjeet:—All right. Let us begin with Mr Rohit and end up with Mr Rahul. That was the original suggestion of Mr Deepak. Do you all agree?

Others:—Yes, yes. Come on Mr Rohit.

Mr Rohit:—Friends, the subject given for our discussion is an interesting and topical one. In effect, it says India must now give up public sector and concentrate on the growth of private sector. The rationale for this is the findings that, by and large, our public sector units have been incurring losses while the private sector enterprises have proved to be productive and profitable. But the question is whether the private sector, which is essentially profit oriented, would come forward to meet all the industrial needs of the country. Experience shows that private sector would prefer to invest only in such areas in which, the returns would be quicker and higher. Thus, the tendency of the private sector has been to manufacture luxury items like colour TVs, refrigerators, electronic gadgets, computers and so on. Secondly, most of these goods are made with foreign collaboration and knowhow, without transfer of real technology to India. This leads to perpetual drain of foreign exchange and perpetual dependence on others. The private sector cannot mobilise enough capital on its own to start many major industries. Profit being the chief motive, a private entrepreneur will prefer to start an industry where the infrastructure is already available. He will not like to move into backward, remote and undeveloped areas. Thus, there cannot be balanced development of all regions. Besides, there are other political considerations too. Our aim is to have a society in which, the gap between the rich and the poor is to be as narrow as is possible. Our dependence on the private sector will go against this goal. Hence, a balanced approach of matching the public sector with private enterprise is necessary.

Mr Rajesh: —I really do not know what to say. I thought, that private sector is good. But Mr Rohit has different ideas. I do not want to go against him. My knowledge is limited. As such, I want to accept his views. But there is a doubt in my mind. Everyone states that private sector is efficient. All private companies make profit. Even Mr Rohit has stated that the public sector is not making profit. You cannot have business without earning profit. I said whatever came to my mind. In conclusion, it is better to accept what Mr Rohit says.

Mr Ranjeet: —Gentlemen, I do not support the proposition which, in effect, tells us to abandon the public sector and go all out for the private sector. This is the American and western viewpoint, echoed by international institutions like the World Bank and IMF. Mr Rohit has already told us why we cannot abandon the public sector altogether. If we do that, the next step would be to give up our planning process and scuttle our Five Year Plans. We know that the Five Year Plan projects are mostly in the public sector. Due to the Five Year Plans we have today become self-reliant in many areas. We have our own steel, cement and fertiliser factories. We have been able to stage the Green Revolution successfully. We have built so many dams with multipurpose benefits like irrigation, power generation, water conservation, flood control and the like. Even in areas like ship-building, aircraft manufacture, automobile industry, railways, thermal power generation, nuclear power generation, oil, etc. We are ahead of many others. Most of these would not have been attractive for the private sector. The operation, methods, management, etc, of the public sector has not been efficient. There is plenty of scope for improvement. We should remove these defects and make public sector as efficient as the private sector. One way to do so is to allow both to compete on equal footing. It is happening now in-the areas of scooters, car, watches, etc. It will force the public sector units to work efficiently and profitably.

Mr Lokesh:—Dear friends, I like what Mr Ranjeet said and I am in total agreement with him. We must have public sector in a democracy. We must have socialism and democracy. Poverty has to be eradicated. We need public sector to attain our goals. In my view, what Mr Rohit stated is also right. In some areas, we can have private sector also. We must advance and make progress. We can do so with the Japanese, Russian and British co-operation. Only with the Russian help our cosmonaut could make the space voyage. Public sector is, therefore, very important.

Mr Shyam:—Friends, I just can not understand how anyone who claims to have knowledge and education, especially in the field of economics, can conceivably speak in favour of the public sector in India. It is a well-known fact that it is India's biggest economic blunder and a monumental mistake. Even the Russians have admitted it, and abandoning communism, they have opted for market economy. All admit that crores and crores of rupees have been wasted on the public sector.

It is a white elephant. The only purpose the public sector has served is to provide politicians with a lot of patronage and power. They can give contracts, jobs and make all the money they want to fight and win the elections, look at Japan, look at Germany, look at South Korea, Taiwan and Singapore. Take any industrially and economically prosperous country. Where are we and where are they? Where is India? There is no equitable distribution of wealth here. It is a myth because we have not made any wealth to distribute. We have only poverty to distribute. One can have as much of it as one wants. Because of public sector, we are in a pathetic economic situation today. Our salvation lies in going for the private sector. You have no choice. It is survival or death. You are welcome to choose and I have had my say and you have been warned.

Mr Jonny:—Friends, I wish to apologise and seek your forgiveness. The more I hear, the more I get confused. First I thought Mr Shyam was supporting the public sector. I mean, in the beginning, when he spoke to me. Now he supports the private sector. But Mr Rohit and Mr Ranjeet favour the public sector. I do not know who is right and who is wrong. The best thing is, therefore, to be neutral. Later, I would like to support the majority decision. That is the safest thing to do. The examiner can not find fault with the majority decision.

Mr Deepak:—Friends, India, after great deliberations, has consciously and knowingly chosen the path of mixed economy to achieve industrial growth and prosperity. Today, in my view, there is not much distinction between the public sector and the private sector, so far as financing goes. Practically, all the private sector enterprises borrow heavily from the public sector banks and financial institutions. Thus all the money and capital rightly belongs to the public. The only difference then is in regard to the functioning of the two and in the sharing of the profits. Secondly, it is wrong to assume that all private enterprises have proved profitable. There are many sick mills while the mill-owners have accumulated fabulous wealth with bungalows, hill estates, foreign cars and deposits in Swiss Banks. On the contrary, there are quite a few efficiently run public sector undertaking. The crucial point then is not public or private sector label but operating the enterprise most efficiently. There are constraints such as lack of managerial skills. These could be removed. If we can run all our enterprises efficiently in both the sector, our growth will be assured.

Mr Rahul:—Friends, I must say, all of you have analysed the topic from all angles and covered all the areas. I only want to submit that we should not be unduly influenced by the western propaganda. One man's food may be another man's poison. What is suited to America, Japan or Germany may not suit us. The same would be the case with Russia or China. We have to see what is best for us. One cannot say that all the countries, which opted for private enterprise have fared well. Pakistan is a glaring example. Secondly, we should not be caught in the net of the multinationals, cartels and monopolies. Above all, we have to become self-reliant. We do not want economic exploitation or blackmail. We should co-operate with the rich and developed nations. We must follow the rules of the new international economic order. The private sector should be told to lead the economy from the front. The profit-making PSUs as well as departments of that government should give support to the privte sector. Free market system has arrived in India. We should use it but carefully, according to our needs and conditions. Finally there is no need to embrace a full-fledged free market system as of now. We can do it later.

RURAL INDIA IS NOT DEVELOPING DUE TO RESOURCE CONSTRAINTS

Mr Nagesh: Good morning, friends! My name is Nagesh Thakur. I want to support the topic. It is true that rural India; is not developing due to resource constraints. India is a developing country. It has not acquired enough resources or growth rate to become a fully developed country. Illiteracy and backwardness are other constraints but resource restraint is the chief inhibiting factor in this context. Thank you!

Mr Asghar: Good morning, friends! My name is Asghar Ali Masood. I would like to oppose the topic. My worthy friend has stated that resource constraints are chiefly responsible in this trend. But I think that illiteracy and backwardness are the chief causative factors. There are good enough resources in rural India. But they are not being utilised. For example, land is in plenty in rural India; so are water, clean air, agricultural products, lumser and natural resources of other types. We are not managing our rural areas well. The rural people do not know how to utilise their resources to generate concrete outputs. Rural management should be an essential part of our school and college curricula. Nearly 70 per cent of India's population lives in rural areas. However, these rural people are at the receving end most of the times. So, I must conclude by stating that we have rural resources but not enlightened villagers who could utilise these resources to make rural India an economic power. Thank you!

Ms Nagma: Good morning, ladies and gentlemen! My name is Nagma Gul. I would like to align my views with those of Mr. Nagesh. If there are no resources, how would they be managed?

Mr Suraj: Rural resources are there.

Ms Nagma: You can speak when your turn comes.

Mr Suraj: But I can give a comment. Can't I?

Ms Neelofer: All right, you can give your comment. Ms. Nagma, he says that rural resources are there. Probably, they are not being managed well.

Ms Nagma: Please let me complete my statement.

Mr Suraj: Do not oppose our comment.

Ms Nagma: I am trying to answer your query. You should know that the primary resources are–land, equipment, manpower, money technology, and methods. These resources are concentrated in the urban areas.

Mr Suraj: Wrong! Land is available in the rural areas of India. Where is the space in any urban area?

Ms Nagma: I understand that. Please note that rural land is cheap everywhere in India, except only a few rural pockets. Money is also not available in rural areas. Had money been available in rural areas, we would never have faced the problem of the migration of rural people to urban areas. Today, every farm or agri-based industry needs money to survive and grow. Similary, technology, methods, manpower and equipment are also in short supply in rural areas. Hence, we are facing a resource crunch, at least in the rural areas of India. Hence, rural pockets of India are not developing. Thank you!

Ms Neelofer: Good morning, friends! My name is Neelofer Dar. I think resource shortage is not a constraint in rural India. The only thing is that we are unable to manage these resources. Money is generated by the farmers in the form of agricultural products of various types. But only a few landlords become rich. Daily-wage labourers and small farmers are always on the brink of extinction. Hence, only a few pockets of rural India are prosperous. Majority of the rural pockets are in shambles. In sum, the rural areas of India are not developing due to the poor management of its resources. The rich-poor divide is chiefly responsible for this phenomenon. If only a few landlords become rich, we cannot conclude that the entire rural India is rich. The resources of the rich landlords must be evenly distributed so that the farmers and landless labourers may be able to become slightly well off. Thank you!

Mr. Suraj: Good morning, friends! My name is Suraj Kumar Verma. I think resource constraint is the major hurdle that is not allowing rural India to reach the coveted goal of prosperity. If we talk of land as a resource, we should know that it would need many other resources to make it productive. The farmer needs tractor to till the land; he does not have the same. He needs electricity to irrigate the land; he does not have the same in adequate quantities. He needs fertilisers to make the land fertile; we know that he cannot afford to buy NPK urea and other fertilisers but has to depend upon natural manure most of the times. If his son wants to start an agro-based project, he needs machines, money and manpower; he does not have any one of them in sufficient quantities. Hence, if land is available and other resources are not in sufficient supply, the land becomes useless. Someone has pointed out that rich landlords enjoy a position of power, as far as resources of these types are concerned. Hence, only a few pockets become powerful. Money earns money; and this tenet is applicable in rural areas as well. As someone has rightly pointed out, if a few pockets are developed, we cannot conclude that all the rural pockets are developed. Hence, our rural areas have been reeling under poverty due to resource constraints. Thank you!

Ms. Neelu: Good morning, ladies and gentlemen! My name is Neelu Pendharkar. I want to state that resource constraint is not a problem in any pocket of India, leave alone rural India. We have, and we can arrange, resources in rural areas as well. Our Five Year Plans have been designed to cater to the needs of rural people. But our planners do not realise the fact that these allocated resources do not reach the rural poor. Thus, the vicious cycle of poverty goes on in the rural pockets of the country.

Let me give you an example in this context. Most corporate sector firms have set up their plants in rural or semi-urban areas of India. BHEL has all of its units located in rural areas, except only a few. Most agro-based industries are located in rural areas. That is because these industries take inputs from the farmers located in their immediate vicinity. A sugar mill will always be set up close to a rural pocket that is known for sugarcane production. Hence, there are factories in rural areas. Despite this dispersal trend, rural areas have not developed. Why is that so? The answer to the question is—only a few people or firms invest money in agriculture or industry. Only a few of them use the latest techniques of engineering and management to develop their respective firms. Hence, only those people or firms develop that use the resources— some one has rightly described the genres of resources— in a best possible manner.

Now, a question arises— if a farmer has the resources, as I have already stated, how should he utilise them? The answer to this question is very simple. He must educate himself and his children. He must use the latest agricultural implements. He must use fertilisers and advanced seeds. He should also start an agro-based industry in his farm. He needs knowledge. He must depend upon the latest technologies. He is not doing anything of this sort. He is using primitive agricultural tools. He is afraid of changing himself. This fact is true about both big and small farmers of the country. Our resistance to change, and not our resource constraints, is responsible for the poor development of the rural areas of our country. Hence, I oppose the topic. Thank you!

Mr Asghar: We have finished the first round. Now, let us get into the depth of the topic. Finally, we will try to evolve a consensus.

Ms Neelu: I think I am on the right track. Many of my colleagues have supported me. If you have any objection, please tell me. I will remove your doubts.

Ms Neelofer: I think only a few landlords are earning in rural areas. Resource constraint is not an inhibiting factor. We have to become better managers of our rural resources. The priorities of the Tenth Plan must be changed.

Ms Neelu: They cannot be changed now.

Ms Neelofer: All right, the Government may change the priorities of the Eleventh Plan.

Mr Asghar: Illiteracy and backwardness are taking rural India back to the Medieval Age. The farmers must educate themselves. Their children should take up the B.Sc. (Agriculture) course to become better farmers. They should not run towards the urban areas of the country. Note that rural migration is the chief causative factor that is perpetuating rural poverty and backwardness. This cycle can be broken only if rural people are educated, trained in modern agricultural methods and informed about resource management skills. Further, do not expect results overnight.

Mr Suraj: In my view, resource constraint is the major problem, as far as the development of rural areas is concerned. In the villages of our country, there are not adequate facilities. Most villages are sans electricity, water, sewage disposal systems, good schools, colleges, vocational training institutes, transport networks, rail networks, medical facilities etc. They cannot grow without resource inputs of the right type and quantity.

Mr Asghar: You are talking about physical resources. I was talking about mental resources. The quality of manpower is not good in rural India. If it is not good, how can illiterate villagers use such resources even if they are provided with the same?

Mr Suraj: You are in the wrong. If they are given such resources, they would be able to do well. They know how to use the resources. But there are not adequate resources to manage.

Ms Neelu: But training also matters. That is what we have been taught.

Mr Suraj: I am not underestimating the importance of training. Tell me, do you need to train a farmer in agricultural practices. He knows much more than all of us in this context. What he needs is fertilisers, tractors, seeds and water. All these are available at a cost. He cannot pay the hefty electricity bills either. This status quo has been maintained for at least fifty years in our country. Poor farmers are the chief groups that are on the receiving end. Our duty is to change their lot at the earliest possible.

Ms Nagma: Resource crunch is the major issue, not resource management. Mr. Rajiv Gandhi became the PM and he did not know a thing about the management of a country. He was declared "a young PM with a vision." If one gets the resources, one becomes capable enough to manage them. If there are no resources, what should we manage? Our urban people are more prosperous because they enjoy more resources than their rural cousins. That is why people go from rural areas of Bihar, Bengal, Orissa, Punjab, UP and MP to urban areas. They would never have gone to the cities, had they been given adequate resources. No one wants to leave his home town, especially our village folk.

Mr Asghar: How can we evolve a consensus at this juncture? No one is ready to budge an inch from his previous stand. We have to co-operate with one another and prove that despite all the differences, the group is a single unit.

Ms Neelu: I think we should concentrate on the education and training of the rural masses. Resources are there but these people have not been trained to utilise to their advantage.

Mr Suraj: I do not agree with you. Our farmers are poor. A majority of them have never enjoyed the facilities that are available to the urban people of India. Many thousand villages of India are yet to be electrified. There is no potable water in any village. Roads are not metalled. Markets are far from villages. The economic cycles of the rural areas move at very slow pace. These cycles cannot match the fast economic cycles of the urban areas.

Ms Neelofer: In my view, the rich-poor hiatus in the rural areas is a chief causative factor in this context. We need good rural managers. An executive, doctor or engineer does not want to go to a rural area. True, there are primary health centres, factories, schools and colleges in rural areas. But the quality of the human resource of all these training and development centres is poor. Hence, the rural areas are suffering. The problem lies in the managerial aspect of rural areas. I think my views are quite similar to those given by Ms. Neelu. So, we are riding in the same boat.

Ms Neelu: Welcome aboard, Ms. Neelofer.

Mr Suraj: Do not try to form a clique in this GD session. Try to arrive at a consensus.

Ms Neelofer: If we carefully analyse your views, you are also riding our boat.

Mr Suraj: Is that so?

Ms Neelu: Yes, but the only difference is that we are focusing on education and training while you are concentrating on the lack of infrastructure.

Mr Suraj: You are in the wrong, Ms. Neelofer. I have stated that resources are available but education and training are not. You have stated that the quality of people in rural areas is bad. I think my views are different from yours or from those of Ms. Neelu.

Ms Neelu: Believe me, you are riding the same boat. We have also said the same thing, albeit indirectly. We have said that resources are available but they ought to be managed with care.

Mr Suraj: So, Ms. Neelu, Ms. Neelofer and I are riding the same boat.

Ms Nagma: Don't be overjoyed! We are opposing you tooth and nail. I still contend that there are no resources in rural India.

Mr Asghar: If my views are carefully analysed, I would be included in the group of Ms. Neelu, Ms. Neelofer and Mr. Suraj.

Mr Nagesh: You are not allowing me to speak.

Ms Neelu: Please go ahead.

Mr Nagesh: There are no resources in rural India. Today, clean air and land are not the only coveted resources. We also need money, materials, methods and manpower to make a village or rural area prosperous. I would like to align my views with those of Mr. Asghar. I admit that illiteracy and social backwardness are other constraints. Further, as some of my friends have pointed out, education, training and managerial skills are also lacking in rural areas. But if adequate resources are provided, even a donkey can become a horse.

Mr Suraj: Mr. Nagesh, we are running out of time. Please come to a conclusion now. Only five minutes are left.

Ms Neelofer: Who would like to conclude?

Mr Asghar: I can conclude the proceedings.

Ms Neelu: He will highlight his own viewpoint.

Ms Neelofer: Never mind, he will do this for the benefit of the group. Mr. Asghar, please go ahead.

Mr Asghar: Oh! I was just joking. If you have given me the opportunity to represent the group, I will do justice to the job. The group has concluded that rural India has some resources like land, air, water, vegetation, mountains and agricultural products. Further, the resources like money, electric power, good manpower, efficient agricultural implements, fertilisers and good methods are lacking in the rural areas. Finally, the resources at the disposal of the rural people are not being managed well. These people must be trained thoroughly so that they may be able to manage such resources in the best possible manner to create wealth. They should not migrate to urban areas. The large firms and MNCs must invest in rural areas. The vicious cycle of poverty of landless labourers and small farmers must be broken at any cost. So, rural India is not developing both due to resource constraints and poor resource management. With these words, I hope none of you has been disappointed by this conclusion. If you wish to change this consensus statement, please give your suggestions.

Ms. Neelu : No, there is no querry to be answered.

Mr. Asghar : I thank you all for participating in the group discussion session. Good bye!

All : Thank you and good bye!

SHOULD OUR SPORTS
STARS EARN UNLIMITED WEALTH

Mr Sinhala: Good afternoon friends! My name is Ramakant Sinhala. If you would kindly allow, I ...

Ms Talwar: Do not play smart, Mister. You are trying to start on your own without getting permission from all of us.

Mr Sen: We cannot fight like this. I would suggest that we have a system of turns. We could start from the middle of this circle of participants.

Ms Shankar: But we are sitting in a U-format and not a circle. So, we can start from one end of this format.

Mr Chandran: But who would start even in this format? There are two eligible persons to do so.

Mr Sinhala: Let the lady start. She is on one end of this U-format. Then, the person next to her would speak. We shall carry on till we arrive at the other end.

All: That would be fine.

Ms Shankar: Good afternoon, Ladies and Gentlemen! The Indian players earn a lot out of the matches played by them against international teams. Sometimes, the winning team earns more than its match-playing fee given by the relevant sports organisation. We are living in a modern era. Everything has been commercialised. Sports events are big money spinners. Favourite sports stars play matches and win some of these. If they win, they get large bundles of money. Even if they lose, they get something. And they play in the name of India! This trend is the direct outcome of the evil effects free market forces. Sachin is the richest Indian player of the world. What about other players? They are languishing and trying to meet their basic needs.

Ms Paul: Good afternoon! My name is Reena Paul. I think Ms Shankar is right in stating that we must not allow our players to earn hefty sums of money in international tournaments. Commercialisation of sports has led to decay of all types of sports norms in the West. It should not happen in India. We should play for the sake of Sportsman's spirit. We should also play for health, fun and entertainment. But we must never play for the sake of money. I hope our sports authorities undersand this vital fact. Money is not being distributed evenly among various sports disciplines.

Mr Sen: Thank you, friends! My name is Subroto Sen. I would prefer to disagree with Ms Shankar and Ms Paul, although both seem to be intelligent ladies.

Ms Shankar: Come to the topic, Mr Sen. You don't have to 'tell' us that we are "intelligent".

Mr Sen: I was only passing a comment.

Mr Sinhala: Mr Sen! You had better not pass any kind of remark on any person. Please continue your discussion.

Mr Sen: I am sorry. I think that money is a great driving force in today's world. It makes man efficient and ambitious. There is no harm in earning money through sports competitions. But there is great harm in effecting the security scam, fodder scam, Bofors scam and all such controversial megabuck scams. Players should earn in sports. But I agree that they should not earn unlimited wealth in such events. In the field of cricket, especially in the one-day series, the cricketers of many nations have earned billions of Dollars. Why cannot the Indians earn this money if the foreigners are earning it with both of their hands? Moreover, look at the sport of cricket today. It has become a sophisticated, fiercely competitive and thrilling sport. I want other sports categories to accept such norms of commercialism. Hockey players are not paid well in India; nor do soccer players. In the UK, the USA and Europe, soccer stars are worshipped, literally. People buy tickets in black to watch their favourite stars clash with their rival teams in European Soccer League. We are earning money only through a few global sports tournaments. Now, Premier Hockey League and Premier Football League have been started in our country. So these sports disciplines would become wealthy. Their sports stars would also start earning money, like their cousins in the field of cricket. The sports stars should, however, have some limits in this context. The regulatory authorities and governments of various nations can define such rules and regulations as can protect the interests of poor sports stars. The government take vital steps in this context.

Mr Chandran: Good evening, friends! My name is Sudha Chandran. There are two types of opinions in the context of the debate. The first group wants sports stars of India to earn the maximum wealth. The other group wants the sports stars to earn only reasonable amounts of money. But my contention is that our sports stars are being paid fees by the sports authorities of those nations in which they play. Why should they be paid hefty amounts of money if they win final matches or sports competitions of various types? And why private firms pay them at all? Obviously, they want the popular film stars to become their brand ambassadors and promote their products. I would say that sports stars should be paid reasonable fees but should never be pampered by unlimited bundles of currency notes. This trend, as stated by a friend in this group discussion session, is prominent in cricket. We must make sports a method of survival and growth of our sports stars. But we must never make it a mode for spoiling them to the core. If these sports stars want to earn lots of wealth, they can set up their business when their sports careers are over. Why should they spoil the game by indulging in sporty mechanisations?

Ms Talwar: Thank you friends! I am Anita Talwar. I am also of the view that sports players should be given reasonable fees and no additional funds for extra laurels earned by them. Teams should also not be given funds, cars, gift hampers or other things by sponsoring firms. An award of "man of the match" could be a plaque. Why is there a need to give a life-size cheque of ₹ 1,00,000 instead of giving a plaque? I do not understand why money sneaks into every issue of human life. Such incentives do not develop the game. Rather, these become the ploys to earn more money. Further, there is competition among sports stars to get berths in the national team. Those, who do not get such berths, feel that they have been cheated. Had money not been used as a method to promote sports, the rejected sports stars could have been told that they were kept out because of their poor performances. But in this era, every player would like to be included in the team because he has to earn money. He would use references, coercion and money to get into the team. So, a vicious cycle of corruption would start; perhaps, it may already have started. Further match fixing scandals forced many star players, namely, Jadeja, Azharuddin and Cronje, to stay out of the sports stadia. In a bid to earn lots of money, sports stars can also lose matches. This evil game behind the game of cricket has been going on since the middle of the eighties. We must put an end to this trend.

Mr Sinhala: Thank you, friends, for giving me an opportunity to deliberate on this vital topic. What is the harm if our sports stars are given cars (like Audi), foreign exchange (like US Dollar or Pound Sterling), funds by private sponsors and gifts of various types and hues? They are talented. They bring Dollars to India. They promote the interests of their families. Perhaps, you are not aware how much foreign teams (of all the sports disciplines) earn by playing even in their league matches. In a free market system, there is no harm in working for money. But sports stars should earn reasonable amounts of money. Sachin Tendulkar has joined the billionaires' club. But hockey stars, football players, swimmers, athletes and other players should also be allowed to earn. For this purpose, sports events of all categories should be organised on a professional basis. For example, international sports competitions attracts a sea of spectators but swimming and hockey competitions (at the national level) prove to be a damp squib. We are paying more attention to cricket and ignoring other sports disciplines. That is why our cricket stars are earning a lot, even in this era of recession! Such trends ought to be reversed. All the sports streams and players thereof must be given adequate chances, financial support and patronage.

Ms Talwar: Just a moment, Mr Sinhala! There are only a few takers of your ideas in this world. And I feel there is none in this group. Why don't these sports stars give some money as charity to their poor brothers and sisters?

Mr Sinhala: They are giving charity money to various organisations. They have helped many poor families.

Ms Paul: I think Mr Sinhala is the odd person out in this group. But we must respect his views. Let us now sum up the debate. I would request Mr Sen to do so.

Mr Sen: Thank you, Ms Paul! Would the group permit me to sum up the debate?

All: Why not?

Mr Sen: Thank you! The group has arrived at the consensus that the Indian sports stars should earn reasonable amounts of money by playing in various international tournaments. The idea is to bring sanity to the world of sports, which, we deem, symbolises the perfection of the body and mind of man. But they should earn to upgrade their standards. They should also give some parts of their earnings to their poor brothers and sisters of India. They can also start profit oriented business when they are past their prime. These business firms would help several thousand Indians earn and survive in the newly created free market economy. Thank you!

All: Thank you!

FDI IN RETAIL SECTOR—A BOON OR BANE

Mr Nagarajan: Good afternoon, ladies and gentlemen! My name is Sathish M. Nagarajan. I hope we would be able to start this group discussion in the nick of time. May I start the proceedings right away?

Ms Ravi: I think we should start from the youngest person in the group.

Mr Kapoor: That is a strange idea. You would tell us now that you are the youngest person around.

Ms Ravi: Please maintain the decorum of the GD session.

Mr Shekhar: Please do not try to create a bad impression of the group. Moreover, this concept would take time to execute, though Ms Ravi has a point. We can start from the alphabetic order, as is normally the custom.

Mr Nirmal: But that would also take time.

Ms Ravi: Then, we can start according to the numbers of our interview letters. I hope you would like the idea. The person with smallest number on the reference number would speak first.

All: That would be fine.

(Everybody opens his letter and hands it over to Ms Ravi. Ms Ravi hands the letters over to Mr Nagarajan after sorting them according to the ascending order of reference number).

Ms Ravi: Let Mr Nagarajan give the name of the first speaker now.

Mr Nagarajan: The smallest reference number is that of Ms Khanam.

Ms Khanam: Thank you! My name is Ayesha Khanam. The Union Cabinet's decision to allow 51 per cent foreign direct investment (FDI) in multi-brand retail has cleared the entry of global super-market giants in India. FDI in retail is a boon or bane depends upon the answers of the questions—(i) Whether it will help farmers and to be precise small farmers, (ii) whether it will improve supply chains and help lower food inflation, (iii) how does it impact the livelihood of traditional food retailers.

Mr Nagarajan: The next higher reference number is that of Mr Shekhar.

Mr Shekhar: Thank you Mr. Nagrajan! Friends my name is Lalit Shekhar. Ms Ayehsa Khanam has rightly raised three questions against FDI. We will examine them one by one. As far as benefit of Farmer and Particularly small farmers is concerned in my view, they will not be benefitted by this. This has been evident from the operations of domestic fresh food super markets in India. Their entry and operations have not yet made any difference to the producer's share of profit so far. Further they will buy only the produce of their choice only on their monopolised prices forcing the farmer to sell the remaining produce at throw away prices at Mandi.

Mr Nagarajan: Now, it is the turn of Mr Surjeet.

Mr Surjeet: Thank you! My friends, Ms Khanam and Mr Shekhar may not be aware of more facts and I do not agree with Mr. Shekhar that farmers will not benefit from the FDI in retail but I am of the view that the farmers will benefit more from it as they will be able to get better prices for their products because of the elimination of the intermediate channels in the procurement process. The money thus saved will be shared by farmers and consumers bringing benefit to both of them in the process.

Mr Nagarajan: Now, it is the turn of Ms Ravi.

Ms Ravi: Thank You Friends! my name is Vidisha Ravi. Now that we have known the views on benefit to farmers. Let me highlight a Policy

Point that the stores will source at least 60% of their farmer produce requirements from small farmers. A small farmer is defined as one with up to 10 hectares of land. There are hardly 1% farmers in India who have more than 10 hectares of land. How will this Policy benefit small farmers in real terms when they do not meet the minimum land criteria of the policy?

Mr Nagarajan: Now, it is my turn to speak. However, Mr Kapoor, who would be the last one to speak, can take this turn.

Mr Kapoor: No, thank you! You have perforce become a compere.

Ms Ravi: You should be ashamed to state that, Mr Kapoor. Mr Nagarajan is trying to streamline the proceedings. These could have become chaotic, had he not offered his service. Moreover, he is offering you his turn to speak.

All: Mr Kapoor, that is bad on your part.

Mr Kapoor: I am really sorry, ladies and gentlemen. I think I should speak in the end. I deserve this punishment. Let Mr Nagarajan speak according to his turn.

Mr Nagarajan: Thank you friends! We have discussed the impact of FDI in retail on farmers, now we will discuss its impact on supply chains. My views is that the super market expansion also leads to employment loss in the value chain. FDI will have negative impact on small retailers. It will badly affect the whole-sellers and retail shopkeepers whole involvement will become zero in bringing the things to consumers. Thus it will force them to close their business and they themselves alongwith their employees will be jobless.

Mr Kapoor: Hello Friends! My name is Rakshit Kapoor. I do not agree with Mr. Nagrajan on the point the FDI in retail sector will do harm to retail shopkeepers rather, it will teach the local retailers about real competition and help in insuring them give better service to their customers. It is obviously good for local competition. Moreover the retail stores operate in a different environment catering to a certain type of customers and they may and they will continue to find new ways to retain them.

Mr Nagarajan: Mr Nirmal, it's your turn now.

Mr Nirmal: Thank you Mr Nagrajan. Now that we have discussed two important points on FDI let's discuss another important point whether FDI in retail will help lower food inflation. It is evident from the role of FDI-driven food super markets of many countries like Mexico, Nicaragua, Argentina, Kenya, Thailand, Vietnam etc. that the Supermarket prices for fruits and vegetables and often basic food were higher than those in traditional markets. Thus consumers are forced to buy food products at highly inflated prices.

Mr Nagarajan: Mr Nirmal, you are the last speaker, would you like to sum up the discussion?

Mr Nirmal: Sure, Mr. Nagarajan! Friends, all of us a arrived at the conclusion that FDI in retail sector in India is not in the benefit of Indian people. Particularly small farmers, small-retailers and whole-sellers and lastly the consumers who will have to buy the food products at inflated prices controlled by big monopolistic super-markets bringing misery and joblessness to their fellow brothers.

Mr Kapoor: Is that all?

Mr Nirmal: Yes I have delivered the consensus view.

Mr Kapoor: That is not the consensus, Mr. Nirmal.

Mr Shekhar: Mr. Nirmal, you should have incorporated the views of all the participants. You have simply repeated your views. Now let Mr. Nagrajan to wind up the proceedings.

Mr Nagrajan: Friends, in addition to what Mr. Nirmal has summed-up. I would like to say that FDI in retail sector in India will lead to healthy competition in business of retail of food products. This will improve the quality, service and availability of the food products to Indian masses. There will be a wide range of products and stores to choose from. Those, who are quality and service conscious, will not hesitate to shell out a little more price for it while the others may as well be happy with their old friendly retail shopkeepers.

Mr Nirmal: Mr Kapoor, are you happy with the final consensus statement now?

Mr Kapoor: It is amazing, Mr Nagarajan has done a good job.

Mr Nirmal: I am sorry, I should have incorporated all the points.

Ms Ravi: Never mind. Man learns from his mistakes and lapses.

Ms Khanam: Any more queries, please?

All: We have none.

Ms Ravi: Now, that none of us have any queries. We shall agree with the what Mr Nirmal and Mr Nagrajan stated in the consensus statement.

Mr Surjeet: Yes, we all agree with the consensus statement. It reflects the views of the entire group. Ms Khanam can wind up the GD now.

Ms Khanam: Thank you Ladies and Gentlemen. With the consensus decision which was delivered by Mr. Nirmal and Mr. Nagrajan, we wind up the GD session. I thank you all for your active participation.

All: Thank you!

Expert Comments

Mr. Nagarajan has the following qualities of a good leader.

(a) Courage to initiate and take up the task to break the ice.

(b) He seeks voluntary support from his colleagues and takes collaborative decision. He wins favour of most of his colleagues.

(c) Courteous

(d) Organiser—as he allocates or decides task among his group members.

He also comes up with innovative ideas on the issue. He has a charismatic personality. — *Selected*

Ms. Ravi comes up with arbitrary ideas (and an absurd one in the beginning) but she is creative. She assists Mr. Nagarajan in organising the group. She is courteous. She shows ethical behaviour when Mr. Kapoor a little rude to Mr. Nagarajan. Ms. Ravi could be a contributive group member. Good candidate. She is also a knowledgeable person.

Mr. Nirmal is a responsible person and does not hesitate to participate freely in the group discussion. He incorporates and harmonises the disparate ideas of all the group members very efficiently. He comes up with more ideas on the issue. He shows a balanced approach and has the ability to visualise the problem with its mildest implications. He can contribute well in a group and can be an efficient group hand.

Mr. Kapoor is an honest person. He readily apologises for his mistake. He also presents a well informed speech. But others have performed exceptionally well. So, as compared to them, his candidature remains under consideration. He hasn't shown extraordinary qualities. He appears to be impulsive—a rude remark about Mr. Nagarajan.
—This is a negative quality

Ms. Ayesha Khanam and Mr. Shekhar know facts but they just remain encyclopaedias of facts. They don't offer practicable ideas. Their selection seems bleak, given that Ms. Nagarajan, Ms. Ravi and Mr. Nirmal have performed far better under consideration.

Mr. Surjeet is yet another encyclopaedia of facts. Moreover he begins his speech in a rude manner—"Ms. Khanam & Mr. Shekhar may not be aware ...". He seems to be a proud person and is not capable of sharing good rapport with his team members.   *—So he is rejected*

PRESS CODE—IS IT MUST FOR THE PRESS?

Mr Ganesh: Well, my friends, may I request you to favour me with your kind attention for one moment, please.

Mr Kamlesh: You want to say,"*Friends, Romans and countrymen, lend me your ears.*"

Mr Ganesh: Yes, of course, you are quite right. I see you are an authority on Shakespeare. Well, gentlemen, I request you all to lend me not only your ears but also your hearts.

Mr Naveen:—If I am addressing a group of young ladies instead of these hardened bachelors here, I would say, lend me your hearts inside and outside your lips too.

Mr Gunjan:—I can guess what you will receive. They won't just lend. They will throw their shoes and slippers at you.

Mr Naveen:—I see you are talking about your own experience. They might have even greeted you with rotten eggs and tomatoes besides the other missiles you mentioned. But when I speak to the girls, I get what I want from them.

Mr Kamlesh:—I challenge you. Let us take a bet.

Mr Naveen:—How must are you willing to bet?

Mr Ganesh:—Please Mr Kamlesh and Mr Naveen, you will agree that both of you have become rather personal and emotional. Let us now relax, smile and start tackling our subject.

Mr Rajender:—You are quite right Mr Ganesh. Let us not waste time on other matters please. No, Mr Ganesh, you wanted to tell us something but got distracted. Please tell us what you had in your mind about our task in hand.

Mr Ganesh:—Thank you Mr Rajender. Well, friends, since we have been given only half an hour to complete our GD, I suggest we start with Mr Naveen and go on in a clockwise order to Mr Gunjan, Mr Kamlesh and soon till Mr Alok gets his turn and gives his views on the subject. This would be the first round during which each can speak for not more than two minutes. We can manage the time factor, if there are no interruptions and each is allowed to present his ideas without any disturbance or interference.

Mr Kamlesh:—What happens if I don't agree with the views expressed by the member or speaker? May be he is something incorrect. Let us say he quotes Tennyson but attributes it to Shakespeare. Should I intervene and point out the mistake?

Mr Rajender:—No, we are not supposed to intervene. We can point out the mistakes when our turn comes and we present our own views.

Mr Kamlesh:—But many of you are going to speak after me.

Mr Ganesh:—Please don't worry Mr Kamlesh, after the first round is completed we shall have a second one, when each will get one minute to voice his criticisms, rebuttals, after thoughts and so on. Finally, after the second round is over, there may yet be a few minutes left to have an open house.

Mr Rajender and Mr Kamlesh:—That is fine, let us start.

Mr Naveen:—No, no wait a minute. I have a better idea.

Mr Kamlesh:—I know you will come out with something silly as you did earlier. Please keep quiet. We can have your pranks later as advised by Mr Ganesh.

Mr Naveen:—Will you shut up Mr Kamlesh? I have every right to express my views. Then it is for the group to decide. I told you I have better ideas. I am not a nitwit like you.

Mr Ganesh:—Please gentlemen, why quarrel for nothing? Certainly Mr Naveen, we would like to hear your views. Please go ahead.

Mr Naveen :—Gentlemen, I totally disagree with what Mr Ganesh has suggested. It is completely wrong.

Mr Rajender:—Okay, okay, tell us what do you want. What is the alternative you suggest?

Mr Naveen:—Why don't you suggest an alternative?

Mr Rajender:—My dear friend, how does that question arise? It is you who do not agree with the plan outlined by Mr Ganesh. All others, including myself, have accepted his suggestion. Am I right, gentlemen?

Mr Kamlesh, Mr Satish and Mr Alok:—Yes, yes.

Mr Rajender:—All right. Now those who do not agree with Mr Ganesh's plan, please raise your hands. There you are Mr Naveen. If you have an alternative, please let us have it. Otherwise, let us go ahead with what we had decided earlier. You see the time is running out.

Mr Naveen:—But you have already made sure that no one would accept my plan. Therefore, I refuse to talk about it.

Mr Ganesh:—Oh! Come on Mr Naveen. I told you myself that I will accept your plan, if it is a better one.

Mr Kamlesh:—I say, we are wasting time. I guarantee that he has no other solution. Leave alone a better one.

Mr Naveen:—Shut up. I challenged you before, but you backed out. What is the bet now?

Mr Kamlesh:—We are here for the GD test and not for poker games. Friends, you could see Mr Naveen is obstinate and obstructive. If he does not start, I recommend we begin with Mr Gunjan and proceed further.

Mr Ganesh :—That doesn't appear to be correct Mr Kamlesh. I appeal to you Mr Naveen, please start and outline your plan of action.

Mr Naveen:—No, no. It is of no use. If they don't want a better idea, it is their pleasure. I am not keen to open the discussion. Now you can start it yourself as suggested by Mr Kamlesh.

Mr Gunjan:—The subject, in my view, deals with newspapers. I don't read newspapers much. I like cinema and my hobby is photography. If you ask me, the newspapers make a mountain of a molehill. That is all.

Mr Kamlesh:—Well gentlemen, the subject of our discussion is whether the Press code is a must for press in India i.e. it should observe self-restraint. I would say the question should be whether the Press in India is free? I think the Press is now free. It was not so during the emergency. Now, what is the guarantee that there will not be such emergencies in future? Already restrictions on freedom of the Press have been imposed in certain states,

I support the view that freedom of the Press is a must for the survival of democracy in India and a Press code should be evolved and strictly followed by all.

Mr Rajender:—Friends, the subject pertinently asks whether the Press in India should observe self-restraint. Assuming that the Press in India enjoys full freedom, the question to be debated is whether such freedom should be unrestricted and total, or whether it should be subject to certain restraints, whether imposed from inside or outside? If one takes the view that Press in India is not at all free, then the question of any restraint does not arise at all. It would then mean that the Press is gagged. I don't agree that the Press in our country is gagged now. Some papers have indulged in irresponsible reporting and hence the concerned State governments have attempted to impose restrictions. But the reaction is sharp, because of the emergency experience. The alternative therefore is self-restraint. The restraint should come from within and there should be a code which should be honoured.

Mr Satish :—Gentlemen, in my view the Press in India has been given too much freedom, which quite a few newspapers are abusing. Mr Rajender referred to a code. There is no code or restraint, we have too much of yellow journalism. Ask any cinema actor or actress and they will tell you how they are being maligned. All that to increase circulation, earn money and power. The same is the case with politicians. Now the industrialists are also becoming largest of such attacks. The existing laws, relating to libel, etc, are so loose that the newspapers can get away with anything. You also know that many magazines are obscene and are practically pornographic. Hence, I would say we need restrictions, self-restraint, I think, no one will observe and none could on force.

Mr Ganesh:—Friends, you all will agree with me that at this point of time the Press in India is quite free and the only limitations are those of ownership by big newspaper chains. There is keen competition and people are becoming more newspaper conscious. An aftermath of emergency, the Press is also quite alert and zealous about its freedom. We know that the opposition were in power, but they lost it pretty soon. The newspapers belonging to the opposition are over critical besides resorting to exaggeration. Sometimes people are quoted out of context giving misleading information. In other words, it could be deliberate misreporting. Financially, with newspapers mushrooming in thousands each day, survival becomes a major problem. In this situation, and with all the corruption and political pressure it is true that self-restraint won't work. Hence in my view, the Press should evolve a code and then leave it to the authorities to enforce it, may be, through proper legislation. The courts are there to see that the freedom of expression guaranteed by the Constitution as a Fundamental Right is not infringed.

Mr Gopal:—Well, you see, I agree with what our friends have said so far. I have nothing against anybody. It is good to observe restraint. That's all what Mr Ganesh has said. I have nothing to add now. Thanking you for given me the chance.

Mr Alok:—No right or freedom is absolute, not even the Fundamental Rights. There are always some implicit restrictions. The Constitution does cater to reasonable restrictions. What I do to others, others can do to me. But if you allow government to impose restrictions or even enforce restraints embodied in a code, it can result in abuse and discrimination. Besides the government has already the patronage of advertisement. Hence I do not favour government interference.

Mr Ganesh:—Come on Mr Naveen, we are waiting to hear your views. Please let us have the benefit of your ideas.

Mr Naveen:—Well folks, I told you before and I repeat it once again. I don't agree with all this. Everything has been wrong and you people did not choose to listen to me. I can prove that all what you people have said is totally wrong. But I have decided not to say anything, just to register my protest. You can come to any conclusion you like, but I am sorry. That's all.

COMMERCIALISATION OF EDUCATION—AN AVOIDABLE EVIL

Instructions : There is pandemonium/chaos in the room. Everyone is trying to address the whole group. Everyone wants to initiate and demonstrate his/her leadership skill (obviously they have undergone mock GDs else where and they have been instructed to do so). Thus, we have a group of enthusiastic and exuberant speakers, all vying with each other to become initiator, organiser, scheduler, controller—in one word—a leader.

What should be the right approach. Politely address each of those who is speaking—call him/her by name. (Calling someone by his/her name creates a dramatic impact on the person so addressed. That is why always learn the names of your group members before the session begins. It is not an easy task, so you may have an edge over others in this respect). Politely urge each of them to give you just a few seconds. Don't give out the impression that you want to lead or initiate. Your success is in the subsidence of the chaos. As soon as the hall becomes quieter. Choose someone, you feel, has an impressive personality and request him or her to initiate and plan the proceedings of the session. This is also an important characteristic of leader—to quieten and to delegate. Even if X determines the proceedings, but he/she is your choice. Now start canvassing for him/her so that the whole group, with minor dissents, accepts your proposal. Your leadership quality manifests in the fact the you have successfully co-ordinated with your colleagues and by delegating to Mr. X, the opportunity to lead, you have shown that you are not self-centred or narcissistic.

Keep assisting Mr. X throughout the session. Be courteous to all and come to rescue Mr. X whenever he faces opposition from a group member.

Reinterpret his words or behaviour to mellow down the bitterness that might have generated. When your turn comes, see if someone is getting impatient. If so, then offer your chance to him or try to soothe him down. Look into the eyes of the person who is speaking and wear a smiling (cheerful) countenance. Remember, what your colleagues have said because you must come up with something new and original. If nothing new strikes you then incorporate their ideas in your speech and harmonise them in order to transform the theory into praxis. But don't forget to thank them for their ideas that you borrowed. Try to pick the opportunity to conclude, if possible. If not, then give way to someone who is willing but don't forget to advise him/her as to what type of conclusion you are expecting—(Be polite and modest throughout the session). Don't talk in asides or in whispers. Don't be extra-indulgent with your immediate neighbours. This is a negative quality.

The participants are Mr. A, Mr. B, Ms. C, Mr. D, Miss E and Mr. F.

Mr. F:—Pardon me Mr. A............

Ms. C:—Please give me a moment

Miss E:—I request you to listen to me, just for a second.

(There is unpleasant noise—incoherent and loud.)

Miss F:—Please Miss E, I hope, you won't mind being an impartial organiser. Please determine the sequence of the proceedings and I promise to follow that. I expect, my friends in this room will agree to it.

Mr. A:—Why do you need an organiser? The common convention is to start in an alphabetical order.

Mr. F:—I agree, but there has to be someone to decide the succession of names in alphabetical order. If you would do that, we don't have any problem. Does anyone of us have any objection? (addresses the whole group and looks at each of them in quick succession).

Ms. C:—No, I want to be the first speaker and thereafter I would invite each member going clockwise from me.

Mr. F:—This way, everyone will want to be the first speaker and this will lead to chaos. I think, alphabetical order, as Mr. A has suggested and Miss E has agreed, will be appropriate. [Note : Mr. F has cleverly brought Mr. A and Miss E on his side. Rest of the members would not support C. Moreover, nobody else has any better idea to put forward].

Mr. F:—My friends, please allow Mr. A to make the schedule. We will write our names on a chit and handover to Mr. A. Thank you friends.

Mr. A:—Dear friends, I happen to be the first speaker, if we go by the alphabetical order. If any one has objection, please forgive me and let the session continue in the same because we are left with only twenty three minutes now. Each one of us will have three minutes to speak and if there is same time left, we can have a second round of one minute for each speaker. My time starts now!

Friends, we know that coaching institutes and tutorial classes are mushrooming across our cities. They charge exhorbitantly. Most of them are run by untrained instructors or unemployed or incompetent people. Their only aim is to make money. Quiet a few institutes are authentic, no doubt, and they employ qualified teachers, but ultimately all of them, however, fleece the parents. Even private schools are charging exhorbitant fees. Now a days, we don't have teachers. Rather we have professionals and subject specialists. Honest teaching cannot be seen. This has happened because of increasing competitiveness, our focus on specialisation and failure of the State machinery in providing for proper education. The poor are the biggest victims of this commercialisation of education. They don't have access to expensive teaching and government schools are in a pathetic condition. Thanks.

Mr. B, now its your turn, dear friend.

Mr. B:—Friends, I agree with Mr. A. At least the necessary elements of a civilized society, e.g., food, shelter, clothing and education should not be commercialised. I know, these private schools and coaching institutes have to bear enormous costs to keep operating but they must devise concession schemes for the underprivileged. Excessive commercialisation of education may aggravate the socio-economic inequality with which our country is already suffering. If government schools are revamped and made more efficient, I think these coaching institutes and private schools may continue and co-exist with the state run institutions. I think commercialisation will not hamper our socio-economic growth in such case.

Mr. A:—Mr. C, dear friend, its your turn.

Ms. C:—(Fumbles and seems to be taken aback).

Mr. F:—Ms. C, please take your time. We can wait for a few seconds or you may choose to be the last speaker.

Ms. C:—Oh! Thanks Mr. F. But I will continue.

Mr. F:—Great!

Ms. C:—Friends, commercialisation is a natural consequence of economic growth. We must not forget that education, like medicine, is a part of Service Industry. What's bad if our qualified, but unemployed youth or our visionary youth take up the profession of teaching. Aren't we trying to promote self-employment. Few critics may say that most of them are unqualified. I agree and I request the government to issue guidelines in this regard. There could be 'minimum standards' that these institutes must fulfill in order to gain license. Its just economics, my friend. Demand is more than supply. The government cannot supply to all of them, so the private sector has been allowed to operate freely in this field. So far as the poor are concerned, I agree with my venerable friend Mr. B and Mr. A, that govt. school must try to enhance their efficiency. Thank you for bearing with me.

Mr. A:—Mr. D, its your turn now.

Mr. D:—Thanks Mr. A and Friends, Mr. A, Mr. B and Ms. C have exhausted the topic. I appreciate their keen study. In addition to what they have said, I must say that education can be categorised into basic and specialised. So far as basic education, i.e., school and undergrade, is concerned I strongly oppose commercialisation because we have to have adequate resources for making provision for this. In case of specialised education I don't mind co-existence of the public and private sector. I have observed that these coaching institutes, purposely, present a bad picture of government schools and colleges. Moreover, most of teachers who visit these institutes also happen to be government school teachers or college teachers. Don't you think this is cheating? On the one hand our tax-payers are financing these teachers and on the other, these teachers are fleecing the credulous parents. I think the examiner meant to raise the issue of nexus of 'unscrupulous teachers' and owners of coaching institutes when he said "commercialisation of education". This kind of commercialisation must be checked. Thanks all of you.

Miss E:—(Stands before Mr. A could call out her name). Dear friends, everything has been spoken. If I say something for the speaking sake, it would be beating about the bush. I wonder what will Mr. F contribute. I can just give my opinion that the nexus of our unscrupulous teachers and the owners of coaching institutes must be discouraged. Like we have two types of food markets, namely, open market and fair price market (i.e. public distribution system), we can also have two types of education providers, namely, public institutions and private institutions. Let them co-exist. But the private institutions should not unjustly enrich themselves, especially because most of them get subsidies from the government— Subsidised provision, cheaper land, tax sops etc. They owe to the society, so they must reciprocate with sympathy. This unjust and unfair commercialisation of education is bad. Thank you All.

Mr. A:—Mr. F, its your turn now.

Mr. F:—Dear friends, all of you spoke so well and your arguments were so strong that I didn't want to intervene when a few of you exceeded your time limits. Perhaps Mr. A was also so overwhelmed/spell bound by your eloquence that he missed that. I can see that only nine minutes are left. Would you allow me to conclude with the group consensus along with my own ideas which will only corroborate what all of you said.

Mr. A:—Yes sure Mr. F.

All:—Please go ahead.

Mr. F:—Thank you all, Friends, all of us agree that there is no harm in the co-existence of the public and private institutions. The private institutions have heavier liabilities like corporate tax, maintaining state of the art facilities, Maintaining high standard of sanitary conditions etc. So they are compelled to charge higher fees. But, as my friends rightly pointed out, the unscrupulous teachers conniving with coaching owners have spoiled the system. Quite often these teachers advertise their private tutorials in schools and colleges. In fact being a college or government school teacher in their strategy because here they get their prospective 'consumers'. This is unethical. Let there be two markets but there should be no immoral pilferage from one market to another. Both of these should provide equal education, so that for studying in government schools one is at par with the rich studying in private schools. If this degraded form of commercialisation is allowed to persist, we will face social and economic injustice in its horrendous form. All of us were unanimously against 'commercialisation of education'. Obviously because the examiner himself indicated that it is an avoidable evil but I must say that it is not privatisation that is evil or mere commercialisation that is evil. The avoidable evil here is the unethical and immoral commercialisation as my learned friends have already pointed. I too, vehemently propose to avoid the nexus between government teachers and private coaching institutes. It was nice being with all of you. Thank you friends. See you again!

SAME SEX MARRIAGE – RIGHT OR WRONG

There is pandemonium/chaos in the room.

Mr. C:—Hello friends! (loud voice) listen to me. Your speech is incoherent. Please don't speak all at once.

Mr. D:—Hello friends! Hey! What's your name? You in that yellow shirt, please calm down. Let me say something.

Mr. F:—Excuse me friends. Please maintain silence. Let us speak in turns.

[**Note** : Every body is trying to address the whole group and so the chaotic situation].

Mr. A has been watching this conundrum for a while. He stands up and exhorts his immediate neighbours Mr. E and Ms. X also to stand up. He urges them to come forward and help him to calm down others. He approaches Mr. C and asks Miss X to approach Mr. D and Mr. E to approach Mr. F. The three urge them to quieten just for few seconds. The other three calm down. Mr. A, quickly, picks this opportunity to addres the whole group. He already has the support of Ms. X and Mr. E and being with manpower for support, he is able to acheive what he desires.

Mr. A:—Friends, without wasting your precious time, I must request Ms. X to formulate the sequence in which we shall speak, or if Mr. F wants to do the same, I hope none of us would have any problem. Please co-operate. We have already wasted our 6 minutes.

Mr. C:—Why Ms. X or Mr. F. Seems you are enamoured of them.

Mr. A:—Oh no! Mr. C. I am sorry, I offended you. Let's elect our co-ordinator, in that case. Agree friends? Let's write our preference on a chit. I am out of this, so that only five of you are left. No one will write one's own name. The one who gets majority vote, will be our honourable co-ordinator. Mr. C will count the votes.

Mr. C:—But this will take same more time.

Mr. A:—Please let it be so, for we will be wasting more time in deliberations. Start friends! (others comply).

Miss X garners majority votes. C declares the result.

Miss X:—Thanks all of you. I propose that we speak in the ascending order of our roll members. Let me see your admit cards.

Mr. C, congrats, you are our opening speaker. Please go ahead.

Mr. C:—Friends, same sex relationships are not new to our culture. Its just that the western idea of individual liberty has inspired a few of our fellow brethren to become vociferous about their unusual sexual indignations. I firmly believe that these people also have the right to life and the right to choose their life partners. The Delhi High Court has also come forward to support the cause of these people who are condescendingly referred as 'queer'. The High Court has said that 5.377 of the Indian Penal Code, which makes their relationship an unnatural sexual offence, be reviewed. I must say that as we are born males or females, few of us are born homosexuals. It is biological. If we castigate them for their natural instincts, we would be doing what the colonisers did with the Black people in Africa. We should not involve morality here. I think same sex marriages are not wrong or unethical.

Thank you friends.

Miss X:—Mr. A, it is your turn now.

Mr. A:—Mr. C has given strong arguments in favour of same sex marriages. I believe, he is right. We have been unfair to various classes such as SCs, STs, women. Similarly, we have been unfair to these so called 'queer' class. Like the Black people fought for their deliverance, we agitated for our liberty, the backward classes struggled for their recognition, our 'queer' brethren are also raising their voice for their identity. Even they are human beings and have human rights. They have the right to life which includes the right to live with dignity. Usually these people are targeted for ridicule (more often in film and other media). The common ideology is that these people are immoral and in fact diabolical. Aren't we discriminating against them for no fault of theirs? Our constitution, unequivocally, says that no one should be discriminated against only on the grounds of caste, colour, creed, sex, religion. Aren't we discriminating against these people as the ground of 'sex'. Its true, heterosexuality is a usual phenomenon. But as my friend Mr. C pointed out, homosexuality is not new. Even this has existed since the ancient days moreover, homosexuality is not an intentioned inclination. Its a natural instinct, purely dependant an our genes. Oh I am sorry, I spoke so long. I have something more to say but I will wait for the second round.

Thank you friends.

Miss X:—Friends, its my turn now. Mr. C and Mr. A have wonderful ideas and I am sure rest of you will be equally eloquent. I am personally a devout opponent of same sex relationships, not on ethical grounds or other discriminatory considerations. I feel, to a great extent, showing that you are the 'other way' has become a fashionable pursuit. Few people are glamourising it in the name of metro sexuality, as a result of which, our present generation is getting confused about its sexual inclinations—psychological conditioning may wreak havoc and even heterosexuals may go for homosexual experimentations. I agree with the Delhi High Court's decision but then relationship is distinct from marriage. Marriage is an institution and has legal connotation, apart from religious or communal implications. The whole branch of the personal law, which is based on the customs and usages of a community, will be ruptured. New issues such as their representation in the legislature, their property rights—as dependents, reservation in jobs etc will sprout up.

Few people may try to take undue advantage by frequently oscillating from heterosexuality to homosexuality. I think, in most of the cases, psychiatric counselling may solve the problem. Please don't forget that legitimiting same sex marriages will increase the problem of experiments with alternate sex everywhere. I sympathise with their cause, but I don't support the idea of such marriages. Let they be in relationship only.

Thank you.

Mr. F, its your turn now.

Mr. F:—What shall I speak? You manipulated it somehow that you all got early opportunities to speak. Now, that everything has been said, all my points will appear to be repetition. See I jotted down these points in the very beginning, as soon as the examiner had left but now you will accuse me of plagiarising. Its you luck guys! Thanks, I won't say anything Huh! Mr. E and Mr. B I pity you!

Mr. E:—Oh! Thanks for concern Mr. E but I think I might still be able to add to what my learned friends have already said. Friends, Miss X has opposed same sex marriage and my other friends have vehemently supported it. I realise that Miss X and my other friends share their concern for these 'other' people. In fact, I found no opposite strains in their speech.

I feel we need to harmonise the disparate ideas in order to emphasise the common theme, that is, the plight of our queer brethren. I feel our country is not politically, legally and socially mature enough to bring about a radical change such as allowing same sex marriage. We need more time so that our people are sensitised. Otherwise such marriages may face the wrath of the society. Such individuals may get ostracized– something that cannot be controlled by making laws. Our people must become mature. We will need to make exhaustive changes in our own legal fabric and we also need to have the requisite political will power. Presently, the Delhi High Court has given the much needed relief by decriminalising such relationships. As far as marriage is concerned, let's wait for some more time lest we should create a horrible confusion. Miss X is right as few people may have been seen glamourising it. I insist that these people should sensitise people rationally.

Thank you.

Mr. B:—Please excuse me friends, I am not feeling well. I need to see a doctor.

Thanks.

IS MORAL POLICING JUSTIFIED

Mr. B:—Please friends, please allow me to speak. Please listen to me.

Mr. C:—Mr. B, hey friends let me speak ... O ... listen to me. (raises voice)

Mr. D:—Friends I think moral policing is justified...

Mr. B:—Mr. D, no one is listening to you. Why the hell have you started speaking on the topic. Let's decide on the order of speakers.

Mr. D:—I know, no one is going to listen. They want to show off that each of them is a leader—the one who can initiate—including you. Just speak whatever you want and your responsibility is over. All of us are leaders so don't expect decorum. Thanks to these coaching institutes which guide them to become aggressive initiators!

Mr. A:—(who had been watching the whole scene silently turns towards Mr. D)

Mr. D how true you are? I think, we must show our natural selves, instead of emulating what these coaching institutes have instructed. You seem to have nice observation. Mr. B, you are right. We need to have an order, otherwise the whole session will fail and we will be rejected (indicates toward D, B and himself) for no fault of ours.

Mr. B:—Right!

Mr. A:—Then let's approach our other friends and being three in member we may well, be able to form a pressure group of ours.

A, B and D speak out in unison. Hey friends! Please pay attention. Mr. C, we hope you will kindly allow us to determine the order of speakers.

Mr. A:—Let Miss X determine the order of the speaker.

Mr. C:—Shall I ask you, why Miss X and not me?

Mr. A:—I am sorry. I shall be equally pleased to have you as our co-ordinator would you mind Miss X?

Miss X:—No, not at all. But I have a suggestion. If Mr. C agrees, then can we have the sequence of speakers in the ascending order of our roll numbers.

Mr. C:—Seems you want this particular order because your roll number is the smallest and you want to be the first speaker. If I am the co-ordinator, then I must decide, how it should be. No suggestions please.

Miss X:—Oh! I am sorry, I appeared so selfish to you but actually it occurred to me naturally, may be, because it's a usual convention, I observed during my pervious GD elsewhere.

Mr. C:—It's okay. Let us determine the order on the basis of the alphabetical order of our names. Let me see your admit cards. Oh! We have already lost precious ten minutes in indecisiveness. Mr. A please start the session.

Mr. A:—Thank you Mr. C and my dear friends—for your co-operation. Moral policing is not a new phenomenon. It has been practised in India for centuries, with gruesome consequences. Young boys and girls have been the usual victims. Our society has always, rigidly, interfered with our likes and dislikes—what to wear, how to talk, how to behave differently with different classes of people, how a man should live and how a girl or a woman should live. If ever anyone dared to flout the orthodox works, he or she was eliminated. This is how our society meted out justice over those hapless adventurers. Woman who dared to question the social norms, were branded as witches. After Independence, our constitution guaranteed us the liberty to determine our way of living to the extent of our legal rights and subject to the reasonable restrictions imposed by law. Our life and liberty can be taken away by the procedure established by law and not by any fanatic individual or orthodox parties. Our parents and teachers are there to guide us when we are minors. But when we attain majority, we are the masters of our own selves. I strongly believe that no one, except the law—meant for public policy, has the authority to take away our individual liberty.

Thank you friends!

Mr. C:—Mr. B, its your turn now. (Mr. C laughingly says, it seemed Mr. A was not going to stop...!)

Mr. B:—Friends, I agree with Mr. A. I strongly resent the so called moral policing by the political parties and the hypocrits who are themselves morally degraded. They resort to violence and other draconian measures. We live in a civilized society where we practise the 'rule of law'. Article 21 of our constitution specifically lays down that we have the 'right to life' and it cannot be taken away except by the procedure established by law. We have the right to freedom which includes the right if freedom of speech, right to move anywhere in territory of India, right to do any trade etc. These rights are subject to reasonable restrictions and these restrictions can be imposed only by the law and no one else. So, these people who claim to be keepers of morality must be severely penelised for violation of the fundamental rights of the citizens of India. They don't have the right to kill intercaste couples or young boys and girls roaming together or religious converts.

Thank you friends.

Mr. C:—Friends, most humbly, I present myself, for its my turn now. Moral policing means controlling public morality by the self acclaimed pressures of morality. These are usually a pack of backward thinking—conservative people who are actually the malcontents of our society. These people need an issue that appeals to our illiterate, superstitions and orthodox people so that they continue weilding power in their hands. By appealing to the basic instincts of men they are able to control their lives. To same extent, moral policing may be necessary. For example, in small towns people have cloistered mentality and they may not be comfortable with the idea of a girl befriending a boy, there the parents have to keep a check on their daughters otherwise their marriage may be hindered. A little moral policing is also required to prevent a minor from becoming a delinquent adolescent or a derelict. But this type of moral policing should be done by our parents, peers, teachers and our elders. I detest the violent methods that are usually adopted by the conservative political parties.

Thanks a lot friends!

Mr. D its your turn now.

Mr. D:—Friends, recently I read in a newspaper that a political party targeted girls who were wearing Jeans. Some colleges have prohibited girls from wearing western outfits in the college premises. I think this is disgusting. Do you know, how do these scoundrels justify their attack on the hapless girls? They say that, because of these western outfits, there have been increase in the number of eve teasings, molestations and rapes. Do you vindicate this opinion? I feel it is the eye of these teachers and the vulgar minds, that tells one obscene and the dress that a woman wears. Won't they blame their own voluptuousness and voyeuristic tendencies? How would they explain rape of a girl child who is five or six year old? What dress that innocent child should wear? I think this is not morality. Morality lies in self restrain. Let everybody decide how he or she should spend his or her life. We must take care that no one is injured or harmed by our life style. Except that we are free to do anything. I am strictly against the demarche of moral policing.

Mr. C:—Would you like to say anything Miss X? Unfortunately, we have said everything and you will only be going into unnecessary repetition.

Miss X:—Mr. C, thanks for being the co-ordinator of our group. I compliment you for your power to prognosticate, but I think, there is still something I could say. Shall I?

Mr. C:—Ya sure Miss! Its your turn anyway!

Miss X:—Friends, moral policing is an anathema to our society. We live in a democratic country where everyone must abide by the law. If we allow individuals or groups to regulate public decency or moral behaviour, we will be heading towards anarchic mobocracy. Then every powerful group will, arbitrarily, lay down its own ideologies or principles and force others to comply. Various powerful groups will emerge, each standing for its own rigid ideology and quite often they may have conflicting claims. We will be governed by our whimsical mighty leaders. Do we really want this to happen. I observe, almost all of us are against the diabolical concept of moral policing. Friends, we don't have much time left for the second round and I am afraid, I shall have to harmonise our ideas and reach the consensus, as quickly as possible. Being the last speaker, I take this opportunity to conclude that the group, unanimously, opposes the concept of moral policing which is but another name for mob justice. This is illegal and unconstitutional. This may lead to compartmentalisation of our society in narrow domestic walls and unlike what Shri Rabindra Nath Tagore meant, we will be perpetually doomed to live where the mind will always live in fear—fear of persecution and fear of uncertainty as what would be moral for one mighty group may be immoral for the other. I think, individual growth will be casualty. There should be a reasonable balance between individual liberty and the society. None should suppress the other. Thank you friends!

CAPITAL PUNISHMENT
UNCIVILIZED WAY OF PUNISHING

Mr. A:—Dear Friends, Good Morning. I am A. I see that we have been talking in asides for five minutes. Do you feel, it would be better if we spoke to the whole group, one speaker at a time. That way, we will be interacting together and it would be easier to reach the group conseusus in the end.

Mr. D:—You are right Mr. A. Let us have you as our co-ordinator. Would you mind organising the sequence of speakers.

Mr. C:—Why Mr. A. There are other eligible and efficient people sitting here. I can see that Mr. B has a pleasing personality. He could be our co-ordinator.

Mr. D:—In that case, Miss E and Miss F are also equal contenders. I wonder how you choose 'pleasing personality' as a criterion for selecting a co-ordinator. I invited Mr. A because he broke the ice.

Mr. C:—Lets have an election.

Mr. A:—Oh! Mr. C that will consume our precious time. We have already lost nine minutes and only 21 minutes are left. Lets do one thing. I am out of the race. I hope Mr. D and Mr. C are also not willing to be in the race. Sorry I presume so because both of you are proposing other members' name. Thus there are 3 people Mr. B, Miss E and Miss F. They are equals and no discrimination meant! I think, let the one be the co-ordinator whose name comes first in the three folded chits (shows) I have just now made. Mr. C please pick one of these.

Mr. A:—Congrats, Miss E you are our hon'ble co-ordinator.

Miss E:—Thanks, Mr. A and Mr. C. I think we go by the convention of the alphabetical order of our names. So Mr. A, you be the first speaker. There are 18 mins left so each of us will speak for 2.5 minutes and last 3 minutes will be for the group consensus.

Mr. A:—Thanks Miss E.

Friends, capital punishment is an inhuman way of awarding punishment. We don't have the right to take away someone's life. I agree that few criminals one incorrigible and they are sadists to the core. They are detrimental to our society. Still I feel that there is the posibility of reforming them. In the rarest of rare cases, where the offence committed is so barbaric that the offender's mental depravity shakes the very foundation of a civilized society, we can allow capital punishment, our hon'ble supreme court has also said that capital punishment should be awarded only in the rarest of rare cases. In almost all the European countries capital punishment has been abolished. I think we can also do away with this practice. Thank you all.

Miss E:—Mr. B, its your turn now.

Mr. B:—Please forgive me. I have not formulated my opinion so far. Please allow me to be the last speaker.

Miss E:—Mr. C, would you grace the group with your wisdom.

Mr. C:—Thanks Miss E. Friends, Mr. A seems to be sympathetic towards hardcore criminals. Perhaps he might change his mind, if some criminal victimises him or his kin. Then I will see whether he is able to maintain his rationality.

Miss E:—Please don't be personal Mr. C.

Mr. C:—Those criminals can never be let free. They cannot be reformed. Their mental perversity makes them dangerous and we can't take the risk of letting them free into the society even after long incarceration. There are serial killers who may remain dormant during imprisonment but actually they feign submissionness. As soon as they are released they might indulge in their distorted pleasures. How can we endanger social tranquility in the name of human rights. Now, few human rights champions say that these criminals can be subjected to life imprisonment instead of putting them to death. I ask them, will they pay for the upkeep of these antisocials? Why should the honest tax payers pay for those who have given them insecure days and nights? Thanks all of you.

Miss E:—Mr. D its your turn now. Please enlighten us further on the issue.

Mr. D:—Friends, there are times when we have to strike a balance between individual liberty and social security. So far as I know, capital punishment is supported by the rationale that it produces a strong deterrant effect on the prospective offenders and they are prevented from giving effect to heinous crimes. But there is some lacunae in this argument. In the European countries, where capital punishment has been abolished, crime rate has not increased. Rather, because of the executive's alacrity and judicial promptness, crime rate has decreased over the past fifteen years. On the other hand in the USA, where capital punishment is still in practice, the crime rate has ironically increased during this period. How would you explain this anomaly? I believe, it is not the fear of death but the certainty of punishment that deters a prospective offender. If we enhance our alertness and if the judicial process becomes fast, I am sure, the deterrence effect will be more effective, so far as taxpayer's money is concerned, we can devise employment opportunities for the prisoners— may be we can promote their participation in cottage industries. In this way they won't be a burden on the tax payers.

Thank you friends.

Miss E:—Friends, we all witnessed wonderful view points on the issue in question. I see that Mr. D and Mr. A have opposed the practice of capital punishment. I too feel that this is an unjust punishment and against the tenets of all religions. This is more a retributive action than discharge of justice. I understand how victims and their kins would feel when the perpetrator of crime is put to death. They feel justice has been done. But this is their angry minds which seeks revenge and vengeance. I agree that there are a few reckless criminals who would never try to reform themselves. Perhaps in their case— the rarest of the rare case— we may resort to capital punishment because when individual interests conflict with those of the society, the law must prevail. Mr. B would you like to speak now?

Mr. B:—No, thanks Miss E. I am a bit puzzled.

Miss E:—Its okay Mr. B. I think there is no reason to get embarrassed. All of us get puzzled at some point of time in our lives.

Friends, I think we must conclude with the group consensus now. Only 3 minutes are left. Anyone interested.

Mr. A:—You have almost done that Miss E. So I request you to go ahead with it.

All:—Please continue Miss E.

Miss E:—Thanks all of you. We have expressed our opinions differently but the common strain in all of them is that capital punishment should be avoided as much as possible. This is, no doubt, an uncivilized way of awarding punishment but in the rarest of rare cases, when the society is rendered sans an alternative, this mode of punishment can be adopted. Mr. C has dissented from the majority opinion. We share his concern and I think his ground of objection is countered by Mr. B's argument. So the group consensus is in not favour of capital punishment unless it is the rarest of the rare situation.

Thank you all!

See you all very soon!

MEDIA TRIAL

Mr. A:—Hello Friends! I am A and I have come from...

Mr. C:—Excuse me dear sir, we haven't assembled here to listen to your autobiography. Let us start our discussion on the topic the examiner has just now pronounced.

Mr. D:—Ha Ha! Mr. C, please don't demoralise our friend. He seems to have come from a rustic coaching institute where they teach you how to introduce yourself.

Mr. A:—Dear friends, I see you are knowledgeable, humorous and co-operative. I will come to the point. We have to start our discussion but there must be a predetermined order of speakers, so that all of us have fair opportunity to speak. Miss X, would you be our co-ordinator.

Mr. C:—Oh you are playing politics. I intercepted your 'epic' so you are trying to rope in others in your camp.

Miss X:—Oh Mr. C, you appear to be too sensitive. May I propose Mr. B's name?

Mr. B:—No, No Miss X. Thanks but consider me out of this. I will speak but I must not co-ordinate, I need some time to think over the issue.

Miss X:—Then Mr. C, you appear to be the best man at the helm. Would you please...

Mr. C:—Sure, I will be the co-ordinator. I think we can start in alphabetical order. First, A, then B and so on. Let me see your admit cards.

(Announces):—Mr. A, please stand up and give us your opinion restricting it to the matter that is relevant to the topic.

Mr. A:—Mr. C, thanks for your instructions. But I will enjoy my literary freedom while I am speaking. Friends, media trial is a recently developed expression. Media is meant for impartial reporting. It is like a mirror to the society. I support the idea of freedom of press and I admire it for its important role in protecting democracy. But I am distressed at the idea of Media Trial. Trial is a judicial proceeding and it should be conducted by people who are legal experts. Trial in the name of investigative journalism is an abuse of the qualified privilege that our media has been accorded with. As soon as a matter comes within the jurisdiction of the executive authority and to the judicial authority, media should not do more than the reporting of the events. If it publishes viewpoints of the witness, interview with accused and opinion of the police personnel, it will spoil the judicial proceedings by vitiating it with partiality. When the accused faces a deluge of questions posed by our reporters, he is forced to give unguarded answers. It appears that he is really guilty of the crime whereas he may have been guilty by a lighter crime. Every person should be presumed innocent unless he is proven guilty in a court of law.

Thank you friends.

Mr. C:—Mr. B, its your turn now.

Mr. B:—Thanks Mr. C. Friends, I agree with Mr. A. Media Trial is detestable. It is contempt of court. When a matter is sub-judice, media should not interfere with the proceedings. Sometimes, the Media also tempers with evidences and witness. Media Trial creates unnecessary pressure on the police and the judges, because of which, they may mete out injustice. Suppose a witness has not seen the accused properly, but due to incessant telecast/publication by the media, the witness may confirm his identification. As a result of this, the accused may not get the benefit of doubt, which is his right. When the accused is acquitted by the court, people may not accept him as innocent person because the media has already branded him as an offender. His reputation is permanently damaged. The judges are also human beings. If a particular accused is castigated incessantly at a public forum, they too may fall prey to undue influence. Such biased judges may not be able to do real justice. Thank you friends.

Mr. C:—Its may turn now. Friends, I understand that Media Trial has its own drawbacks. But we must not forget that the cases like Jessica Lal case, Manu Sharma case, Mattoo case, cash for questions scan, P.D. Dinakaran case, etc., could not have been brought before the public, had our media not been pro-active. The media kept these issues alive so the state authorities were under a constant pressure to bring the offenders to the books. Therefore, I favour Media Trial.

Mr. D, its your turn now.

Mr. D:—I can't say much but I feel Mr. C is right. Every thing has its pros and cons. We can keep a check on the negative fall outs of the Media Trial but we cannot make it silent. This is for democracy, my friends.

Thank you.

Mr. C:—Your thoughts are very poor Mr. D. You could have chosen to speak in the end. Anyway, Mr. E, would speak now.

Mr. E:—Thank you Mr. C. Media Trial is a negative aspect of the free press. This is not, what I feel, responsible journalism. I thank media for reporting crimes. This is useful for the public. Media must concentrate on public purposes. We call it the Fourth Estate because it is an indispensable pillar of democracy. If sovereignty lies in us then the media is our instrument through which we exercise sovereignty. This is the forum where we keep vigil on our government and control those who are at the helm of affairs. But when the media starts conducting trials, it is doing something beyond its competence. It is the violation of the rights of the accused, rights of his relatives, rights of the witnesses and rights of the judiciary. Witnesses become prone to the perils posed by the accused, once they are highlighted. Recently, a crazy fellow attached Dr. Rajesh Talwar, father of Arushi Talwar who was killed at her home some time ago. The media presented the news in such a manner that any reasonable person would think that Dr. Talwar was the killer. When the police as well as the CBI, found nothing, they dropped the charges against him. Thus Dr. Talwar was neither an accused, nor a committer. Still this crazy fellow thought that he was the culprit, so he attached him. This is how most of the people felt. Why? Because of the media hype. I strongly believe that Media Trial is an abuse of the freedom of press.

Thank friends.

Mr. C:—Miss X, now, its your turn. We are left with 6 minutes. So I urge Miss X to continue her speech upto the conclusion incorporating the group consensus.

Miss X:—Thank you Mr. C. Friends, I agree with Mr. E, Media Trial is an undesirable phenomenon. Every sector has its own functions to discharge. Our constitution expects the legislature to make laws; the executive to implement the laws and to implement the policies; and the judiciary to interpret the laws as well as to do justice. Similarly the press has the duty to inform us. They should present untampered reports before us. Forming opinion is our prerogative. If the journalists show their own bias, people will not get the correct picture of the situation. Trial is the prerogative of the judiciary. The legal experts are properly trained. The accused has the right to be represented by his counsel. If he cannot afford one, the court provides him a legal representative. The court takes its decisions on the basis of concrete admissible evidences. Witnesses cannot tell lies in a court because they are afraid of being punished for perjury. The court may conduct trials in camera, if it deems fit. On the other hand, Media Trial offers no protection to the accused or the witnesses. There is no deterrance to present the witnesses from lying before the Media. The media may create a hype on the basis of inadmissible evidences and mere conjectures. Therefore, I think the media should stick to its prescribed and expected role instead of encroaching upon the jurisdiction of the executive and the judiciary. I also feel that in deserving cases, the media must be held for contempt of court. Mr. C dissented from the group consensus. The majority opinion is against the practice of Media Trial. Now a days, impartiality of the media has also become questionable, especially because the cut-throat competition among the channels and the newspapers because of they focus on sensationalisation of the news. Also, they depend on the revenue generated from the advertisement, so I doubt they might play second fiddle to their paymasters.

Thank you friends.

See you very soon!

NOTE

Selection is done on the basis of the following virtues:

Leadership Skills + harmonious personality + polite words + original ideas + team spirit/group behaviour + clear perception of the issue.

One must also demonstrate the capacity of coherent and impressive articulation. A candidate need not be perfect but the preponderance of the forementioned virtues will be highly influential in the selection procedure.

www.ingramcontent.com/pod-product-compliance
Lightning Source LLC
Chambersburg PA
CBHW050555170426
43201CB00011B/1699